Also by Matthew Gabriele
and David M. Perry

The Bright Ages: A New History of Medieval Europe

Oathbreaker

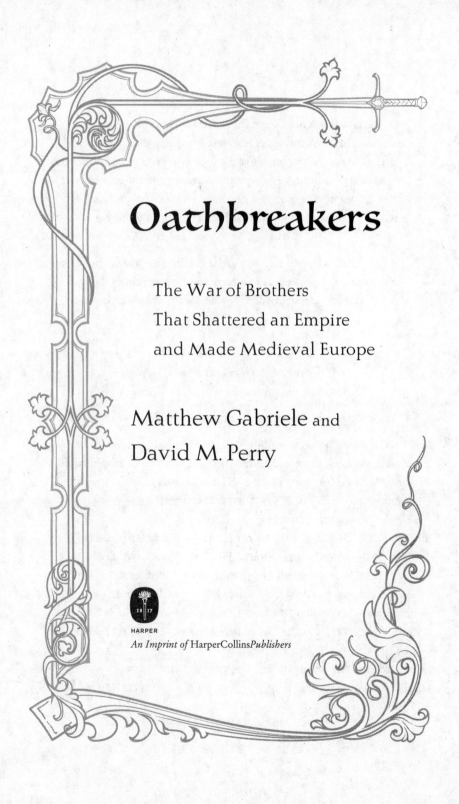

Oathbreakers

The War of Brothers
That Shattered an Empire
and Made Medieval Europe

Matthew Gabriele and
David M. Perry

HARPER
An Imprint of HarperCollins*Publishers*

HarperCollins books may be purchased for educational, business,
or sales promotional use. For information, please email the Special
Markets Department at SPsales@harpercollins.com.

FIRST EDITION

Designed by Leah Carlson-Stanisic
Art by Antonpix/Shutterstock, Inc.
Map illustrations by John Wyatt Greelee

Library of Congress Cataloging-in-Publication Data

Names: Gabriele, Matthew, author. | Perry, David M., author.
Title: Oathbreakers: the war of brothers that shattered an empire and
    made Medieval Europe / Matthew Gabriele and David M. Perry.
Description: First edition. | New York, NY: Harper, [2024] |
    Includes bibliographical references and index.
Identifiers: LCCN 2024022314 (print) | LCCN 2024022315 (ebook) |
    ISBN 9780063336674 (hardcover) | ISBN 9780063336681 (epub)
Subjects: LCSH: Carolingians—History. Lothair I, Emperor, 795–855. |
    Louis I, Emperor, 778–840. | Charles II, King of France, 823-877. |
    Emperors—Succession—France. | France—History—To 987.
Classification: LCC DC70.A2 G33 2024(print) | LCC DC70.A2 (ebook) |
    DDC 944/.01—dc23/eng/20240913
LC record available at https://lccn.loc.gov/2024022314
LC ebook record available at https://lccn.loc.gov/2024022315

ISBN 978-0-06-333667-4

24 25 26 27 28 LBC 5 4 3 2 1

For our siblings

CONTENTS

Act III: Civil War

741   Death of Charles Martel

751   Pepin III "the Short" becomes king of the Franks

754   Pepin III anointed as king at Saint-Denis (outside Paris) by Pope Stephen II, the first time the pope had traveled north of the Alps

768   Death of Pepin III; succession of Charlemagne and his brother, Carloman

771   Death of Carloman; reunification of Frankish kingdom

774   Conquest of Lombards by Franks; disappearance of Carloman's family

792   Rebellion of Charlemagne's son Pepin, later called "the Hunchback"

794   Ermengarde marries Louis the Pious

800   Charlemagne is crowned Roman emperor in Rome on Christmas Day

806   Charlemagne divides the empire among his three legitimate sons in a document called the *Divisio regnorum*

810   Death of Pepin of Italy

811   Death of Charles the Younger; death of Pepin the Hunchback

813   Coronation of Louis the Pious as co-emperor

814   Death of Charlemagne; succession of Louis the Pious

817   Formal division of the empire by Louis the Pious among his three legitimate sons in a document called the *Ordinatio imperii*; supposed rebellion by Bernard of Italy

818   Blinding and death of Bernard of Italy

819   Judith of Bavaria marries Louis the Pious

822   Formal public penance by Louis the Pious at Attingy

823   Birth of Charles the Bald

827   Aizo's revolt in Barcelona

828   Dishonoring of Matfrid of Orléans and Hugh of Tours

829   Elevation of Bernard of Septimania as chamberlain; his appointment as guardian of Charles the Bald

830   First insurrection against Louis the Pious

833   Second insurrection against Louis the Pious

834   Lothar's siege of Chalons-sur-Saône; murder of the nun Gerberga

838   Death of Pepin I of Aquitaine (son of Louis the Pious); disastrous council at Nijmegen that alienates Louis the Pious from Louis the German

839   Transfer of kingdom of Aquitaine to Charles the Bald; reconciliation of Lothar and Louis the Pious; (separate) revolts of Louis the German

840   Death of Louis the Pious; succession of Lothar I as emperor, Louis the German as king of East Francia, and Charles the Bald as king of West Francia

841   Death of Adalbert of Metz at the hands of Louis the German (May); Battle of Fontenoy (June); Dhuoda begins letter to her absent son (November)

842   Oaths of Strasbourg (August); wedding of Charles the Bald and alienation of Nithard from court (December)

843   Completion of Dhuoda's letter (February); Treaty of Verdun (August)

844   Execution of Bernard of Septimania

845   Death of Nithard

Adalard Seneschal under Louis the Pious after circa 830; military commander under Charles the Bald at Fontenoy; protector and uncle to Charles the Bald's wife, Ermentrude

Adalbert of Metz Close advisor to Louis the Pious throughout his reign; nemesis of Louis the German; killed by Louis the German in the Ries Crater shortly before the Battle of Fontenoy (841)

Agnellus of Ravenna Churchman who wrote history of the bishops of Ravenna, which includes an account of the Battle of Fontenoy

Angelbert Noble in service of Lothar I; wrote poem about the Battle of Fontenoy in 841

Angilbert Adviser to Charlemagne; lover of Charlemagne's daughter Bertha; father of Nithard

Astronomer, the Churchman and courtier who wrote biography of Louis the Pious shortly after 840

Bernard of Italy Son of Pepin of Italy; grandson of Charlemagne; led supposed rebellion against Louis the Pious in 817; blinded and died in 818

Bernard of Septimania Cousin of Louis the Pious; appointed chamberlain in 829; accused of witchcraft and proximate cause of rebellion in 830

Bertha Daughter of Charlemagne; mother of Nithard

Charlemagne Frankish king and emperor 768–814

Charles Martel Frankish progenitor of Carolingians; died 741

Charles the Bald Youngest son of Louis the Pious; king of West Francia 838–877; emperor 875–877

Charles the Younger Eldest son of Hildegard by Charlemagne; died 811

Clovis Merovingian king 481–511; converted Franks to Christianity

Dhuoda Wife of Bernard of Septimania; wrote long letter to son when he was a hostage to Charles the Bald in 841–843

Drogo of Metz Illegitimate son of Charlemagne; bishop of Metz; close confidant of Louis the Pious after 830

Ebbo of Reims Enslaved foster brother of Louis the Pious; archbishop of Reims; sided with rebels in 833; stripped and dishonored in 834

Einhard Courtier and biographer of Charlemagne; personal tutor to Lothar I

Ermengard Wife of Lothar I; daughter of Hugh of Tours

Ermengarde First wife of Louis the Pious (794–818); mother of Lothar I, Pepin of Aquitaine, and Louis the German

Fastrada Fourth wife of Charlemagne (783–794)

Florus of Lyons Churchman who wrote poem on the destruction of the empire after Fontenoy

Hildegard Third wife of Charlemagne (772–783); mother of Charles the Younger, Pepin of Italy, Louis the Pious, and six more children

Himiltrude First wife of Charlemagne (768–770); mother of Pepin the Hunchback

Hugh of Saint-Quentin Illegitimate son of Charlemagne; abbot of Saint-Quentin; close confidant of Louis the Pious after 830; killed by great-nephew Pepin II of Aquitaine

Hugh of Tours Powerful noble under Louis the Pious; dishonored after failed expedition to Barcelona in 827; helped lead insurrections against Louis the Pious in 830 and 833; father-in-law to Emperor Lothar I

Irene Byzantine empress 797–802; took throne from her son; created brief marriage alliance with Charlemagne until ca. 780

Judith of Bavaria Second wife of Louis the Pious (819–843); mother of Charles the Bald

Leo III Pope 795–816; crowned Charlemagne emperor in 800

Lothar I Eldest son of Louis the Pious; emperor 840–855

Louis the German Son of Louis the Pious; king of East Francia 840–876

Louis the Pious Youngest legitimate son of Charlemagne; inherited Frankish Empire from father; emperor 814–840

Matfrid of Orléans Powerful noble under Louis the Pious; dishonored after failed expedition to Barcelona in 827; helped lead insurrections against Louis the Pious in 830 and 833

Nithard Grandson of Charlemagne; in service of Charles the Bald; wrote history of the civil war

Odo of Orléans Cousin of Bernard of Septimania; given county of Orléans from Matfrid in 829; killed by Matfrid in 834

Otgar of Mainz Archbishop of Mainz; sided with rebels in 833; enemy of Louis the German

Paschasius Radbertus Monk and follower of Wala; wrote screed against Judith and Bernard to justify rebellions in 830 and 833

Pepin the Short First Carolingian king of Franks 751–768; overthrew previous dynasty (Merovingians) in coup

Pepin I of Aquitaine Son of Louis the Pious; king of Aquitaine; led rebellion of 830; died 838

Pepin II of Aquitaine Son of Pepin I; disinherited by Louis the Pious; led rebellion in Aquitaine until his death in 864

Pepin II of Italy Son of Hildegard by Charlemagne; died 810

Pepin the Hunchback Eldest son of Charlemagne; led failed coup against father in 792; died 811

Thegan Churchman; wrote biography of Louis the Pious circa 837; sympathetic to Louis the German

Wala Cousin of Charlemagne; preeminent adviser during emperor's last years; exiled repeatedly by Louis the Pious

Wiggo Demon

William of Septimania Son of Bernard and Dhuoda; recipient of long letter from mother with advice on surviving at court; hostage of Charles the Bald; killed in rebellion at Barcelona in 850

Oathbreakers

A Feast for Vultures and Wolves

Late in the afternoon on Saturday, June 25, 841, a nobleman named Angelbert fled with his emperor from the battlefield east toward the imperial city of Aachen. Not long into the journey, days before he reached Aachen, he sat in his tent, listening to the groans of the wounded who had been carried in wagons from the field, the whinnies of the exhausted horses, and the clink of metal on metal as patrols warily kept watch for pursuing enemies. Perhaps even before the blood had been cleaned from his blade, he began to write a poem to help him remember what he had seen. What had happened was too important. He needed his audience to remember the horrors of the terrible slaughter he had witnessed—and participated in—at the Battle of Fontenoy.

> *Let not that accursed day be counted in the calendar of the year,*
> *Rather let it be erased from all memory,*
> *May the sun's rays never fall there, may no dawn ever come to [end its endless] twilight.*

We know almost nothing about Angelbert other than what he tells us in this deeply learned and emotive poem: that he was a warrior and ninth-century nobleman. From this little bit, we can reconstruct more. We know that nobles such as Angelbert were no strangers to battle. For generations, men like him had fought together and

crushed their enemies, brought peoples across Europe to heel, celebrated victories, and shared in the spoils of war with their leaders. In
the process, those ancestors had built an empire that spanned Europe
and rivaled Rome at its height. Its frontiers extended from the North
Sea to beyond the Pyrenees, from Brittany's Atlantic coast to beyond
the Danube. They called themselves the Franks.

The Franks had built their empire first and foremost by accret-
ing power through military victory, piling conquered territories one
upon the other until their realm touched every surrounding sea.
Once they had their land, they stabilized their new territory and its
populace through ideological assimilation, providing pathways for
conquered peoples to themselves become "Frankish." And those conquered peoples did assimilate with stunning regularity throughout
the late eighth and early ninth centuries, wanting part of the spoils
of the expanding empire. The Franks won victory after victory; it
seemed clear that God favored them. That truth seemed manifest in
the breadth of their empire.

But the dust, the sweat, and the blood on Angelbert now told a
different story. These God-favored people had turned their swords
against one another. As Angelbert sat composing his poem, he knew
only that it was Frankish blood he would soon clean from his blade.
He must have feared it could be the blood of old friends.

The Frankish political and cultural consensus that had subjugated
a continent across the last two generations had fallen apart at the
seams. Angelbert had come to Fontenoy with the emperor Lothar I,
the eldest son of the recently deceased ruler Louis the Pious. Lothar
had been co-emperor with his father for the last twenty-four years
but was now facing off against his two younger brothers, their respective armies composed of families now torn asunder. Friends who
had so recently campaigned with, socialized with, and loved one another now stared across the battlefield with vengeance in their eyes.

Angelbert wasn't naive. Certainly, he knew there had been turbu-
lence across Francia (the land of the Franks) in the past. The men
of the ruling family had been at odds for more than a decade, and
the late emperor had put down—with some difficulty, it must be

said—numerous rebellious plots over that period. The Frankish people, united in culture and custom and ruling over almost half a continent, had never been divided on this scale though, and even when
division had reared its ugly head, it had never erupted into open warfare. It had never been as bad as this. Until now.

The mere experience of the battle was traumatic enough for Angelbert, but to make matters worse, the rebels had won. His emperor
had been defeated. The world was seemingly upside down. His poem
reflected back from the morning after the battle, weeping and cry-
ing out to the heavens even as he tried to soberly analyze what the
battle meant politically and also theologically. What harbingers did
it summon for an uncertain future? This was the question he tried
to answer. He emphasized that his leader, Lothar I, had lost only because he was betrayed. Lothar's brothers, kings Charles the Bald and
Louis the German, had turned the Franks against themselves. Hell
was open, and the devils were there. They stalked the fields of Francia, reveling in the carnage, the breaking of bonds of kingship, the
scenes of familial murder.

> When dawn with morning light divided off the foul night,
> That was not the Sabbath day, but Saturn's mixing-bowl.
> An ungodly demon delights over the brothers' broken peace.
> War screams aloud as here and there dire fighting breaks out,
> A brother readies death for his brother, an uncle for his nephew;
> Sons refuse to give to fathers what they deserve.
> No slaughter was ever worse on any field of war;
> The law of the Christians was shattered by this shedding of blood,
> Whence the company of hell and the mouth of Cerberus rejoice.

For Angelbert, Fontenoy was a crime—a shattering of not only
the law of man but the law of God. It was a crime so significant, so
pervasive, that the mouth of Hell had to stretch itself to take in all its
new inhabitants.

The poem concludes with the grief of the families for their lost,
suggesting that the toll was compounded by the mourning of not

only their own but those they knew on the other side. Their agony was deepened by the immensity of the violence. So many dead couldn't be buried quickly enough. Both sides had to watch their friends' bodies being desecrated. Angelbert, who says that he, "fighting alongside the others, saw this crime unfold," records vultures and wolves descending on the field to devour the corpses of friends and family. The very earth recoiled from the slaughter as he wrote (using the Latin verb *horreo* ["to tremble"], from which we derive our modern word *horror*) that "The fields tremble, the woods tremble, the very swamp trembles."

Angelbert's audience in ninth-century Francia, those earlier comrades in arms, now one another's murderers, had mostly known one another at the royal court of Lothar's father (and some of them even since the time of Lothar's grandfather Charlemagne). They had socialized and intermarried. They had been educated together. Their training, their profession, was warfare, but their culture was literary and religious, filled with history and poetry and a deep, abiding sense that the Franks played a crucial role in the movement of sacred history. They read the Bible and its commentaries and thought that stories from both Christian Old and New Testaments spoke to their own times. The Franks believed that God favored them so much that they were a new chosen people to replace the old—new Israelites. As such, Frankish authors, writing theology, history, and poetry, read the world around them for signs of God's work. And Angelbert found those signs, even if they weren't comforting.

One of the last lines of the poem is a dirge that echoes. "I shall not more fully describe the wailing and howling [of the Franks]: Let each hold back his sadness as well as he can." Here he is deliberately evoking a passage from the Christian Old Testament, Jeremiah 3, in which the prophet foretells a grim future, saying that Israel's sins will bring a terrible, bloody punishment upon it and that the people of the kingdom will "wail and howl" on the highways. Angelbert had seen that warning come true in June 841. The sins of his people, including (perhaps especially) their wicked rulers, had angered God and called down a terrible vengeance upon the Franks. In this way Angelbert tried to put the battle into a cosmic perspective. And the deafening silence of the poem's end was meant to enable the audience to feel more clearly the despair that their sins had wrought, the terrible punishment they had earned.

The wailing and howling after Fontenoy echoed down across the generations that followed. About a century later, a chronicler remembered that "in this battle the power of the Franks was so diminished, and their famous manhood so weakened, that thereafter they were incapable not only of expanding the kingdom, but also of defending its frontiers." In the twelfth century, a monastic chronicler described the violent conquest of Jerusalem by the Christians during the so-called First Crusade by looking backward for precedents. In 1099, just before the Christians massacred Muslims as they took the city of Jerusalem, that monk noted that a brilliant light illuminated the night sky on the day before the final battle, portending "a great outpouring of human blood." That prophetic sign was important for the author because he said it had happened only a few times before in human history—the first of which had been just before the "lamentable war between the sons of Louis the Pious." In other words, the author—inadvertently, perhaps, but with the benefit of much distance—had clearly seen something that Angelbert could only sense: Fontenoy and the Frankish Civil War had washed away an old world with blood and made something new. Europe would never be the same.

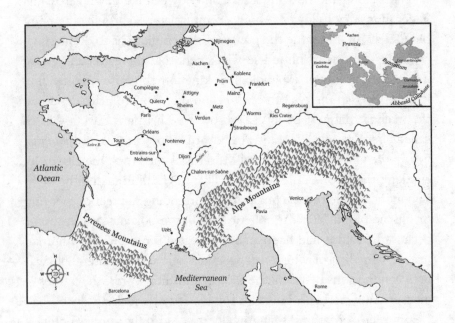

The Carolingian World ca. 800 CE, with selected important locations mentioned throughout the book

Origin Stories

732–750

Over the course of the eighth century, a group called the Franks built an empire with fire and sword. They expanded their borders, subjugated their enemies, and made alliances with their neighbors, including the powerful Byzantine emperors in Constantinople and the even more powerful caliphs in Baghdad. Under their leaders at the time, a family we know today as the Carolingians, the Franks would rule an expanse of land from beyond Rome in Italy to the North Sea and from beyond the Pyrenees in the west to beyond the Danube in the east. On Christmas Day 800, one of those rulers named Charlemagne (from the Latin *Carolus magnus*, or Charles the Great) was crowned by the bishop of Rome as a new Roman emperor.

But like all empires, this one rested on a foundation of lies. The Franks' power was real, yes, but their empire was built as much with quill and parchment as it was with iron and blood. The story they told about and to themselves in their histories, in their theological works, and in their art made it all seem so fated: their destiny as the new Israelites, the builders of the kingdom of God on Earth, seemed to manifest itself all too clearly into the early part of the ninth century. To create this story of themselves, dissension, revolts, and disasters that had been a reality from the outset of the Frankish imperial project were elided, silenced, papered over. They wrote backward from the present—from what they saw as the pinnacle—to make the past a predestined prelude to the present. The story they told themselves, in other words, was one that was never intended to be factual; it was intended to be *true*, to reveal a hidden divine plan they saw for themselves, to demonstrate that they were inevitable.

Apexes are precarious, though. Over the course of the ninth century, the tapestry of the Franks' history unraveled as quickly as it had come together. Military victories became harder to come by. Losses piled up. Fathers oppressed sons, or sons didn't show due respect (depending on perspective). The Franks' intellectual project to justify themselves continued but couldn't ultimately bear the weight of a crushing new reality. A vision of unity persevered even as the functioning of power and society factionalized. Angelbert's agony, written in the midst of a civil war when brothers turned blades upon brothers, leaps from its vellum and across the centuries to show us how the lies they told collapsed in on themselves.

Oathbreakers builds toward the critical years of 841–843, toward the horror of the Battle of Fontenoy. At that time, immediately after the death of Emperor Louis the Pious (d. 840), a civil war erupted within the Frankish realm as his sons fought one another for power. Much of the war was waged by proclamations and military maneuvers that were mostly posturing. Lothar I (d. 855), the eldest of the brothers and Angelbert's patron, inherited the imperial title after his father died and immediately claimed lordship over his younger siblings, Louis the German (d. 876) and Charles the Bald (d. 877). All three brothers wanted to maintain the illusion of unity—a fantasy required if the Franks truly held a special status—but the youngest brothers nonetheless wanted to rule independent kingdoms that had been carved out of imperial territory. Feints and provocations had characterized the last decade before their father's death, yet never had rebellion led to serious bloodshed. They had always pulled back from the brink.

Until they leapt off the cliff.

"Bloodless" became blood-soaked at the Battle of Fontenoy, where

the three brothers met in battle for the first time, in June 841. Angelbert was there and saw it all. Ostensibly, the civil war that came
to its bloody peak at Fontenoy would end with the famous Treaty
of Verdun in 843, often seen as the beginnings of the separate nations of France and Germany. But violence among the descendants
of Charlemagne would continue for generations. That "end" was just
a beginning, and each iteration of the conflict spawned its own set
of lies until the Carolingian Empire was no more and in its place
arose new families, kingdoms, peoples, who would look back on the
mighty Charlemagne and wonder how things had gone so wrong.

To understand how the sons of Louis the Pious arrived at a civil
war that no one had expected yet everyone had seen coming, we need
to begin our story at the moment the Carolingians took power and to
conclude with the legends that arose—largely in modernity—about
the Carolingians and their rule. By listening closely to our sources,
we'll see that the emergence of violence among the brothers during
the civil war was not so much an anomaly as it was a revelation of
a deeper truth, a series of events that punctured a bright, shining
lie that the Franks had been telling about themselves (and largely *to*
themselves). For the Franks, the eighth and especially ninth centuries
witnessed at once continuous violence and near-constant attempts to
create lasting peace in its aftermath; the creation of works of staggering artistic and philosophical genius and movements to suppress intellectual inquiry; political intrigues that would put any Shakespearean
play or TV drama series to shame; and breathtaking acts of charity
and solidarity. Those events also show how fragile even the mightiest
regime can be and how quickly it can fall apart.

Who were those people, the Franks? We know about them and how
they lived initially mostly through ancient Roman textual sources,
which reveal the group to have begun as a loose confederation of
people who lived near the mouth of the Rhine. Slowly, and often with
Roman imperial support, those groups moved westward across the

river and into imperial territory through the fourth and fifth centuries and settled, as largely dutiful Roman subjects, in the region roughly around the modern Low Countries, though deeper into Gaul (modern France) as well. Then, as centralized Roman authority receded back to the Italian Peninsula and eventually across the sea to Constantinople and Asia Minor (modern Turkey), subgroups of Franks established their own regional kingdoms: the largest being Austrasia, in the middle Rhine region and centered roughly around Metz, and Neustria, toward the Loire Valley and roughly centered around Paris. Burgundy, south of Neustria and approximately following the Saône River, was its own kingdom and close to the Frankish orbit, while Aquitaine, west of Burgundy and north of the Pyrenees, never became a kingdom even though it developed its own identity.

In part, after the retreat of centralized Roman authority in these regions, the story of the Franks became the story of their kings and their petty realms, each claiming independence, each still claiming to be part of the Roman Empire. At first there were many kings, but during

The separate Frankish kingdoms around the time of the Merovingians

the fifth century the most powerful of them arose out of Austrasia and was a member of the family known as the Merovingians. Contrary to some modern conspiracy theories that say the Merovingians were descendants of Jesus, the dynasty had its own non-Christian mythology. According to a seventh-century chronicler, the legendary hero-king Merovech, from whom the dynasty derived its name, was fathered by a sea monster who raped Merovech's mother while she was swimming one day. Historians like us are a little doubtful that that actually happened. More likely, that legendary origin story covered up a coup (or some other shenanigans) that brought him to power, an ascent now lost to history.

Nevertheless, Merovech's descendants would consolidate power across northwestern Europe, and their real takeoff as players on the regional stage would occur under his grandson King Clovis I (d. 511). There are two faces to this Clovis or two sides of the same coin we ought to consider when assessing his reign. He was, at least in part, merciless; according to the chronicler-bishop Gregory of Tours, Clovis was prone to smashing his enemies' skulls in when they displeased him. He was also an astute leader who used military power to intervene against his neighboring rulers at key moments, methodically expanding his own authority. He won traditional military victories against his fellow Franks, as well as groups to the south and east, but he also entered a civil war in Burgundy, and then rather quickly exited once he had extracted as a bride one of the ruler's daughters. That marriage reminds us that Clovis was a person who made choices. One of those was the decision, in part because of his wife, to publicly convert to Christianity not long after 500.

That last decision, his conversion, was strategically brilliant, gaining him powerful allies by linking him more closely to the neighboring Burgundians, as well as positioning himself as an ally of the Byzantines, who were still active in Italy at the time. Clovis used those relationships to help him crush the Christian Visigoths in Aquitaine in 507 and defeat rival Frankish leaders to the north and east not long afterward. By the time of Clovis's death in 511, the kingdom of the Franks stretched, under one leader, from the North Sea to the Pyrenees.

It wouldn't last, though. Clovis's four sons would, following Frankish tradition, redivide their father's holdings into their own separate kingdoms, and—also in the Frankish tradition, as we will come to see—the son's descendants would plot and scheme and murder one another for the next couple centuries. The Frankish kingdom would reform as one, split in the next generation, reunite, and split yet again. The kings always led the way in those maneuvers, yet the constant infighting had the perhaps unintended effect of elevating the importance of the nobility *around* the kings, the warrior class. Those nobles staffed and led their kings' armies, secured grants and favors from their rulers, and at times were more than willing to change sides if the rewards were juicy enough.

One such family, with a power base in Austrasia, alongside but separate from the Merovingians, managed to secure for themselves the court position of "mayors of the palace" during the middle of the seventh century. This family, initially known as the "Pippinids" (after one of their first prominent members, Pepin or Pippin I), would soon emerge as the real power behind the throne. It was the Pippinids who led the Frankish armies on behalf of the Merovingian kings of Austrasia, they who doled out spoils, they who moved warriors' loyalties away from the kings to themselves.

By the 720s, the Merovingians were kings mostly in name only. When Theuderic IV died in 737, no one bothered to succeed him. Charles Martel, the head of the Pippinid family and mayor of the palace at the time, was firmly in control. Only in 743, after Charles Martel's death and in the midst of a brewing civil war among his sons, would the royal throne be reoccupied by a young Merovingian named Childeric III. But his reign wouldn't last, either. By 750, a Merovingian was no longer needed. One of the Pippinids, member of a family now known to history as Carolingians (after Charles [Karolus] Martel), having grown tired of being the power behind the throne, took it for himself.

❈

The story of the rise of Charles Martel, hence the story of the Carolingians, begins with a battle. It's a famous battle. In 732, a Frankish
army under Charles Martel—Charles the Hammer—met and defeated,
somewhere between Tours and Poitiers, an Islamic force sent north
by the Islamic governor of al-Andalus, the Arabic name for the recently conquered Iberian Peninsula. That did happen. But the story
of that battle is often set, especially by eighteenth- and nineteenth-
century European historians, in an imagined world divided between
Frank and Arab, Christian and Muslim. And that's just not true.

As recently as the year before the fateful battle at Tours, Martel
had been fighting in Aquitaine to assert power over its ruler, a fellow
Christian. We tend to think today of the Pyrenees as a great divider
within Europe, but then, as now, people moved around. The Christian ruler of Aquitaine had strong ties in Iberia, even marrying his
daughter to a regional Islamic lord there who was in revolt against
the governor of al-Andalus, 'Abd al-Rahman. So in 732, al-Rahman
sent a force across the Pyrenees and into Aquitaine to plunder his
enemy's lands. Let's be clear: it wasn't a war of conquest nor in any
sense a holy war but rather one of politics. The Islamic raiding party
won a great battle at Bordeaux and then headed north. The Christian ruler fled before them and begged Charles Martel for help. And
Charles was only too happy to march south and assert his own dominance over the region. And so, near the city of Tours, the Frankish
army defeated the Islamic force from Iberia.

That was no "clash of civilizations"; it was little more than a skirmish. But in that skirmish, if we look closely, we can see a permeable
early-medieval world in which it was normal for Christians to fight
one another for dominance, normal for Muslims fight one another,
and normal for a Christian ruler to ally himself with his Islamic neighbors. None of those peoples existed in a world of binaries but rather
in one of political, social, and religious complexities. Throughout
Oathbreakers, as we trace the paths of Charles Martel's descendants,
we must always recognize that the Carolingians lived in a world of
many regions, peoples, faiths, and polities. Those regions saw their

own stories playing out, often in ways that impacted the others, but those are not our story.

Still, let's follow the retreating Muslim army south for a moment to see the broader region both as historians know it to have been and as the Franks, our protagonists, understood it, starting with Iberia. For centuries, the peninsula had been ruled by Visigothic kings from one of the many Germanic-Roman hybrid states that emerged in the fifth and sixth centuries, much as the Merovingians had farther north. But in 711, a small invading force of Arab and Berber fighters crossed the Strait of Gibraltar, perhaps to intervene on behalf of one pretender to the Visigothic throne but ultimately serving as the vanguard of a much larger army from North Africa. By 713, much of the Iberian Peninsula had been conquered and transformed into a province of the great Umayyad Caliphate, ruled from Damascus. Iberia was, however, a long way from Syria and so, like many parts of the far-flung Islamic empire, operated as a semi-independent state.

That independence only intensified after 750, when a new dynasty, the Abbasids, overthrew the Umayyads and eventually moved the imperial capital to Baghdad and stretched its sphere of influence far into Central Asia. But one Umayyad escaped from the coup in Syria, fled across North Africa, and eventually (in an epic story but, alas, not ours to tell here) took over most of Iberia and established the Emirate of Córdoba. Sometimes those various polities would be aggressive foes of the Franks, sometimes they would ally with one Carolingian or another, and sometimes they would watch bemusedly from the sidelines. But throughout, the Iberian Peninsula was a land of Christians, Muslims, and Jews; Visigoths, Iberians, Arabs, Berbers, and of course Franks.

The Frankish army of 732 didn't pursue its defeated foes into Iberia. Charles Martel had other, more pressing, concerns closer to his home base in Austrasia. As did his successors, he spent much of his time on campaign, pressing Frankish claims outward in almost every direction. He fought polytheistic Frisians to the north and pagan Saxons to the east, fellow Christians in Burgundy and Aquitaine, as well as the Lombards, who controlled northern Italy and often menaced the bishops of Rome.

The Lombards had moved into northern Italy in the late sixth century and at first competed primarily with the Byzantines for control of regions in the north, centered around Milan, Pavia, and Ravenna. As Byzantine power waned, Lombard power grew and a separate Lombard Kingdom took shape in the south of Italy around Spoleto and Benevento. That squeezed Rome. Without military support from Constantinople in the eighth century, it made sense for the bishops of Rome to look for allies in the Franks as the preeminent power north of the Alps. We will see how that story played out when we turn to Charles's heir, Pepin the Short. The Lombards wouldn't go quietly, though.

Neither would the Byzantines. They held tight to their aspirations of reconquering Italy and restoring the grandeur of the Western Roman Empire. In the eighth century, the Byzantine Empire ruled a reasonably healthy, if diminished, expanse of territories across Asia Minor and southeastern Europe from the fabulous city of Constantinople. Their wealth and prestige as continuators of the Roman Empire ensured their continued political and military influence. Throughout our period, messages, goods, and peoples moved among Byzantium, Rome, and Francia, with all powers very much aware of what the others were doing—so much so, in fact, that Frankish theologians paid close attention to internal religious tensions in Constantinople, and when, in the later eighth century, Byzantium was racked by a religious schism and a group called *iconoclasts*, or icon breakers, who argued against image use in worship, took the imperial throne, they saw a rhetorical opening for the Franks.

The bishops of Rome rejected iconoclasm. It was heresy, they said, to destroy holy images or even to deny their efficacy as symbols in worship. Both sides spent much time writing diatribes against the other, at times even excommunicating the other side's bishops, fighting for power via theology and symbol with just as much ferocity as on the battlefield. Into that breach stepped the Franks. Indeed, it was the new alliance between Carolingians and the papacy, a useful story for both sides about who should be king, that spawned *Oathbreakers*.

❖

European historians during the age of colonialism and imperialism, the eighteenth and nineteenth centuries, saw the Carolingians as bringing order to chaos, as taking the reins from the ineffectual Merovingians and creating something that would necessarily evolve into the modern nation-state. Such modern historians held up a mirror to the past, looking for their own reflections in the people they saw as the best, the brightest, the fiercest, the ones who embodied virtues they themselves claimed. Who better, for those moderns, than the Franks under the Carolingians? But when you're telling a story, every rise has to have a fall, every rebirth is followed by a death. Those modern historians explicitly lamented the missed "takeoff," the chance to establish a new lasting empire in the ninth century, and the fact that the story of the Franks under the Carolingians was "emplotted"— because it was a *story* those modern scholars told and so it needed a plot!—as a tragedy. Tragedies are recognizable in their structure, with a compelling cast of characters, a promise of something great, and then some misfortune that dooms the project, leaving their audience wondering what might have been. In this version of the telling, the Franks had laid the seeds of European greatness that should have fruited but instead, because of the civil war of the 840s, took several more centuries to germinate. Alas and alack.

This wasn't an invention created merely in modernity by starry-eyed nationalists, however. That would be too easy; history is many things, but it's never easy. Instead, it was a recursive fiction, a narrative that doubled back on itself to reinforce its claims. That supposedly necessary ascent was first created by the Franks themselves as part of the Carolingians' self-fashioning that tried to hide how they had violently taken power and had made certain that other events disappeared from the record. And to the end, all the way to the twenty-first century, the stories about that empire's rise and fall have rippled through history, repurposed and retold in ways that support contemporary agendas, often concealing what we can know about the past.

As such, as we move forward, we must be aware that our sources, like most of those from medieval Europe, are not transparent windows into the past. Ninth-century Frankish sources pose particular problems because their authors were very conscious of what they were doing: investing heavily in history, writing in order to ensure that they were remembered as they wished to be. They wanted their contemporaries and successors to think of the Franks as God's new chosen people, whose favor had been proven by victory in battle, intellectual achievements, and a stable politics and culture. Ideology, as much as armies, bound the Franks together in the late eighth and ninth centuries.

Throughout the book, we'll show how we can sift through these problematic sources and still uncover what was really going on. Even as we move toward a bloody civil war and the breakdown of an empire, we won't script it as a tragedy. As we did in *The Bright Ages*, we'll instead show the choices that people had, the reasons they made the decisions they did, and how things could have been otherwise.

Oathbreakers has a cast of characters (many named Pepin, Louis, or Charles). It has misfortunes and triumphs aplenty. But their story was never inevitable, as no human history ever is. We bring together the best current research with a vast array of primary sources from the period in order to be honest about who the Carolingians were, why the empire rose, why it descended into civil war, and what happened afterward. Medieval Europeans were not automatons running a sort of script so that the world would inevitably arrive at European modernity. People in the past were human beings who made choices and who could have made different ones. They didn't always understand the repercussions of their choices, but sometimes they did, and sometimes they lied about them to themselves and others. Our sources from the period can tell us much more about who those people were, as long as we listen attentively to what they were trying to say and try to understand why.

In *Oathbreakers*, we'll see an empire emerge under Carolingian kings, but one that was born from a bloody coup and that, even at its height, was only superficially united by an ideological project based around a particular Christian vision. The ruling family was never postcard perfect. None ever is, despite their protestations. Rebellions and dissent continued throughout. These disruptions were papered over by an intellectual project built upon a politics, culture, and religion that in most cases adapted artfully to changing circumstances. It seemed, both to outsiders and even to the Frankish political elites themselves, that their empire had emerged from great military victories and then was a city on a hill beset by (at times supposedly demonic) external enemies. At the center of power, the Franks created a political and social consensus among their elites and even a common cultural experience centered around the capital.

But then, during a period of acute political and cultural crisis, that ideological consensus ran aground. Latent tensions about the role of the government coalesced into factions, and then, after the ruler died, a disputed succession very quickly erupted into violence. This empire, this violence, and what came next were never inevitable but the product of choices made by people who could have done—and often almost did do—otherwise. But their decisions nevertheless set the course of history.

The story of the Franks in the ninth century is one of an empire and its dissolution, a story of kings and queens, of soldiers and traitors, of priests and witches, but most of all of people trying to understand their world. Throughout it all, the mass of people suffered when aristocrats stopped caring for the public good and pursued their own game of thrones. This is a story and warning that may feel all too familiar to modern readers; political consensus, the sense that even if various powers are striving against one another, the basic functioning of society is secure, can collapse all too quickly with terrible results.

In 843, in the midst of the civil war, a noblewoman named Dhuoda sent a long letter to her son William, who was being held hostage to ensure his father's support for one of the warring brothers. In her preface, she wrote, "Although I am besieged by many troubles, may this one thing be God's will, if it please him—that I might see you again with my own eyes. . . . But since salvation is far from me, sinful woman that I am, I only wish it, and my heart grows weak in this desire." We know rather little about Dhuoda, but we know that she loved and she mourned, just as Angelbert did for his friends and family killed not long before Dhuoda wrote. We also know that she almost certainly never saw her son again.

In the end, the history we will tell of the Franks isn't a tragedy, nor is it a comedy; rather, it is a story that encompasses the full range of the human experience. It's one of love and hate, despair and hope, and one, as Dhouda and Angelbert show us, that's best heard through the voices of those who lived it.

ACT I

An Empire of Lies

CHAPTER I

Discontent and Disinheritance

750–792

The priest lay beneath the altar in the darkened church, listening to men scheme and plot. He knew their voices. Charlemagne (Charles the Great) and his court had spent more than a year residing at the Bavarian palace in Regensburg, using it as a base of operations for military expeditions against the Saxons to the north and from which to assert authority over the fiercely independent Frankish nobles in the region. The court was a small world, riven by factions but still intimate; the men and women in it all knew one another. It was not odd for groups to gather unexpectedly, but not often in a church and almost never in the middle of the night. Only the grace of God had given the priest a moment of warning—an instinct to hide—before the group of nobles could see him. Now only the thin altar cloth concealed him as he listened.

He bit his lip to stifle a gasp as he recognized the voice of Pepin, Charlemagne's eldest son. He nearly fainted as the men spoke, and the reason for the assembly, in the middle of the night in his church, dawned on him. The priest prayed silently, eyes screwed shut, as Pepin told his allies that they would seize the king, his father, and murder him. Pepin would then claim the throne.

Maybe at that the priest gasped a little too audibly in horror. As the meeting came to its conclusion, Pepin ordered the church searched, and the conspirators, poking into every corner, eventually looked under the altar. When they found the cleric, he was sure his days on Earth had come to an end and resolved to try to face the fact bravely.

But in the early Middle Ages it was one thing to plot the murder of a king, quite another to slaughter a priest in his own chapel. What's more, should such a blasphemy be discovered, if the priest were missed, the ensuing investigation or alarm could endanger the conspiracy. So two men grabbed the priest and held him tightly as Pepin offered him a choice: the priest could die right there, right then, or he could swear a sacred oath of silence—which of course as a priest he would be expected to keep. Ashamed and terrified, the priest swore the oath and then collapsed into himself, a wreck, as the nobles and their conspirator prince left the church.

Is an oath made under duress really an oath? the priest asked himself. Would it not be a greater sin to keep quiet than to cling to sacrilegious words forced from his lips? Would it not be better to, in other words, break that false oath? The priest decided, as soon as he was sure the conspirators had really departed, that it would. He would risk his soul to try to save the king.

That same night, the priest ran to the palace. But it was late, and one does not simply walk into the king's bedroom. In fact, the priest discovered that the chamber lay at the heart of the building and was guarded by seven locked doors, all staffed by loyal guards. The great Charlemagne may not have suspected his son's perfidy, but plenty of people might try to harm him and his family. By God's grace, so the story goes, the priest found a way in, wriggling through windows and drainage ditches, ripping his vestments, until, clad only in a linen shirt and undergarments and filthy from head to toe, he found himself at the threshold of the king's chamber, banging on the door.

Within a few moments, court attendants arrived to see who would dare disturb the royal household at that late hour. The women laughed to see such a seemingly deranged individual demanding an audience with the king. They mocked him, then slammed the door and relocked it, intending to simply leave the matter there. But the king was ever vigilant, ever wakeful. He emerged and demanded to know the cause of the commotion. When he heard about the wild man, he sensed that something was amiss and ordered the man to be brought before him. The priest threw himself at the king's feet and told him everything. The plotters were captured and swiftly punished. Some were exiled, all had their property confiscated, and Pepin was sent away to the abbey of Prüm and forced to take monastic vows, destined to live out the rest of his life in penance and seclusion, unable to inherit the throne he so craved.

❧

This attempted coup against Charlemagne, launched by his son Pepin and other Frankish nobles in the year 792, was recorded in several contemporary sources, but the version recounted here comes to us from nearly a century later, written by a monk and historian, Notker the Stammerer. This is by far the most detailed and dramatic account of the plot we have but also one of the most distant from the events in question. Indeed, it's so vivid that we can almost be certain it never happened that way.

There absolutely was an attempted coup in 792. Notker described it as serious in intent but quickly squashed. Charlemagne, as king and father, had no need to make an example of the conspirators by drenching either the city of Regensburg or the region of Bavaria in blood but instead used the occasion to demonstrate his wisdom and mercy. So in Notker's version of the story, the punishment for conspiring to murder the king was that several high-ranking Frankish nobles lost major tracts of land, some were also exiled, and Pepin, who by the time Notker wrote was remembered as an evil, ill-tempered, misshapen, bastard son of a concubine, was packed off to monastic seclusion. Frankish writers such as Notker expanded upon a later description of Pepin as a "hunchback" by turning it into an epithet, using a perceived outward physical difference to serve as a sign of inward moral turpitude, even evil. Charlemagne would then be seen as insightful and willing to listen to his loyal subjects, betrayed by his son but ever watchful and temperate enough in judgment to seek restoration rather than retribution once the danger had been averted.

But the threat to Charlemagne was much more dangerous than Notker let on. First, the conspirators were actually willing to kill him. Second, far from being an unprecedented demonstration of disloyalty by fractious nobles and an unfit son—unfit due to stigma around disability and also his designation as a bastard—this type of maneuvering was not out of the ordinary. The Frankish Kingdom was prone to moments of volatility; Frankish sons of the royal household had a tradition of plotting against their fathers. But the story of the Franks, the story of a people who thought themselves chosen by God as they built an empire, required concealing how tenuous the whole enterprise actually was, both at the moment of the threat and for several generations after.

The idea of a unified Frankish kingdom was always more argument than fact. This is why our sources from the period portray Pepin's actions in 792 as both threatening and ephemeral. The king and his supporters needed to kill the story of disloyalty and instability as much as they needed to kill the plot itself. In the early Middle Ages as today, a ruler might not be able to ignore such a public event, but he could do everything in his power to shape the meaning that people took from the event. Here, the Franks needed desperately to keep pretending that the empire, at least under Charlemagne, was stable and secure, and so that was the story Notker told. But in fact, Pepin's revolt shows that even at its most powerful, its most grand, the Carolingian dynasty rested on a cracked foundation.

The ripple effects of the coup attempt continued for years, though not always poorly for the conspirators. Those who had not been maimed or killed could, with the passage of time and if they had sufficient wealth and political influence, be restored to Charlemagne's favor. The kings of the Franks needed their nobles, in some ways more than the other way around. The same, however, cannot be said for Pepin, who largely vanishes from our sources and into the realm of the imagination—save a notice of his death in 811, a miracle story from 839 about a saint leading the heirs of Charlemagne to a path that could have created a lasting peace, and a Broadway musical produced in 1972.

❖

Before we return to 792 and a son seeking to overthrow his father, hoping to take advantage of the ongoing political and military crises (there were always crises), we must look at how the Carolingians came to power in the first place. Or, better, we need to look at how the Carolingians told themselves a story of how they had come to power in the first place.

We learn that story in large part from a text now known as the *Royal Frankish Annals* (*RFA*). Annals, more or less bullet-pointed lists of years with "important" events listed thereafter, were one of the most common forms of historical writing among the eighth-century Franks. These sources often come across as objective records, but there is a method and a message in each annal entry because the annalist was almost never recording events as they happened. Instead, the text was usually written long afterward—a conscious selection of events meant to highlight them (by their inclusion) or silence them (by their exclusion). In other words, the purpose of the annals was to control how the story was told, a power that medieval authors wielded both eagerly and with considerable skill.

The authors of the *Royal Frankish Annals* were very, very good at framing Pepin's story. Their identities are unknown, but the text was almost certainly created at Charlemagne's court. The writers projected the message of the emperor outward, detailing moments not necessarily chosen *by* Charlemagne but certainly chosen *for* him. Specifically, the *RFA* has an entry for every year between 741 and 829, beginning with the death of Charles Martel and the assumption of power by Pepin the Short, and then ending in the middle of the reign of Charles's great-grandson Louis the Pious (specifically the appointment of Bernard of Septimania as the emperor's chamberlain—remember that name). There's an entry for every year. With two exceptions.

The only years missing from the *RFA* are 751 and 752, the years immediately after Pepin the Short declared his intention to overthrow the Merovingian king Childeric III and take the crown for himself.

Those pivotal years, the founding moments of the Carolingian dynasty, were erased from the permanent and official record, a gaping hole that speaks loudly to us across the chasm of more than a millennium. For many years, even through much of modernity, the story was that Pepin had seized power in a bloodless coup in which the last Merovingian king, already weak and relatively powerless, had shrugged his shoulders and toddled off to a monastery to spend the rest of his life in seclusion. But one of our main sources on this event, and the one most directly connected to the glorious rise of the Merovingians' successors, is empty, an erasure that tells us something important about that transition of power. The great rulers of the Frankish Empire once again hid the violence in the great story of Carolingian ascendance.

But there are no bloodless coups.

So what can we say about Pepin the Short's decision to take the crown from the Merovingians? At the time of the coup, Pepin was mayor of the palace, acting as a sort of prime minister at the Merovingian court—a military leader who mediated between the nobility and the king. But he shared that position with his elder brother, Carloman. Because Pepin at the time had no children but did have an older brother, things actually didn't look all that promising for his future. But fortunes can change in a moment. In 747, for reasons largely unknown, Pepin's brother withdrew from public life to take up the monastic vocation. Pepin's decision to maneuver against the Merovingian king was likely spurred not only by his desire for the throne but also by his need to shore up his position against his brother's family. The immediate impetus was the birth of Pepin's first son, the future Charlemagne, circa 748. That gave Pepin prospects for the future. But the king and Pepin's nephews, who were prominent at the royal court, stood in his way. So Pepin found other allies, namely the bishops of Rome, who were willing to work with him because they needed allies against the Lombards.

By 749, Pepin felt secure enough in his position to, according to the *RFA*, send a delegation to the bishop of Rome to ask a loaded question: the delegation wondered aloud about who should rule a kingdom, those who held the title by birth or those who wielded "actual power." This was surely a rehearsed moment, and so Pope Zachary (d. 752) astutely read the room and answered that of course it should be the latter. This was all Pepin needed. The Frankish delegation returned happily to Francia and, according to the last entry before the gap in the annals, Pepin was "peacefully" elected king by the Frankish nobles in 750 and the Merovingian king was sent to a monastery. That's where the *RFA* goes silent. The entries resume with 753, when Pepin won a great victory over the Saxons, heard the news of his half brother Grifo's death, and later that year forged an alliance with the new pope who had succeeded Zachary.

We really don't know a lot about what happened in 751–752, but it seems safe to guess that the intervening years were violent and so intentionally silenced by the *RFA*. For example, we know that in 753, in addition to the death (or maybe murder) of his half brother, Pepin's nephew Drogo of Metz was also sent to a monastery. That meant that, conveniently, all of Pepin's familial rivals were now out of the way and his place was secure. That same year, the pope not only wrote to the Franks telling them (again) to back Pepin but even crossed the Alps himself to parrot the line. The next year, at a lavish ceremony at Saint-Denis, an important church and monastery just north of Paris, Pope Stephen II anointed Pepin with oil, resurrecting the ritual that had, according to tradition, been used to sacralize the biblical kings of Israel but had almost never been used in medieval Europe prior to that moment.

Taken together, these little snippets do not convey the idea of a secure and stable transition of power from the Merovingians to Pepin. Instead, they speak to a violent and prolonged, but textually hidden, civil war. And while some civil wars are fought with huge armies in pitched battles, others involve daggers in the night, sudden ambushes, and shocking betrayals. We can't know which it was in 751–752, but we do know that once enough blood had been shed, all efforts in 753–754 under the new king were dedicated to smoothing over the transition with both quills and swords. The Franks were beginning to tell themselves stories, cloaking the disorder of their times behind a wall of vellum.

But time can be a flat circle. Not quite two decades later, another
Frankish king needed help against his rival brother and another pope
needed help against the Lombards. Pope Stephen III (768–772) had
ascended to the papacy through chaos and bloodshed, installed on
the throne of St. Peter by a faction of Roman administrators and
bureaucrats who had successfully defeated—and in one case tortured
and maimed—two other would-be popes. Their backers show the
complicated politics of Rome at the time. One of Stephen's rivals
was supported by the local nobility, a powerful force that controlled
the day-to-day functioning of the city. Unfortunately, that candidate
was the one who was blinded and whose tongue was cut out. This
happened not infrequently in early-medieval papal elections.

Yet by the time Stephen III was elected, the Lombards, despite
Frankish pressure, had not surrendered their aspiration to extend
their influence toward Rome. That became a particularly acute problem in 768, the same year Stephen III took the papal throne, because
Pepin the Short died. His sons, Charles (long before he got even close
to the greatness that would later lead him to be known as Charlemagne) and Carloman, immediately settled into an uneasy co-rule.
There was tension, in no small part because Charles was rumored
to be considering putting away his current wife in order to marry a
Lombard princess and thereby gain a powerful ally. So Stephen immediately wrote the brothers a letter about the proposed nuptials.
He was, to put it mildly, not pleased with the idea. "The Devil alone
could have suggested a thing, since this would not be a marriage,
but a shameful association. It was madness to attempt a union with
the noble race of the Franks and that fetid brood of the Lombards, a
brood hardly human." He continued on to fulminate against the evils
of divorce and threaten the Frankish rulers with excommunication.
Stephen III really, really didn't like the Lombards. But it was what
came next in the letter that interests us here. The pope claimed that
the marriage proposal was also a bad idea because Charles and Carloman were both already "united in marriage to beautiful Frankish
women, to whom you ought to hold tight in love."

The beautiful Frankish woman united with Charlemagne was

none other than the noblewoman Himiltrude. Later authors, almost always writing after the failed coup attempt in 792, would describe Himiltrude as, at best, a concubine and their son, Pepin, as a bastard born out of wedlock. But we need to understand that medieval heterosexual relationships (like most marriage traditions in history) were not a simple binary between single and married. Instead, we should think of early European medieval marriage as existing on a continuum in which relationships could exist in all kinds of formal and informal ways. For Frankish elites such as the Carolingians, marriages could be formed or unformed swiftly and without too much stigma. That would begin to change later in the Middle Ages as the Church hierarchy began to insert itself more formally into couples' relationships. But certainly in the eighth century in Francia, sexual relationships and the status of the children they produced were, let's say, flexible. This meant, too, that the ability of children to inherit could also be flexible and depend greatly on the needs or politics of a specific moment. So whether Pepin—or the child of any noble—was "really" legitimate or not depended primarily on that ruler's desire and his power to execute that desire. In other words, legitimacy and marital status were arguments to be made, rather than states that simply existed. And in 768, Pope Stephen III called Himiltrude a beautiful Frankish wife who had given Charles a son and heir.

In the end, Charlemagne ignored Stephen and married a Lombard princess. But we know very little about that marriage—not even the bride's name—because it lasted only a year (we told you early medieval marriage was flexible). By 771, Charlemagne's brother was dead and Charlemagne's focus had turned back to the Frankish heartlands and securing his brother's kingdom for himself. Therefore, his next wife was a Frankish noblewoman named Hildegard, whose family held important lands in his brother's former domain. Together, they had nine children in just over ten years, including three sons: Charles, Carloman, and Louis. We'll hear much more about them in the next chapter, but briefly, the eldest of them, Charles (called "the Younger") spent his years near the imperial court but never married and died without children while his father was still alive. The youngest, Louis, became "the Pious" and was the only one to outlive his father, thus inheriting the empire.

The middle child, Carloman, is more interesting for us right now because he didn't keep his name for very long. In the year 781, Charlemagne left his eldest sons—Pepin the Hunchback, age thirteen, and Charles the Younger, age nine—at his palace in Worms and took his other two sons—four-year-old Carloman and three-year-old Louis—to Rome to celebrate Easter. On its face, this made sense. Medieval childhood was often thought of as divided into stages, with infancy extending to about seven, then childhood from there until about fifteen. As such, Carloman and Louis were both infants and needed a lot of looking after.

We can imagine the scene of the two toddling little children, dressed in finery, attending Mass in the old St. Peter's Basilica. The mammoth basilica had been built more than four hundred years before by Emperor Constantine I. It was cold and drafty, and the smell of heavy incense hung in the air. Perhaps they stood quietly by their father's side, alongside their parents and minders, or perhaps they behaved like normal children their age and refused to be still or be quiet. Medieval children liked to play. Medieval parents, even or especially powerful ones, might look on fondly. Even in church.

The ritual continued regardless, appealing to all the senses, one of many moments in church, council chamber, and battlefield that we'll encounter over the course of our story. The Mass began with chant and then a great procession passed, led by Pope Hadrian I (772–795). Latin chant echoed throughout the space, amplified by the acoustics of the stone. The sweet smell of incense intensified. Everything seemed to be building toward something. Charles and Hildegard were beaming but tense. The children were delighted or bored. But they were the main attraction; toward the end of the service, the pope went to his honored guests, holy water and holy oil in hand, to anoint the young ones, "the Lord Pepin to be king of Italy and the Lord Louis to be king of Aquitaine." Carloman had become a new Pepin, rebaptized by Hadrian I as the child's parents looked on proudly. And yes, this is our third Carolingian Pepin, our third Carloman, and our third Charles. And there will be more.

Historians have been debating the impetus behind the name change for a long time, and we will likely never know some of the details. But names signaled intent. There is some evidence that the whole thing started as Pope Hadrian's idea. Pepin the Short had defeated the Lombards and given some of the captured territory to Pope Stephen II in the 750s. Then in turn, that Pepin had been anointed king by the pope in 754, thus cementing the legitimacy of the Carolingians' coup. Three decades later, with Charlemagne ready to place the toddler symbolically in charge of Italy, renaming the child Pepin could have been an attempt to symbolically renew the Frankish-papal alliance while making it clear to the Lombards that they were on the outside looking in.

But Charlemagne, too, was alert to the importance of names. He had surrounded himself with philosophers such as Alcuin of York, who believed in the Neoplatonic connection of symbol to thing. Renaming in this way is a kind of magic, in this case a ritual alchemical transformation of a child into his grandfather, into the embodiment of the idea of Frankish rule over Italy. In taking on the new name, the child was literally being changed. Carloman was a family name, but one associated with Charlemagne's dead brother. Pepin was a king's name and the name of a papal ally. Both pope and king got what they needed from the ritual.

But as names are given, they can also be taken away or at least eclipsed. We haven't forgotten that there already was a son named Pepin in Charlemagne's family. It's unclear in 781 what Charlemagne's plans were for his eventual succession, but the king was probably in his late thirties, so we can guess, both from what he had experienced with his father and from what happened later, that he was indeed thinking even at this time about how to divide power across a wide territory. The baptism and coronation didn't necessarily mean that

Charlemagne planned to cut the elder Pepin out of the succession entirely, but it probably didn't seem great from the latter's perspective. His royal name, his pride of place as elder son, his identity were being threatened as news came back to him from across the Alps. The elder Pepin may have been many things, but he surely wasn't naive.

We can't know for sure why Pepin the Hunchback might have participated in or led or been roped into a coup attempt against his father eleven years later, but it's not hard to imagine him reading the writing on the wall, recognizing the threat that sharing his name meant for his fortunes, and so he was at least willing to listen, a decade later, when a group of Frankish nobles approached him about a regime change.

It's easy to look at a king and a court and see unity. But in the lightning flashes of violence and plot, the fissures in the facade become visible; we can see the people, the families, the generations, the factions, and all the ways a political project can be at risk of collapsing. This will be true again and again in our story, often with husbands, wives, and children playing a key role in determining the shape of factions. So let's back up to be clear where we are. Pepin the Hunchback, son of Himiltrude, was born in 768, and as we emerge from 781, he's yet to be formally placed into the realm's governance structure. His younger brothers, the sons of Queen Hildegard, have already been granted kingdoms of their own. When their mother died and Charlemagne married his fourth wife, Fastrada, she continued to back Hildegard's children and favor them over the elder Pepin for reasons that aren't entirely clear. It seemed to be a tense but manageable state of affairs in the decade after that fateful Roman adventure. But a great vortex of events came swirling around in 792. The facade cracked, and the dynastic edifice almost came tumbling down.

In the Frankish Kingdom, factional lines often broke regionally. As we noted, Austrasia and Neustria had their own identities, but more striking were places such as Aquitaine, Burgundy, Saxony, and in this case Bavaria, home to the city of Regensburg. The Carolingians had taken control of Bavaria only in 788. The duchy had been a bit of a thorn in the Franks' side. It was ruled by a powerful family that stood on a par with the Carolingians themselves and also intermarried with them. Charles Martel's daughter had married Duke Odilo of Bavaria, so when Charlemagne took the region in 788, the person he had removed from power was his first cousin. The former duke was confined thereafter to the Monastery of St. Goar, a dependent house of the Abbey of Prüm. Direct control of the duchy by the Carolingians massively expanded their control over the region but brought with it other problems, including hostile non-Christian groups farther to the east (including the Slavs and Avars) and a seminative, resentful aristocracy with now-disrupted lines of patronage and access to power. When the plot was uncovered in 792, Charlemagne had been in Regensburg for more than a year, dealing with both of those issues.

But there's another reason why Charlemagne would have been in Regensburg in 792. That year was also important because his son Pepin of Italy (formerly Carloman) would turn fifteen and therefore reach his majority. He would, in other words, be able to act on his own, create his own court and advisers, and rule Italy on behalf of his father. It was a critical moment, and such birthdays, for Carolingian children, would be acute points of tension for the next several generations.

The gathering of Charlemagne's family in Regensburg likely had a dual purpose: to elevate both Pepins, the one in Bavaria and the other in Italy. A small Mass book that dates to that time reveals just this. It contains a list of those who deserved the churchmen's prayers, including Charlemagne and Fastrada, as well as all the children. There, listed below Pepin "of Italy" is a Pepin *rex* (king). These are the kinds of small, critical details that seem insignificant but reveal much wider worlds. Peering through this tiny keyhole, we see a court in transition. The latter King Pepin was Pepin the Hunchback, and that Mass book was created at the precise moment—very shortly after 790, if not in 792 itself—when that son was being groomed to take control of Bavaria, likely now raised, as Aquitaine had been, to the status of a kingdom within the Frankish realm.

But then it all went so very wrong.

None of that happened, and instead, Pepin the Hunchback lost his position and nearly his life. In large part, we know how serious the plot was because the *RFA* entry for 792 doesn't include a single mention of the plot or its consequences. It was added by a later reviser, writing in the early ninth century and tied (for reasons we don't need to go into right now) to Louis the Pious. By then, the Franks had their story straight. Both the reviser of the *RFA* and Charlemagne's biographer Einhard, writing in the 820s, noted that the immediate cause of the plot was the "cruelty of Queen Fastrada." Einhard added that the plot hadn't been Pepin's idea but rather that he had been lured into it by the promises of some Frankish nobles. Certainly, as he was the eldest son and by that time a full adult of about twenty-four years old, some of the aristocracy would have been looking to the future and (not foolishly) hitched their star to Pepin. Just before the fateful events Notker imagined in the church, Pepin the Hunchback had probably been granted some power in Bavaria that did not quite amount to a royal title but was close.

We need to understand the coup attempt, therefore, as revealing tensions both between factions of the royal family and between an outlying region of the kingdom and the heartland—a pattern we will see again and again. All contemporary sources agree that the plot was serious and may have involved a plan to kill Charlemagne, but the object was probably the disposition of Bavaria. Most likely, Charlemagne changed his mind and moved to limit Pepin the Hunchback's position in Bavaria, if not strip him of power entirely. Maybe that was in part after Fastrada made the case for the sons she favored—either Charles the Younger or, more likely, the just-adult Pepin of Italy. The Bavarian nobles saw their stock plummet and so suggested that Pepin the Hunchback take radical action, conspiring to elevate him to kingship themselves. Fatefully, he acquiesced. As we'll see repeatedly, Frankish nobles were only too happy to use the disaffection of the king's children to do their dirty work. We have to look at the whole court, men and women, high clerics and secular lords, and indeed the whole empire stretching out over western

Europe. It was made up of people with agendas and regional loyalties that sometimes led to war.

But not this time; the plot was foiled. And in a way, maybe Notker was at least in part right about how it had been revealed; the reviser of the *RFA* said specifically that a Lombard named Fardulf had been rewarded with the abbacy of the tremendously important Monastery of Saint-Denis when he went to the king with the news. Perhaps Fardulf was the terrified priest of Notker's story, as close as we can come to even a possible identification. We do know that Notker was wrong about the consequences of the failed coup. Blood did flow from the necks of some who had been involved. Other conspirators were stripped of their lands. Pepin himself was sent to Prüm to live out his days as a monk while the king showered loyal nobles with wealth in the following year.

Decades later, brother would fight brother and the intellectual surety of the Carolingian world would collapse. The savage internecine violence of Frank against Frank will be seen as terrible and extraordinary. And it was. But the cracks in the towering edifice of their empire had been there from the start. Those who had succeeded in overthrowing the Merovingian kings in an act they demanded be remembered as bloodless, those who had snuffed out a threat against them in a coup they claimed was just the workings of a deranged and misshapen bastard, all laid a thin veneer of unity over those cracks. Maybe the creators of the empire believed that the rhetoric of common purpose, if projected broadly enough, would eventually become true.

Indeed, empires require projection, not only of force across wide tracts of land but also of an image of stability. The rulers of the Franks proclaimed themselves to be God's chosen people. They wrote histories, chronicles, biographies, saints' lives, legal documents, and other documents to tell both the present and posterity a story about a unified people united in a common purpose under a great ruler. They staged great rituals, sent emissaries far and wide, sponsored

magnificent artistic and intellectual activities, and even welcomed
an elephant sent by the Abbasid caliph in Baghdad to Charlemagne's
court in Aachen. But beneath the facade of unity and power lay fissures that burrowed deep into the foundation of Frankish society,
bubbling up again and again in dispute, deception, and rebellion.

CHAPTER 2

Fathers and Sons

800–814

The earliest version of the twelfth-century poem known as the *Song of Roland* tells a legendary story about a real event, specifically the Frankish defeat in the Pyrenees in 778. In the reality that spawned the much later fiction, Charlemagne had been invited into Iberia by the Islamic ruler of Barcelona, who needed help against other Islamic rivals in the region. There the Frankish army muddled around for a bit, won a few small victories in support of its Islamic allies, and then headed back north. But on the way back across the Pyrenees and into Francia, Charlemagne's rear guard was attacked and defeated by local forces, Christian Basques objecting to being invaded from the north. The Basques used their local knowledge to strike effectively at the tail end of the much larger Carolingian army and succeeded in killing a number of prominent Frankish nobles.

But in the retelling from centuries later, Charlemagne and the Franks are in Iberia for conquest and conversion and the battle lines have been drawn more starkly. Gone are the real, historical, complicated politics that saw shifting alliances of Christians and Muslims. In its place is a holy war. Now the Franks' enemies have been transformed from Christian Basques to a unified force of Muslims from Iberia, North Africa, and as far away as Baghdad. The legendary Charlemagne of the *Song of Roland* stands very clearly at the head of all Christendom, God's champion on Earth. He's over two hundred years old and directly communicates with the angels. Yet he still faces serious internal dissent to his divinely ordained rule and ultimately still has limits on his power.

As the poem opens, only one Iberian city holds out and *seems* about to surrender. But dastardly deeds are afoot. At a diplomatic meeting between Christians and Muslims, Charlemagne is betrayed. Promises are made that convince the Franks to return home in victory. But this is all a ruse. Charlemagne's nephew Roland, in charge of the Christian army's rear guard, is trapped by a massive Islamic army in a mountain pass and the army annihilated.

Unlike in the actual events of the eighth century, this defeat becomes a victory in the poem. The rear guard falls after a heroic last stand, but then, as legend has it, Charlemagne charges back across the mountains to wreak terrible vengeance upon his enemies and ends up conquering all of Spain, forcing the Muslims to convert or be killed. At one point, angels even pause the sun in the sky so that Charlemagne can slaughter his enemies, in an allusion to the Book of Joshua.

Scholarship on the poem tends to focus on the interreligious warfare, but it is also a story about the instability and betrayal at the heart of the Frankish court. The ambush of the rear guard in the *Song of Roland* is ultimately the responsibility of a powerful Frankish noble named Ganelon, who betrays both Charlemagne and his nephew Roland to the Islamic ruler in a fit of pique. But when this treason is finally revealed, even "Charles the king, our great emperor"—God's chosen, a man conversant with angels—cannot act directly against the traitor because his council of nobles is ambivalent about the case. They hem and they haw, and they kind of see Ganelon's point. Justice is eventually served, but the poet makes clear that the exercise of power and violence—even in a fictional world of angels on the battlefield and miracles to favor God's chosen people—is a high-wire act that needs to be negotiated between a ruler and his nobility, regardless of that ruler's title.

During his lifetime, as in the later poem, Charlemagne held

multiple titles that allowed him to rule over a broad swath of people. He inherited the title "king of the Franks" from his father, consolidated it when his brother died, took the title "king of the Lombards" when he conquered that group in the early 770s, then resurrected the title "Roman emperor" in the West when Pope Leo III (795–816) placed a crown on his head during Mass in Rome on Christmas Day 800. For the remainder of his reign after that day, he used all three titles together on his decrees: "Charles the most serene augustus, crowned by God, great and peaceful emperor guiding Roman power, who is also by the mercy of God king of the Franks and Lombards." Each title gave him power over certain communities, but his power everywhere was far from absolute and he constantly faced both external and internal threats.

As we saw in the last chapter and will see in this one, the power of a Frankish ruler (even as an emperor) was a bit of a paradox. That power was immense but always limited, despite the stories the Franks liked to tell about, and to, themselves. The acquisition of the imperial title mattered because it confirmed for the Franks their belief that God was with them. But saying that they were chosen by God, surprisingly, didn't actually solve the problems of competing family loyalties that dogged the Carolingian dynasty, nor did it resolve the tension of a ruler who had to rely upon a powerful nobility that wielded its own violence and desperately craved status, too.

❈

For much of the European Middle Ages and, frankly, much of modernity, the resurrection of the title "emperor" was seen as a high-water mark in Charlemagne's reign—a sign of not just the Franks' ambitions but also their attempts to create a proto-nation-state. But it turns out that when you really dig into Charlemagne's actual practice of rule, things didn't radically change after he was crowned emperor. Early-medieval titles of rule could of course mean nothing if, for example, your powerful nobles decided to stage a coup or your out-of-favor son became a node of discontent and tried to have you murdered. But even when

titles didn't bring more power, they did matter as symbols of authority. Charlemagne very clearly sought titles not only because of how he
hoped they could insulate him, if not inoculate him, from threats but
also for what they enabled him to do.

In the case of the imperial title, as the *RFA* tells the story, Charlemagne had come to the eternal city in 800 because the pope was in
trouble. Again. The year before, the citizens of Rome—or at least
a faction that thought someone else should be pope—had attacked
Pope Leo III, blinding him and tearing out his tongue, and thrown
him in prison. Nevertheless, Leo managed to escape his cell, scale
the city walls, and flee north across the Alps to Charlemagne's court.
Performatively outraged at the pope's treatment, Charlemagne sent
an army to accompany the bishop of Rome back to Italy and then
followed them south the next autumn. In the interim, Leo apparently
got better. Tongue and eyes somehow now intact, he welcomed the
king into Rome in late November 800. With Charlemagne now in
the city, again according to the *RFA*, he set the Church in order, received symbolic gifts from emissaries sent by the Christian patriarch
of Jerusalem, and then witnessed the pope swearing his innocence.
The visit culminated on Christmas Day 800, when, during Mass in
St. Peter's Basilica, the pope placed a crown on Charlemagne's head
and the people of Rome sang with one voice, "To the august Charles,
crowned by God, the great and peaceful emperor of the Romans,
life and victory!" As emperor, Charlemagne concluded his visit by
administering justice, forcing the conspirators against Leo into exile.
He then left the city and headed back across the Alps in early 801.

Other contemporary sources by and large confirm the outlines of
the event. But we should immediately doubt some of the details—
tongues and eyes tend not to grow back, for instance. That said, it
seems very likely that in 799 the bishop of Rome was indeed attacked
by a rival faction in local politics and fled north. Throughout the early
Middle Ages, Rome was notoriously fractious, with various powerful
families vying for control over the bishopric (which of course held
secular as well as theological power). Pope Leo III was himself a Roman but not necessarily of the high nobility, and it seems likely that

relatives of his recently deceased predecessor, Pope Hadrian I, were unhappy with Leo's ascent and wanted one of their own on the papal throne instead. That faction from Hadrian's family almost certainly instigated the attack on Leo III.

During his long pontificate, Pope Hadrian I had consciously turned his focus northward and away from Byzantium, the Eastern Roman Empire, on which the papal gaze had for so long been fixed. The Franks offered a new center of power that could serve as a counterweight to Byzantium. That said, the Byzantine Empire continued to haunt Italy like a ghost. Since the fifth century, the Italian Peninsula had seen various Romanized Germanic peoples fighting one another for control. But Byzantium had endured and at times controlled much of Italy. By the seventh and early eighth centuries, the city of Rome still looked primarily to the emperors in Constantinople for (at least theoretical) protection. But there was constant tension on theological points, and that, coupled with the realities of other political powers on Rome's northern borders, eventually shifted the papacy's focus to the Franks and an alliance that began in earnest in the 750s. This is all to say that by the time Leo III came to power in 795, the relationship with the Franks was long established; it was natural and understandable that he would look to Charlemagne for help.

We know the rest of the story. Charlemagne did help, sending Leo back to Rome with a Frankish army, then following the next year to administer justice and restore the pope to his position. He became emperor on Christmas Day, when the pope placed a crown on his head and the assembled Romans and Franks shouted their assent. We should note that this last detail is an important one, as only an acclamation by the populace (a perhaps fictional expression of the general will) could make a Roman emperor, following precedent that dated back into antiquity. This detail also reveals that the coronation was clearly a well-planned, carefully stage-managed event, from Charlemagne's arrival in the city to the ritual itself. Much as eyes and tongues don't grow back, crowds of Romans didn't spontaneously gather and chant "Life and victory!" to visiting Frankish kings. Charlemagne and his circle had been planning it all since about 798, and the attack on the pope in 799 provided the perfect pretext to move forward.

But another part of the decision to move forward with the imperial coronation had to do with rather chaotic events far away in Constantinople. In the late third century, following half a century of civil wars and with the hopes of bringing about some stability, the Roman Empire had been split in half, each with its own ruler. Though nominally connected to each other, each region functioned more or less independently with its own line of succession. At least, that's how it was supposed to work. In reality, the system tended to lead to more civil wars. Western and Eastern emperors vied for full control of the empire and sometimes took it for themselves. But the structural fiction was important because it enabled continuity in times of particularly acute crisis, such as when the last Western emperor was deposed in 476. When that happened, for example, the East just kept chugging along and several Germanic rulers simply pledged their allegiance to the emperor in Constantinople. Even centuries later, when we reach the era of Charlemagne, though Byzantium's power in Italy had waned significantly, Franks and Romans still paid a lot of attention to imperial dramas in the East.

In 797, the Eastern empress Irene, who first served as her son's regent during his infancy and then, by refusing to cede power, became a sort of co-ruler with him for about a decade, had her son blinded and took power for herself. In the grand scheme of intrigues that occurred in Roman history, those actions by themselves weren't so shocking. What does seem to have been shocking both in Byzantium and in the West was a woman ruling on her own, without at least the fiction of a man in the wings.

Charlemagne and Irene had long enjoyed friendly relations, even possibly arranging a marriage alliance between his daughter and her son around 780. But the friendship soured suddenly when Charlemagne broke the engagement off in 787, right before the wedding. This probably happened because he felt slighted after Frankish bishops weren't invited to a council in Constantinople to resolve an important theological matter. It was a medieval slap in the face.

Indeed, the tension was confirmed shortly afterward when open hostilities between the Franks and Byzantines erupted in southern Italy.

Relations could have been restored a decade later in about 797, when Empress Irene's son sent emissaries to the Frankish king to ask for support against his mother. Charlemagne was noncommittal, but they had arrived too late anyway; the son had been blinded and deposed and Irene was fully back in control by the time the Franks' response arrived in Constantinople. That said, once Irene took power for herself, the pace of communication back and forth between Charlemagne and the East generally picked up. Part of that was due to Irene's looking to shore up support for herself and protect Byzantine interests in Italy against further Frankish military intervention, but another part was the Franks' taking the initiative to enter the world stage as a major power by revivifying the long-dormant western half of the Roman Empire.

Those envoys demonstrate once again that medieval Europe was a permeable space and its people were very much part of a wider world that extended across the Mediterranean, even into Egypt and modern Iraq. For the Franks, the envoys were clear signs of their expanding horizons, attempts to assert themselves as a significant power in the wider world but also to check what they saw to be Byzantine "haughtiness." At the end of 799, Charlemagne received emissaries from the Christian patriarch of Jerusalem, who came bearing relics from the Holy Land. The same source records that in early December 800, another emissary Charlemagne had sent to the patriarch of Jerusalem returned to Charlemagne in Rome bearing "keys of the Lord's Sepulcher and of Calvary, also the keys of the city and of Mount Zion along with a flag." These symbolic gifts were meant not only to place the Holy Land under Charlemagne's protection but also to assert that the stewardship of the Christian sites belonged to the Franks, not the Byzantines.

Charlemagne continued expanding his role in the broader world by looking even further to the east, to the Islamic Abbasids, based in Baghdad (and whom Frankish sources often called "Persians").

At times allies and then enemies of the Byzantines, the Abbasids ruled an empire that stretched from modern India across almost all of North Africa. For Charlemagne, however, friendly relations with them were a form of prestige diplomacy, intended to enhance the rulers' standing in the eyes of their subjects by sending and receiving emissaries and gifts. And what gifts they were. Before Charlemagne left Italy after his coronation, emissaries from Baghdad reached him in Ravenna with news that the caliph had sent the Frankish king an elephant. That, too, was symbolic; an elephant was a gift that had once been sent between ancient Romans and Persians and as such was a recognition not just of mutual respect but also, in the Franks' eyes, of parity of status between caliph and king. Romans and Persians had once warred with each other and exchanged lavish gifts; that was now happening again.

It's no coincidence that the *RFA* reported so much of the diplomacy preceding the coronation in Rome. If Charlemagne was, as we think, planning to become emperor, then demonstrating his claim to *imperium* was in part accomplished by being perceived as an equal to great leaders, such as Irene and the caliph Harun al-Rashid. Sending and receiving gifts, the more sacred or more exotic the better, was seen as something a man of great status would do. A later document originally created circa 808 (though the actual manuscript is from a bit later) demonstrates this quite well. Drawn up on Charlemagne's explicit instructions by emissaries he'd sent to Jerusalem, the text is an inventory of all the churches in and around the city. It's a fascinating bit of social, religious, and economic history that reveals (among other things) diverse sets of Christian communities surviving, maybe even thriving, under Islamic rule. There was even at least one Latin-speaking monastery—thus more directly connected to the Frankish world—on the Mount of Olives. But more specifically, the structure of the document, which carefully records the size of churches' roofs, as well as the exact number of churchmen serving at each location, reveals Charlemagne's intentions; he considered those churches to be under his care. The gifts that arrived from the patriarch of Jerusalem in 800—keys to the city and its important churches and a banner—were mostly symbolic, to be sure, but symbols represent a reality. Charlemagne took his responsibility as a Christian emperor seriously. The Franks were quantifying the churches' need so that they could properly care for what was *theirs*. Indeed, records of a council in 810 record a discussion about "the alms that had to be sent to Jerusalem on account of God's churches that need to be repaired." This was almost certainly in response to Charlemagne's mission to the city a few years before.

In the end, it seems that with a woman on the throne in Byzantium, Charlemagne and his advisers thought it was a moment to expand his power in the West. In 800, the city of Rome was in disorder. There was no ruler in Italy. An imperial title allowed Charlemagne to claim power that was both real and intellectual, covering not only his ability to dispense justice against antipapal conspirators in Rome, to press claims in southern Italy (sending his son Pepin, formerly Carloman, on campaign in that region from late 800 to early 801), but also even to symbolically protect the faraway city of Jerusalem. That was all done at a moment when because of Irene's precarious position after her coup, the Byzantines were in no position to do much about it, certainly not militarily, but realistically not even diplomatically.

But Charlemagne wasn't a fool. He never claimed that he was usurping Irene's position. Instead, he was stepping into a void in the West, claiming, with the help of the pope, authority in Italy and a hegemonic title that would sit next to (but above) his other ones. The most common title he used on his decrees was clear about this: "Charles the most serene augustus, crowned by God, great and peaceful emperor guiding Roman power, who is also by the mercy of God king of the Franks and Lombards." He was an *augustus*, a great honorific. His power came from God, but he was not an emperor "of the Romans" (like those in Constantinople). Instead, he was an emperor who exercised Roman power. The distinction was subtle but important, and it gave the Franks an opening to expand their authority and grandeur without permanently severing their ties to Constantinople.

✻

The imperial title gave Charlemagne an intellectual weapon in legitimizing his exercise of power in the various regions of his empire. But did the resurrection of the title "emperor" actually change the nature of the Frankish realm? Could that ritual stabilize a dynasty founded by a coup?

Before 800, Charlemagne's court was a magnet for some of the most brilliant minds in Europe, with scholars from Ireland and England crossing the English Channel and others from Iberia crossing the mountains to attend the Frankish king, who stayed primarily at his palace at Aachen, though he often spent months or even years in regional capitals. His armies constantly pushed outward, defeating Danes, Muslims (and Christians) in Iberia, Lombards and Byzantines in Italy, Avars in eastern Europe, and Saxons in northern Germany, among others. Spoils of war and tributes from neighboring kings flowed freely to Aachen, where they were doled out to the Church as charity and to Frankish nobles as guarantors of their loyalty. He exchanged emissaries with the Byzantine emperors in Constantinople, winning their grudging respect, while also sending and entertaining much friendlier delegations from the Abbasid caliph in Baghdad. Even before the coronation in Rome, Charlemagne had landed in a position of relatively unrivaled power over almost all of Europe. So in trying to figure out what actually changed when an imperial crown was placed on his head by the pope, scholars have tended to focus their attention on the man himself and how differently he acted after he acquired his new title.

Though the idea that a monarch could act with absolute power was a creation of early modernity, even then it was always a fiction. A king or queen always had a court, regional nobles, their families, spouses, princes, princesses, offspring and lovers, families, and always a number of bastard offspring, who might hold their own prominent positions and key offices and have their own factions. Then, too, there were the men on the make, those seeking access to the king, and of course a vast array of servants, laborers, enslaved people, artisans, and more, who are often difficult to locate in our surviving sources but were there in large numbers and lived complex, fully human lives. That mess was what the *Song of Roland* expressed all too well, and it was in these tangled relationships that so much of our story emerges and so many of the cracks in the foundation of Carolingian rule, cracks opened by violence and coups, slowly widened over the years to come. Because a king never ruled alone.

Charlemagne and his court were adept at adaptation, at finding ways to incorporate disparate regions and continue to manage them on a Europe-wide scale. He centralized but didn't standardize. Part of his success had to do with his near-constant motion, his willingness to move among the palaces scattered throughout the realm and to make himself present to those who ruled regions in his name, as well as his near-constant presence at the head of his armies in the field, spending time himself on military campaigns on the peripheries of places under Frankish control (especially Saxony but also Italy and Iberia). Campaign season, roughly from late spring until early autumn, would have been a particularly appropriate time to try to bend the king's ear. One could impress him by killing in his name. They would do what he told them.

And the Franks were very good at killing. Charlemagne never forgot that his family had taken power in a bloody coup against the previous dynasty, and he never forgot that some of his nobles, along with his eldest son, had plotted against him. He therefore tried to limit how violence could be used and thus limit where power might accrete, to mitigate against the concentration of influence and power in other people, be they his children or powerful regional aristocrats. To distribute authority and power, he often assigned more than one person to an important task, such as co-leading armies in the field or acting as part of a team of emissaries to a foreign ruler. For example, the *RFA* related that Charlemagne had assigned the campaign against the Avars in 796 to none other than his son Pepin (d. 810), king of Italy (whom we first met as Carloman), and to his brother-in-law Duke Erich of Friuli. The campaign was successful, so not only were the laurels shared, but the plunder was sent back to Charlemagne, who "after receiving it and thanking God, . . . sent Angilbert [not the same person as the poet], his beloved abbot, with a large part of it to Rome. . . . The rest he distributed among his magnates, ecclesiastic as well as lay, and his other vassals." Pepin and Erich acted as checks on each other, each ensuring that the other didn't control all the plunder or use it to create his own network of patronage. The spoils flowed to Aachen. And all patronage flowed from Charlemagne himself, guarding against rivals' creating nodes that could amass power. Pepin and Erich may have won the battle, but Charlemagne celebrated the victory.

Charlemagne's fingers were in everything. His was a "high-touch" rulership. He never forgot that power had been allowed to coalesce away from the Merovingian king and around his father, as mayor of the palace. He was determined to avoid the same fate. Pepin the Short as king, and now Charlemagne, had both learned that lesson, removed the intermediary, and attempted to make themselves the only gravitational force in the Frankish solar system. That applied to the king's children as well. Charlemagne kept all his sons and daughters close to hand but never allowed them to create their own power bases. He made sure that he was in control.

Yet because his presence was everywhere, that style of rule at least gave his subjects the sense that he was available and that others could access that power. Aachen was the de facto capital for about the last twenty or so years of his reign and so a place where one could find the king and court. That center became a magnet for all the nodes of power spread throughout the different areas under the Franks' control, the court a community that many people aspired to belong to and a place from whence power emanated. Charlemagne's courtier and biographer Einhard, who wrote about a decade after his subject's death, told the story of the king's love of the hot springs around Aachen and his regular swims there. Einhard continued to say that the great Charlemagne not only allowed his sons to bathe with him but also often invited his friends, other nobles, various followers, and bodyguards. It seems odd to include this anecdote, perhaps, but the point was first to show off Charlemagne's physical vigor (he was a dude, after all), but second, and more important, to show that that activity was a point of access to the king and his inner circle. In all politics, decisions are often made before they are formally and publicly "made." The ninth century was no different. The people in the bath were the important people who formed relationships that moved the empire. The bath was a closed circle of power but one that hinted at its permeability. You, too, could bathe with Charlemagne! You, too, could, maybe, not only wash with him but gain his favor!

That royal bath became more full as Charlemagne aged. He reproduced prodigiously. He had at least nineteen children by at least eight different women, five of whom were his formal wives. Of those women, we know precious little. The sources are often silent. At that level of society, marriages were political, means of forming or cementing alliances, and very rarely conceived of as anything else— even if the relationship could (and did in Charlemagne's case) grow into both one of affection and a real partnership. That also meant that wives could come and go, depending on the changing needs of the ruler, and certainly at that time without the involvement of the Church. So let's move quickly through the family, marriage after marriage, child after child, starting not with Charlemagne himself but with the death of his father, King Pepin. Because one of the issues for the Frankish elites was that there were only so many spots next to the king but lots of people who wanted to claim them. We'll return to the ones who play roles in our drama, but now is the moment to get a sense of the size of the whole company, even the chorus in the back.

Charlemagne took power upon the death of his father, Pepin the Short, in 768. But he didn't inherit alone. Just before his death, Pepin had hastily divided the kingdom between his two sons and arranged marriages for both. The younger, Carloman, had been given lands mostly to the south and been married to a Frankish woman named Gerberga. Charlemagne, as the eldest, had been given the Frankish heartlands (around the modern Low Countries), and lands hugging the Atlantic coast. His wife was a Frankish noblewoman named Himiltrude. Pepin died that year, and his wife, Bertrada, the mother of the two princes, showed favor to Charlemagne by choosing to live with him. In 769, Himiltrude bore a son, whom we met as Pepin the Hunchback. All seemed well for Charlemagne, and the fact that he named his firstborn son Pepin, after his father, signaled that the child stood to inherit at least some of Charlemagne's titles.

But Queen Bertrada seems to have had other plans for her eldest son. In 770, she went to Italy and convinced King Desiderius of the Lombards to wed his daughter to Charlemagne, extending Frankish power over the north of Italy through a marriage alliance. Charlemagne unceremoniously put Himiltrude aside and sent her to a convent. But love, or at least marriage, is fickle. The union lasted perhaps a year, upended when Carloman suddenly died and his wife and children fled to the Lombard kingdom to seek refuge from Charlemagne.

They were right to flee. Charlemagne moved quickly and ruthlessly to take his brother's kingdom for himself. He sent his Lombard wife—we don't even know her name—back to the Lombard capital at Pavia so he could marry a Frankish woman named Hildegard in early 772. She came from a powerful family from Alemannia, a region east of the Rhine and an important part of Carloman's former lands. The goal of Charlemagne's wife swap was twofold: First, the marriage alliance provided reassurance for Carloman's former nobles that when Charlemagne seized Carloman's lands, he would prioritize the interests of their families, keeping the Rhineland at the center of a reunited kingdom. Therefore, there was no need for the nobles to defend the rights of Carloman's sons to inherit from their father. Second, because the Lombards were sheltering his nephews, Charlemagne needed a provocation to attack them and eliminate the potential threat to his reign. Expelling the king's daughter, breaking the marriage tie, did the trick. And it worked. Almost all the nobles in his brother's former kingdom pledged loyalty to Charlemagne, and just a year later, in 773–774, he marched a combined army into Italy, crushed the Lombard Kingdom, and took it for himself. Carloman's wife and two young sons "disappear from the record." Most likely they were murdered at Charlemagne's orders.

Immediately after the conquest of the Lombard capital of Pavia,

Charlemagne sent for Hildegard to come with his two sons, the afore-mentioned Pepin (aged probably four or five at the time) and Hilde-gard's firstborn (aged about two), Charles the Younger. This was a public display—an opportunity for Charlemagne to demonstrate the creation of his own dynasty at the exact moment he snuffed out his brother's. Then the dynasty grew. Hildegard had at least eight more children, though only five of them survived infancy. A daughter, Rotrud, was born in 775, then Carloman (the boy later renamed as Pepin) in 777, Louis the Pious in 778, Bertha in 779, and Gisela in 781. Again, the names of children meant everything.

For the women, names denoted links outward to other elite fam-ilies, visible symbols of the webs of alliance among the great Frankish magnates that held the realm together. Or at least they were supposed to hold the realm together. Rotrud was named after Hildegard's grandmother, Bertha after Charlemagne's mother, and Gisela forged another link to Hildegard's family. For the men, they denoted dynasty. Pepin was, at first, already taken, so Charles was chosen for Charlemagne's second son. Carloman referenced his brother's legacy—at least for now. The name Louis was even more ambitious, as it's a version of "Clovis" ("u" and "v" were the same letter in Latin), the most famous king from the previous Frankish dynasty. Their last child, Hildegard, was born in late 782 and was named after her mother, who died shortly after childbirth at age twenty-five. It was a moving tribute, made more moving when that daughter followed her mother in death just a month later.

It is a common trope that medieval Europeans didn't care for their children, but this is disproven again and again in our sources. It seems clear that there was likely some real affection between the king and Hildegard and genuine anguish for his lost daughter. We see that in the naming, but we should also take seriously the fact that Hildegard often traveled with her husband—something Charlemagne's mother had not done with her husband—perhaps a sign that their relationship was more than a political formality. That behavior would be repeated with Charlemagne's next wife after Hildegard's death.

Fastrada, married to Charlemagne in 783, came from another

prominent East Frankish family linked to the city of Mainz, on the Rhine River. She has an unfortunate reputation in Einhard's record for being cruel. This may or may not be true, but she was clearly an astute politician. It was likely she who helped engineer the dispossession of Bavaria from Pepin the Hunchback in favor of Hildegard's sons, which led to Pepin's revolt in 792. She did clearly favor certain of her stepsons over others, which didn't sit well with elements of the Frankish aristocracy and led to great trouble. But at the same time, Einhard's take could also have been a way of deflecting blame from Charlemagne for making the decision to marginalize Pepin the Hunchback. Einhard's comments also provided a not-so-veiled warning to any other emperors about what might develop if the power of women at court were left unchecked. Indeed, the arrival of a new queen always meant a shuffle in the way power operated. New advisers came to court and new centers of power formed around them, which could be (and often were) a threat to the established dynamics. Sometimes this reshuffling got people killed.

In this case, Fastrada, at the age of eighteen, quickly stepped into the role of matron, pregnant almost immediately, but perhaps more important she was stepmother to several children ranging from roughly ages thirteen to two. All those children, from several different mothers, had powerful extended families who were quite wary of seeing their access to the king and court marginalized. As such, we really ought to marvel at Fastrada's canny diplomatic skills. Throughout her eleven years as queen, she certainly kept things from getting worse as factions grew in lockstep with the size of the Franks' realm. In part, she was able to move within the court as a peacemaker of sorts because she never ended up having a son of her own (instead, two daughters). But when her eldest stepson, Pepin the Hunchback, revolted in 792, it shook the Carolingian world and cleared the path for Hildegard's sons, Fastrada's favorites, to claim their place foremost in their father's affections. As bad as it was, though, we really should realize that it could have been so much worse, setting off a longer-term resistance to Charlemagne in Bavaria or among Pepin's mother's family. But it didn't. And an extraordinary coin, 21 millimeters (less than one inch) in diameter, is a tiny piece of evidence that Fastrada likely had something to do with stabilizing the empire after the revolt.

That coin, minted circa 793, showed the king's name as "Charles, king of the Franks" on the front and on the reverse hers as "Queen Fastrada." Early-medieval coins were expressions of power as much as systems of exchange. Control of a mint was reserved to certain levels of authority and therefore jealously guarded, with very intentional images used to complement other ruling policies. To put a queen's name on a coin was unprecedented among the Carolingians, and its timing so close after Pepin's revolt the preceding year raises all sorts of interesting questions. Was it a contemporary attempt to deflect blame for the revolt just the year before? Was it a recognition of her heretofore maybe more informal political role at court, both as mother and as diplomat among competing factions? In many ways, it seems more likely that it was the latter—a recognition of how highly esteemed Fastrada had been all along, but with curious timing.

A 791 letter from Charlemagne to Fastrada addressed her as his "beloved and very lovable wife," wishing she would write more often, and making clear that while he was on military campaign she was responsible for the performance of the litanies (prayers for the army). That might not seem like much at first glance, but letters in premodern Europe were never private. They were highly stylized, public performances. This letter was meant not only for Fastrada but also for those around her, with Charlemagne using the odd circular phrasing about his care for Fastrada as a signal to the entire court that she was an avatar for him while he was away, that she was entrusted with a task—and not just a menial one. The mention of the litanies, ritualized prayers that would ensure God's favor on the battlefield, were making clear that Charlemagne trusted her with a responsibility of the highest order.

Fastrada died in 794, not long after the coin was struck, and was buried at Mainz. Charlemagne married once more, a woman named Liutgard, likely circa 798. She bore him no children, but at her death in 800 (before the coronation), she was celebrated in poetry for the political skills that Hildegard and Fastrada had also both evinced.

After her death Charlemagne had five more children by various women, none of whom he married. Three of them were sons. They were given Frankish but not royal names (Drogo, Hugh, Theodoric), making clear that they were not meant to inherit the kingdom and would never be a threat to the eldest ones, those in line for the throne: Hildegard's sons Charles the Younger, Pepin II of Italy, and Louis the Pious.

❖

After Pepin the Hunchback's revolt against his father in 792, Hildegard's three children held pride of place at the court and would stand nearest the throne. But things became a bit more complicated among the siblings as their father began to age, and the boys began to reach adulthood. By the time of Charlemagne's coronation as emperor, for example, his son Charles the Younger was twenty-eight, Pepin of Italy (formerly Carloman) twenty-three, and Louis the Pious twenty-two. Moreover, both Pepin and Louis had households of their own—wives and several children each—and more formal responsibilities as kings in their own right at the peripheries of the realm. Pepin was tasked with managing Italy and Louis with Aquitaine. But what was Charles in charge of?

The sources are infuriatingly silent on Charles the Younger. He remained primarily with his father, never marrying, nor (to the best of our knowledge) having any children. A poem from the time hinted at his homosexuality by way of explaining why he had no heirs, not as an accusation. Another contemporary source suggests that he didn't wed because he'd earlier tried to engineer his own marriage alliance, which had earned him the ire of his father. What we do know is that he was active on military campaigns but never formally assigned a place to rule nor even a regnal title until much after his younger brothers. He may have been assigned lands in Neustria circa 790, and a papal source—but notably no Frankish text—says he was crowned king in Rome on Christmas Day 800, just after his father became emperor. But this, too, is curious, because it's not clear what he was crowned king of. Even then, references to him as "king" in any sources after 800 are scarce.

It is really only in 806 that we see a bit more when formal provision for all the sons' futures was made in a document called the *Divisio regnorum* (Division of the Kingdom). The document is in some ways unique but in others quite normal. That is to say that dividing the kingdom among the ruler's sons followed Frankish tradition all the way back to Clovis I; what was new was that it was written down, formalized, solemnly witnessed by churchmen, and (it was hoped) its provisions given binding power by all who witnessed it. And what did it say? Very simply, the text made Charlemagne's three sons co-rulers with one another and assigned each of them a region: Louis remained primarily with Aquitaine, Pepin with Italy (and Bavaria), and the young Charles got the heartland of Francia. All three were noted as kings, but none was emperor. That title was reserved for Charlemagne.

With good reason, we might be tempted to see the early ninth century as a high-water mark for Charlemagne and the Franks. The boundaries of the empire were at their greatest extent. Several crowns sat comfortably on Charlemagne's head. Tribute and gifts flowed to Aachen from north, south, east, and west. Aachen was a magnet for the greatest minds in Europe. He was surrounded by his daughters, who helped administer the court. He had three hale and hearty (and loyal) sons, each with his own portfolio to govern.

But then the emperor's children started to die. Pepin of Italy died in summer 810, his sister Rotrud in that same year, Charles the Younger in December 811, and Pepin the Hunchback suddenly in his monastery at Prüm, also in 811. It's notable that those deaths are so closely clustered together. There was a great cattle plague that swept Europe in 809–810, and at least one source suggested that it moved between animals and humans, which means that the disease may have been responsible for some of those deaths. There are other possibilities, though. We know almost nothing about Charles the Younger's death: not how he died, where he died, or where he was buried—an odd omission. Pepin the Hunchback's death followed quite closely, giving us reason to raise our eyebrows. A much later ninth-century source from Prüm, where Pepin had been confined, related that Charles the Younger and Pepin the Hunchback had been rather close, at least until the coup attempt. We can't put too much weight on this later account, as we can never be sure of its sources, but we do need to acknowledge that this Pepin, even confined to a monastery, was still a legitimate, potential heir. And he did die rather suddenly. By the beginning of 812, Louis the Pious was conveniently the only legitimate son still alive and set to inherit the empire. Our eyebrows are duly raised.

Even then, the elevation of Louis as sole heir proceeded slowly. There was little action on that front throughout all of 812, and it was only in fall 813 that Louis was summoned to Aachen from Aquitaine for a general council. The lack of movement demonstrates some ambivalence, even at that late stage, about Louis's position as heir to his father. Did that come from Charlemagne himself, those around him, or both? We can't be certain. We do know that at play in this moment were decades of aristocratic jockeying, with nodes of patronage that had formerly orbited around other sons now altering course toward Louis. Some would never fully reposition themselves, as we'll see in the next chapter.

Regardless, the die was cast by late 813, when Charlemagne himself placed a crown on Louis's head and named him co-emperor, while Louis's nephew Bernard (Pepin of Italy's adult son, Charlemagne's grandson) was named king of Italy. All our sources agree that at the time, Charlemagne was not in great health. He seems to have taken the entirety of 813 to prepare for his passing, ordering five general councils to be held across the breadth of the empire to ensure that the Church was in good order. Yet, curiously, Louis didn't stay at Aachen and was instead sent back to Aquitaine almost immediately. He was away from the court when Charlemagne died in his palace at Aachen just a couple of months later, in January 814.

There was no period of mourning. The emperor was buried in his palace chapel the same day he died. Almost certainly, the event had been foreseen and meticulously planned and then executed promptly when the day came. His daughters, who had remained with him at court, likely managed the ceremony alongside Charlemagne's most recent lovers and his most trusted advisers, Archbishop Hildebald of Cologne and Charlemagne's cousin Wala. But again the new emperor, Louis, was nowhere to be seen. He was in the region of Tours when he heard the news about his father's death and moved deliberately, rather than swiftly, toward Aachen. He likely had no idea what would await him when he arrived.

CHAPTER 3

Sisters and Nephews

814–823

In about 812, a falconer arrived at Charlemagne's court in Aachen, an emissary to the emperor from his son the king of Aquitaine, Louis the Pious. While waiting for a response to take back to Louis about "certain urgent matters," the falconer was corralled by members of Charlemagne's court, who urged him to speed home and bring Louis to Aachen. Charlemagne was ill.

The falconer outlined all this to his king upon his return; Louis received the news with great concern. His advisers urged him to go to Aachen immediately, but, after praying for guidance, he decided to delay "so that he would not give his father cause for suspicion." Suspicion of what? It's unclear. Ultimately, Louis decided that the sufficient period to wait to visit his aging father would be two years, and in preparation, he spent the intervening time pacifying rebellious nobles in Aquitaine. In the end, Louis didn't have to wait that long. Charlemagne, of his own accord, recognized his failing health and summoned his sole surviving (legitimate) son to court. During the summer of 813, father instructed son on how to rule over the entire realm before crowning his son himself, then sending him away, back to Aquitaine. Louis was home in November 813, a new co-emperor of the Franks.

Charlemagne died just a couple of months later, in late January 814. After his rapid burial in the palace chapel at Aachen, a messenger was sent from the court to let Louis know what had happened. Louis was the sole surviving (again, legitimate!) son of the emperor, yes, but Aachen was a world away from Louis. The men in Charlemagne's court had been powers behind the throne in the emperor's old age, not unlike the Carolingian mayors of the palace under the Merovingians. Would they decide to step up and take the throne for themselves?

Louis had to move both quickly and slowly: quickly to assert his rights; slowly so as not to put his person into the hands of those who might prove disloyal. As he moved northeast toward Aachen, his first stop was the city of Orléans, where he called on its bishop. Theodulf had been an integral part of Charlemagne's inner circle, an intellectual well respected at court since the end of the eighth century, with a powerful network of relationships that could smooth the transition to power for Louis if there were indeed any trouble. There was no trouble at Orléans, at least. Theodulf met his new emperor outside the walls as a sign of respect and welcomed him into the city, where he celebrated Mass with and for the new Frankish ruler. So far, so good.

The bigger test of loyalties would come as Louis got closer to Aachen, closer to the men and women who had run the court under his father. But Louis had a plan, simple but effective, to sniff out trouble. He paused his journey and just waited, saying nothing formally but by his behavior demanding that the magnates come to him instead of the other way around. Had anyone at court hoped to shift the power dynamics by waiting for the emperor to come onto their turf, the gambit failed. The court instead acquiesced to the silent demand, seemingly without complaint. They went to Louis willingly, led by Charlemagne's first cousin Wala, a relative who had often served as the late emperor's right-hand man. Louis regarded Wala as the key to winning over the court generally. Wala was, after all, a Carolingian himself, a direct descendent of Charles Martel. So when he went quickly to Louis and pledged his loyalty, the transition of power seemed over, the path to the throne seemed clear and open.

With exceptions.

At some point before he reached the imperial palace, Louis was supposedly scandalized to learn of the behavior of his sisters, who had never married but had had lovers and borne children. Really, there's almost no chance that Louis had just learned of their behavior. It was a pretext—a chance to flex his new imperial muscles. And flex them he did. He sent Wala and other leading nobles back to Aachen to set things in order in preparation for his arrival, to arrest "a few who were particularly debauched or whose scornful arrogance was treasonous." Louis showed his newly acquired raw power by deploying a top figure of his father's entourage to break up certain elements of his father's remaining entourage. Louis was making the court his own.

Our sources are cagey on how many people were caught up in Louis's theatrical outrage over his sisters' impurity, over his pretended anger at the men who had debauched them. But it was bloody. A man named Odoin tried to escape the king's justice by killing one of Louis's loyal confidants and grievously wounding another count. Odoin was later caught and run through with a sword while trying to escape, but Louis took the escape as an act of defiance, a sign that the treachery ran deep. When he arrived at Aachen, he decided to blind another captive named Tullius as retribution. But having shown the fist of iron, he now sheathed it in a velvet glove. He pardoned the other men who had been arrested. He banished his sisters from court but sent them to properties bequeathed to them by their father. A king needs to be both ruthless and merciful, and Louis was setting the tone of his rule.

Having dispensed justice—having rid himself of some potentially troublesome residents at court via a fair bit of murder—the emperor finally entered the palace. We're told that he was received with joy by his extended family and indeed by all the Franks. He held a great assembly, inviting the powerful of Aachen, the powerful from around the world who had come to the capital, to gather. There he gave great charity to relatives and to churches across the realm. He responded to emissaries sent by the Byzantine emperor and sent his own diplomats east, and also received his nephew Bernard (his brother Pepin's son), who had come north as king of Italy to assure Louis of his loyalty. Louis received his nephew joyfully and sent him home confirmed as king, a ruler at once independent in his own region but ultimately submissive to the emperor. He ended the grand assembly that accompanied the transition of power by calling a great council for later that year in order to empower his men across the empire to right any wrongs that had been perpetrated under his father and ensure that the law was being duly enforced.

The transition was complete. Louis was the sole ruler of the Franks.

❈

Everything we know about those events comes from sources written long after they happened. Frankish history was written, as we remember, to be *true* rather than simply factual. In this case, the account above comes to us from a text known as *The Life of the Emperor Louis*, written not long after his death in 840. One way of looking at that distance is to say that the Astronomer, the name given to the anonymous author, benefited from hindsight, looking back across Louis's entire reign. But another way of looking at that distance from the events is that the author was settling some scores.

We call this particular author "The Astronomer" because, as he recounted in his book, the emperor Louis once asked him if there was a divine sign behind a comet that appeared in the late 830s (and we'll get to that comet soon enough). The fact that Louis asked the Astronomer about this celestial event also means that the author was likely at court and thus well informed about its goings-on. This makes the Astronomer's account of the transition of power in 814 particularly compelling, perhaps even the report of an eyewitness. Yet there are a couple ways in which the Astronomer's framing of Louis's accession is rather odd, as you can likely tell from our recounting. When read carefully, the author can't quite make up his mind. The transition went slowly, and it went quickly. It went smoothly, and it was drenched in blood. Everyone acquiesced, and some people resisted. The narrative both makes Louis quite active in seeking to succeed his father and suggests that the succession had been Charlemagne's idea all along. So, like a Cubist painting, the Astronomer tried to show different visions of events all at the same time. The Astronomer tells us that Louis arrives at Aachen twice—first just before the treason of Odoin and Tullius and then again after their punishment, when the emperor is (now) universally acclaimed by his family. This inconsistency reveals a level of circumspection in the text about how smoothly the transition went.

And when we think about the claim that Louis decided to wait two years before he went to Aachen to see his ailing father, we're forced to ask: Was it really the case that Charlemagne sent for his only surviving (legitimate) son during the winter of 813? Wouldn't it make more sense that Charlemagne—specifically his court, who, we remember, were the ones who supposedly gave Louis's falconer the message in the first place—was fine with Louis staying in Aquitaine until after the emperor's death? Louis the Pious's deliberate, cautious march toward Aachen makes a lot more sense if we read through the Astronomer's veneer of inevitability. He likely was right that some of the nobles at court didn't like the idea of this, let's be frank, outsider taking over, bringing his own men with him, displacing long-established positions, and upending formerly stable networks of patronage and power. And they were right to worry. Louis used the court against itself, sending Wala and other nobles (along with his own men) to Aachen ahead of him to round up those he deemed intransigent, including his sisters and certain nobles almost certainly connected to those women (it is possible that Odoin and Tullius were his sisters' lovers, and it is perhaps unlikely that they had ever been going to survive Louis's arrival).

The "truth" that the Astronomer's version of the transition of power intends to convey, as many medieval European sources do, is Louis's right to rule, the matter-of-fact assent of the most powerful men at court, the ease with which Louis was able to slot into his father's role in dispensing charity and dealing with foreign emissaries. But the transition of power that occurred after Charlemagne's death, portrayed as orderly and proper in the Astronomer's telling, was contentious and precarious enough that the cracks in his rhetorical facade shine through, revealing both ongoing and new familial and political tensions. Once again, at the moment of transition from one emperor to the next, we see a foundation of lies.

Unlike his father, Louis was the sole surviving legitimate son when he inherited the Frankish realm, but he was not the only son, nor was he the only legitimate child; his sisters had been at court their entire lives and been intimately involved in the affairs of state. Also unlike his father, Louis already had adult sons from his marriage to Ermengarde in 794. His eldest children, Lothar and Pepin, were nineteen and seventeen respectively in 814, while his youngest, Louis, was eight. Louis the Pious had never been Charlemagne's favorite and was facing a skeptical elite that had helped his father rule without him for decades, but he was nevertheless the sole ruler and had to chart his own path.

❖

Why, other than to show off his power, did he feel the need to drive his sisters out of court? He justified his purge on the grounds of right order, decorum, and a need to create a sexually pure space. But the real reason was that those women were a significant threat to his tenuous position as heir.

His rationale wasn't necessarily antagonistic to his true purpose; "purifying" things is almost always about power. But ironically, being purged based on accusations of impurity reveals exactly how integral early-medieval women could be at the highest levels, as well as how rivals could use medieval misogynistic ideas against powerful women. We saw Charlemagne's mother weave alliances for her son, and we know that throughout his reign, women suffused Charlemagne's court. His five successive queens were responsible for ordering the palace during their respective tenures, assisting with the distribution of gifts to nobles and churchmen alike, and seemingly charged with ensuring proper religious rites to safeguard the king and the realm as a whole. Fastrada, for example, was explicitly designated that critical role in the 791 letter. But after his last wife, Liutgard's, death in 800,

Charlemagne's daughters came to occupy the heart of the kingdom's politics. Though he entrusted them with many spheres of tangential power, his daughters (there were at least eight) were never allowed to marry, likely because Charlemagne feared potential rivals with a claim to Carolingian blood.

A poem composed in the late eighth century by Bishop Theodulf of Orléans offers us clues to how important those women were in Charlemagne's court. He described the daughters as participating in numerous rituals and court-related activities—not just banquets and domestic events but even activities traditionally reserved for men, such as the hunt that the king would typically take with his advisers. Several of them even accompanied Charlemagne to Rome for his imperial coronation.

And though none of them was allowed by their father to marry, they definitely weren't necessarily chaste; for example, one of the eldest daughters, Bertha, had a long-running relationship with a close counselor of the king's named Angilbert—the same person who had carried gifts of plunder from Charlemagne to Rome, not the Angelbert who wrote a poem on the Battle of Fontenoy decades later—that produced three children, including the nobleman Nithard, who would become an important chronicler of the 840s. That relationship caused no scandal and in fact likely helped elevate Angilbert into Charlemagne's inner orbit. In the early ninth century, he was a highly respected member of court, a close confidant of Charlemagne, and became the lay abbot of the Abbey of Saint-Riquier, a position that carried wealth and influence.

It seems clear that other sisters were active in that way as well, promoting their favorites to their father, using their networks of patronage and promises of access to the king to push their own agendas. In other words, during the last decade or so of Charlemagne's rule, his daughters were the keepers of the king's inner sanctum; they became power centers in their own right, having built up their own networks of patronage and information. Notker's anecdote about women guarding Charlemagne while he slept during Pepin the Hunchback's revolt was closer to the truth than many realize. Indeed, there are hints that in the early 800s, as Charlemagne aged and succession became a pressing concern, the sisters took sides among their still living brothers (Charles the Younger, Pepin of Italy, and Louis the Pious), hoping to steer their father toward their particular favorite. What doomed Odoin and Tullius was likely the fallout from those machinations against Louis by his sisters.

For Louis the Pious in 814, the position of his sisters and the networks of patronage and power each had constructed among the elites of his father's court was deeply threatening. He had spent his life alienated from that court, perhaps familiar with the major players generally but not in control of it nor really connected to any of the power centers that orbited around it. His sisters controlled that. It must have been unclear, as he received the news of his father's death and began his careful march toward Aachen, if his sisters would deny him access to the treasury or even prop up a rival or try to have him killed.

But purity, or at least the perception of court purity, had its own importance beyond its utility as a rationale for a political purge. For Louis, as for most Franks of the time, court purity reflected perceptions about the state of the empire as a whole. Laxity and corruption—whether sexual, economic, or political—at the center would pervade everything and touch all areas. The Franks saw themselves as the new Israelites and looked to the sacred past for models of how to behave in the all-too-earthly present. The Franks had told themselves, as they expanded their empire and conquered their enemies, that God must be on their side. Yet that carried responsibilities, and violation of those responsibilities had severe consequences. Just as Joshua was responsible for making things right with God, so Louis saw himself stepping into that role in his own time.

This understanding—the power of concerns about sexual purity when deployed as a political weapon—would come back to haunt Louis later when his enemies realized they could wield it against him, but we'll get to that part of our story soon. For now, it seems he understood that as a new ruler he needed to deploy whatever tools he

had at his disposal. Attacking the court's moral laxity when he arrived
at Aachen was a convenient way to marginalize his sisters and, by
extension, those they patronized and held favor with. Louis's idea of
righteous kingship gave him, he thought, an unimpeachable reason
to bring in his own people to replace his father's, even if we understand the accusations as slanders rather than facts. In Louis's mind,
the women who ran the court had to be removed from the palace
before he could take his rightful place, and a public (even if sincere!)
concern for purity allowed him to do this.

So the sisters were sent away to convents, effectively removed
from court and any potential romantic entanglements with the nobles and courtiers left behind. And it wasn't just his sisters and their
inner circle; Louis then banished several archbishops who had been
close associates of Charlemagne in the last few years of his reign,
and even the aforementioned Wala, the key to the court who had
submitted to the new emperor, as well as Wala's brother Adalhard.
In so doing, he created space for his new inner circle of advisers.

But this ostentatious display of power, not so shockingly, didn't
settle things for good. There were still members of the Carolingian
family out there who could make claim to parts of the empire. Wala
was a descendent of Charles Martel and, under Charlemagne, had
acted almost as a "mayor of the palace." Bernard of Italy was Charlemagne's grandson; he had been crowned king of Italy and confirmed
in that position by Charlemagne and Louis the Pious in quick succession. Adalhard, also a blood relative, was a close adviser of Bernard's
and had played the same role for Bernard's father (Louis's brother).

And there were still more Carolingians. Two of Louis the Pious's
sons were adults, and provision had to be made for them. The answer
for these two seemed simple enough, though, and Louis dispatched
them to regions at opposite ends of the empire. Lothar, the eldest,
was sent to Bavaria and Pepin to Aquitaine. Louis the German (the
youngest, only eight at the time) remained at court, all following the
precedent set by Charlemagne.

Because there were so many Carolingians, Louis needed to add
some measure of security to his crown, and he followed precedent

there, too. In 816, he once more leveraged the Frankish relationship with the papacy and called the new pope, Stephen IV, to Reims to recrown him emperor, superseding the diadem that his father had placed on his head in 813 when Charlemagne had crowned the prince Louis as co-emperor. Now, the pope traveled to Reims, in Francia, to crown Louis as sole emperor.

Louis wasn't done, though. Everything he had done to marginalize the threats posed by family members so far had been, in a way, informal. There had been no administrative oomph behind his actions. That changed in 817 when he took steps to divide the empire more formally among his sons, once more following a precedent that had been set by Charlemagne in the *Divisio regnorum* (Division of the Kingdom) in 806. Ostensibly, the events of 817 were spurred by a bad accident Louis suffered at Aachen, after a wooden arcade suddenly collapsed on top of him and his entourage while they were leaving Mass. He was fortunate, the *RFA* says, to escape with only minor injuries, as many around him were more seriously hurt. Perhaps that near-death experience made him reflect on his mortality and worry what would happen to the empire after he was gone. Perhaps. More likely, given how deliberately he seemed to move when confronted with other consequential decisions, he'd been thinking about doing something like this for some time.

In the few years between his assumption of power and that accident, things had been going pretty well for Louis. Warfare on the borders of the empire continued, but, again for a noble class that defined themselves by their military prowess, that was a good thing. The Franks involved themselves in a Danish succession dispute, pushed further into Iberia against the Muslims, and roundly defeated uprisings by the Basques in the southwest and Sorbs in eastern Europe. He'd also maintained good relations with Rome, with his nephew Bernard of Italy acting as a loyal servant in carrying out the emperor's orders and extending the Franks' power both in Rome and farther south against the Byzantines. Popes Stephen IV and Paschal I continued their predecessors' policy of sending the emperor gifts to ensure his protection upon their ascent to the papal throne. As noted just above, Stephen IV even scurried from Rome to Reims and all too willingly put a crown onto Louis's head to confirm him as Roman emperor. It all seemed very much business as usual for the empire.

Instead of a rash decision or a reaction to an accident, the council at Aachen that would formally divide the empire in 817 was a strategic move. Louis the Pious needed his sons' help in maintaining the extremities of the Franks' territory, but he also recognized that they were adults and ready to lead in their own right. The process of formally assigning a line of succession, and the document that arose out of it known as the *Ordinatio imperii* (Ordering [or Arranging] of Imperial Power), officially gave positions to his three current sons. His youngest, Louis the German, became a king in the eastern part of the empire, centered around Bavaria, while the middle son, Pepin, was a king in the West, centered around Aquitaine. Lothar, as eldest son, received the imperial title and the Frankish heartlands on either side of the Rhine in northern Europe, as well as Italy.

In some ways, that confirmed the status quo. Lothar and Pepin, of course, were already kings. But the *Ordinatio imperii* did shuffle territories around, moving Lothar back to the heartland in order to make space for Louis's youngest son in the east. It also ensured that his sons, in theory people he could wholeheartedly trust, were in the regions where he'd recently had some trouble: Pepin could handle the Basques and Muslims, Lothar could handle the Byzantines and Romans, and Louis could be deployed against the Sorbs and Slavs.

All attendees swore to abide by the decisions of the council on the succession. They included not only Louis's sons and the bishops who, by their prayers and rituals, had attempted to ensure the purity of the proceedings but the great nobles as well. This last group had come to the convocation on behalf of whichever son of Louis they'd hitched their star to (and also to argue for their own interests). The nobles' opinions and attitudes mattered greatly. We, like the Carolingians themselves, shouldn't forget that they had come to power as high nobles who had staged a coup against the Merovingians, a legitimate ruling dynasty. It therefore shouldn't surprise us that Louis at least initially took the *Ordinatio imperii* so seriously that he made the nobles reswear to abide by its terms two more times (both in 821). Parchment was one thing, the iron of the nobles' blades another. They were seen as the primary enforcers of the divine and imperial order.

Though it may seem as though Louis the Pious was focused on ensuring that his sons kept the kingdom in the family, a closer look at the *Ordinatio imperii* suggests that the emperor's primary concern wasn't his sons' positions but about making things "right" with God. It's telling that the document lays out a clear hierarchy, one that operated quite differently from the one Charlemagne had set down in 806. In that earlier document, made moot by Louis the Pious's brothers' deaths, all of the sons were to be kings in their own realms. Charles the Younger had received perhaps a "better" share than his younger siblings, but there had been no implication of a unified empire that would remain together afterward.

But in 817, the emperor sat above his brothers. Lothar became the co-emperor with his father (crowned by Louis the Pious himself, as his father had done before) and sat above his brothers, allowing the Franks to remain a united front against external foes. Important decisions were ultimately the emperor's to make. In that way the *Ordinatio imperii* was not just ordering an empire but also defining a family. It drew a much harder line between legitimacy and illegitimacy while also attempting to put boundaries up around the font from which that legitimacy flowed. Only the sons of Louis, king and emperor, from lawful marriage would inherit. And the fasting and prayers and churchmen who accompanied the council where the document was drawn up were all meant to clearly show that this was not merely what the ruling dynasty wanted but the will of God.

But the will of God didn't mention Bernard of Italy even once.

When Louis the Pious became co-emperor with his father in summer 813, Charlemagne confirmed his grandson Bernard's position as king in Italy. Then, as we know, when Louis took power in 814, he once again confirmed that position for Bernard. Bernard is noted as accompanying Louis the Pious into Saxony on campaign in early 815 and then being dispatched to Rome to deal with an uprising there.

He carried that out flawlessly and secured the papacy. But Bernard's fortunes changed pretty quickly after that. His biggest supporters at Aachen in the last years of Charlemagne's reign had been Wala and Adalhard—who were, as we know, both immediately exiled after Louis came to power in 814. That cast Bernard under some suspicion. More damningly, he had a son in 815 and named him Pepin, likely after Bernard's father (Louis's brother).

Everyone knew that was a Carolingian royal name, one of great importance going back several generations. Such a symbolic name could feel like a threat to the new emperor. And it did. Bernard was cut out, and quickly. There's no mention of Bernard in any of the major sources of Louis's reign for 816–817, even though two popes died in rapid succession in those years and Bernard was Louis's man in Italy. In the *Ordinatio imperii*, Bernard was out for good. Not only was he excluded from attending the council itself, the document specified that Italy was from then on to be under Lothar's purview. Bernard could only read that snub as a provocation, and as later events would seem to prove, Louis almost certainly meant it as such.

Bernard was indeed provoked and took swift action. But as with most of the stories from the time, competing narratives obscure what actions actually took place.

There are four different versions that explain the conflict between Louis and Bernard. Most spectacularly, a biographer of Louis the Pious by the name of Thegan said that Bernard wished to depose the emperor and take the throne for himself. A different, much later source from Italy said that Bernard had been a good ruler who hadn't done anything wrong and that the whole thing had been a put-up job engineered by Louis's wife, Ermengarde, who hated Bernard. But we can pretty immediately discount both those claims. Bernard would have had to have been out of his mind to revolt in 817. What could he possibly have thought he'd accomplish from Italy? And then, on the other side of the spectrum, it's a well-established trope to blame the wife for a king's decision. Indeed, both claims mirror those made about Pepin the Hunchback's revolt in 792.

But something did happen, and we can indeed say that Bernard wasn't going to acquiesce without some kind of fight.

Perhaps somewhat closer to reality, the *RFA* and the Astronomer both said that shortly after the *Ordinatio imperii* of 817, Bernard closed all the passes through the Alps into Italy and confirmed the loyalties of all the peninsula's city-states to him. Both sources say that Bernard had been swayed by the counsels of evil men and intended to set up an independent kingdom in Italy. But then they immediately retracted their own statements. The *RFA* tempered its claims by saying that the dire report about Bernard's actions and intentions that reached the emperor at Aachen "was partly true and partly false." So perhaps both accounts conveyed actual details but hedged (or fudged) the reasoning behind them. If he actually did it, Bernard may have closed the passes as a precautionary measure to lock down his own support on the peninsula until the emperor's intentions were made clear.

But let's step back and try to find some facts among all those medieval "truths." What we have is a powerful Carolingian left out of the succession plan. He's at the very least resistant to submitting to a potentially ignominious fate but almost certainly not considering doing anything drastic. But then the sources converge into a single story about what happened next: Louis reacted as if Bernard had rebelled, gathering an army and heading south. Bernard must have been terrified and optimistic at the same time. After all, he was a crowned and confirmed king and less than two years before, he'd been by his uncle's side and dispatched as a trusted aide to protect the pope and take care of trouble in Rome. He had reason to hope that the whole misunderstanding would quickly be resolved. Before the end of 817, he went to meet his uncle, the emperor. To assuage any worries, Bernard didn't march north with an army, taking only his household guard with him.

Uncle and nephew met at Chalon-sur-Saône, south of Dijon. Was he surrendering and admitting his guilt, or was he simply there to meet his uncle and clarify their new relationship? In the end, it didn't matter. Bernard was arrested along with the supposed ringleaders and taken back to Aachen before any real conversation could take place. Early in 818, they were all sentenced to death. In a fit of mercy, Louis decided to simply blind Bernard rather than kill him, but it didn't go well, and Bernard died in agony three days later. The Astronomer dryly noted that Louis felt bad about that outcome. Did he really feel bad, or was this another moment of selective remembering by the author, looking back from much later in the reign? We wonder. But we do know that Louis's rage at Bernard's supposed audacity was widely felt. Several important nobles who were loyal to Bernard suffered the same fate, Louis's illegitimate half brothers (including Drogo of Metz and Hugh of Saint-Quentin, who will become very important later) were sent away from court to monasteries, and some important bishops (including Theodulf of Orléans, the trusted adviser of Charlemagne who had welcomed Louis into his city and smoothed the path of his ascent to the throne in 814) were deprived of their offices and exiled.

Now we see what was really going on. The *Ordinatio imperii* had not only formally ensured the succession, guaranteed by the Franks' swearing of sacred oaths, but also provided a pretext for clearing the rest of the field of any remaining Carolingians. But it's clear that Bernard wasn't supposed to die. It's not that Carolingians necessarily wouldn't kill family members; Charlemagne most likely had his nephews killed, and the sudden, convenient death of Louis the Pious's brother Pepin the Hunchback is, after all, a little suspicious. Blinding, however, was an older Roman punishment that initially represented a tyrant's injustice and fury but was transformed in the early European Middle Ages into a symbol of a ruler's mercy—his willingness to let a rival live. That was the model Louis the Pious was following, and he said so specifically. For the first time, it was deployed against a Carolingian. It was supposed to be merciful. Louis was Pious.

But note two important things. First, Bernard died. Intentionally or not, Louis the Pious had murdered his nephew. In addition, Louis had broken his oath. He had promised in 813 to honor Bernard's rule in Italy, then confirmed it a year later. Then he took it away in 817. And now Bernard was dead by Louis's decree.

That was a fact not lost on contemporaries. Around 820, a visionary text was composed that directly criticized Louis the Pious for his
actions against Bernard. The "Vision of the Poor Woman of Laon"
was almost certainly written by a monk at Reichenau Abbey in modern Germany, perhaps even by its abbot, Heito, who had been an
adviser to Charlemagne. Regardless of its specific authorship, the
vision channels "in the district of Laon [just northwest of Reims, in
modern France] a certain poor woman who was once seized by a
state of ecstasy." Those types of texts became particularly important
in this and the following generations as modes of indirect critique,
of churchmen using their believed connection to the divine in order to call down dire warnings for those in power. They were often
peripheral to the primary political conversations going on at court
but served as a mirror for princes and were significant for a ruling
class that thought seriously about the need to maintain God's favor.
Neither fact nor fiction, they operated in a third space in which—not
unlike the histories themselves—they were intended to say something
true, not necessarily something real.

The Poor Woman, led around the afterlife by a robed monk, sees
not only the saints in repose but also some of the most powerful men
in Francia in torment. Charlemagne, referred to, interestingly, as a
prince of Italy rather than as the emperor of the Franks, is suffering
in unspecified torment, but her guide assures her that he will soon be
released because of the prayers organized by Louis the Pious. That
seems positive enough for the Carolingians, but then things get dark
and the rest of the vision is a searing indictment of Louis the Pious.
After Charlemagne, the Poor Woman sees one of Louis's closest advisers held down by demons as they pour molten gold into his mouth
and mock his greed. Queen Ermengarde, Louis's wife, has three
boulders attached to her, dragging her into the depths. She cries out
to the Poor Woman for help, for Louis to organize prayers for her as
well. And just in case Louis doubts Ermengarde's anguish, the guide
tells the Poor Woman to reference a conversation Ermengarde and
her husband had privately in their garden not long before her death.
He will remember, and he will then understand.

Next, the Poor Woman encounters a wall through which she can't pass. On the other side is the terrestrial paradise, and on its walls she "read and found that the name of Bernard, once king, was inscribed in letters more brilliant than any other there." Continuing to read, she sees that "the name of King Louis was so faint and almost obliterated that it could scarcely be seen." Shocked, she asks why. Her guide somberly tells her that "the killing of Bernard led to the obliteration of that name." He also tells her that the king has to be warned of what she saw in that vision and so, reluctantly, the vision ends with her gaining an audience with Louis and telling him everything.

Dream visions like that one provided Carolingians with a reasonably safe way to comment on current events, placing critiques of the king literally out of this world. But the visions rarely provided good news for the people in power; no one ever gambols through the fires of Hell and then comes back and says that everything is fine. Every part of that particular vision is about Louis's murder of his nephew in 818. Charlemagne is called a prince of Italy, reminding the vision's audience that it was he who gave Italy to his grandson Bernard. It was therefore not a title Louis could take away. Louis's adviser, drowning in molten gold, is wretched because of his court's rapaciousness, seizing Italy from its rightful ruler. What else, the author seems to have wondered, was Louis's move against Bernard if not greed? The revelation of Ermengarde's "private" meeting with Louis before her death in 818 hints strongly that she is whispering into the emperor's ear, goading him on to violence on behalf of her sons, Lothar, Pepin, and Louis. And for the sake of those three sons, she is being pulled into the abyss by three rocks. Finally, Bernard emerges as akin to a martyr. His name shines brighter than any other on the wall of life.

The vision is a critique, yes, but at a distance—safe, unlikely to generate the direct wrath of the king. Therefore, we might better understand it as a helpful admonition rather than a full-throated condemnation of Louis's rule. The emperor's name is almost obliterated from the wall, but it's not gone and as emperor he can organize prayers to save (some of) the damned: his father and wife. He can set right what went wrong because the vision's real ire was at

Louis's greedy counselors who had led him astray. As the scholar Paul Dutton so deftly summarized, "to make one powerful friend was to spawn a hundred jealousies." That was the curse of life at court.

That it was a poor woman, one on the lowest rung of the ninth-century social ladder, who had to speak truth to the emperor is evidence of how troubled the times were, a world turned upside down. The vision assured the reader, though, that God had gifted the emperor a path back to redemption. The question now was what he would do with it: Would he find wise counsel, or would his name slowly fade from the walls of Paradise?

Far from settling things in 818, putting away the last potential Carolingian rivals to his and Ermengarde's sons, Louis's treatment of his nephew—a recognized Carolingian king—induced powerful ecclesiastics and secular nobles to raise their voices in protest. Louis needed to atone for his sins. As if that weren't bad enough, world events seemed to confirm the suspicions contained in those admonitions. There was plenty of evidence that God was angry with the Franks. Louis's wife, Ermengarde, died just six months after Bernard of Italy in 818, and the emperor began to lose many of his closest advisers—some of whom had been with him since he had been king, under his father, in Aquitaine—at just that time.

Louis tried to right the ship. His first step was to remarry. In 819, at the age of forty and on the advice of his counselors, he decided to find a second wife. At the beginning of that year, the sources report, many of the most noble, most beautiful, and most eligible women from the empire descended on Aachen, and in the end the emperor selected and married Judith of Bavaria. At the very least, the Astronomer's account of this "bridal beauty pageant," the author still being more interested in truth than in fact, is a conscious allusion to the Book of Esther. In that biblical book, an Israelite woman named Esther is selected (by pageant) to wed the king of Persia. She then exposes a dastardly plot by one of the king's evil advisers and saves the

Israelites. Looking back from his perch at the end of Louis's reign, the Astronomer knew well what no one at the time had: that that promising marriage would, in the next decade, expose the nefarious doings of some of Louis's advisers. Thegan did agree, however, that Judith was very beautiful, so perhaps that part of the story is in fact true.

Judith's family was well connected to nobles east of the Rhine, particularly in and around Alemannia. Her father, in fact, was related to one of the powerful Bavarian nobles who had caused trouble with and for Pepin the Hunchback and Charlemagne back in the day, but now that family had, as so many others, reintegrated, and was back at the center of Carolingian power. Its members were useful to Louis, who continued his quest to unify and settle debts in the service of his kingdom. Indeed, those in Judith's parents' circle slowly began to join the emperor's, adding yet another stage to the shifting presences and influences around the royal court in the period just after Bernard of Italy's death. Maybe this reset of his court would help the realm, with a newly reinvigorated court and new queen as a model for the Franks as a whole?

Nope.

The *RFA* reported that there was a persistent revolt in Pannonia (roughly around present-day northern Croatia and Bosnia and Herzegovina), war had restarted with Muslims in Iberia, pirates were tormenting the Italian coast, and a great pestilence had torn through humans and cattle and ruined crops. That was all in the year 820. Louis's spiritual adviser, the monk Benedict of Aniane, died in early 821. Things seemed only to be getting worse.

Louis had to try again.

Later in 821, a great assembly of Franks met at Thionville, just north of Metz in modern France. The ostensible reason for the gathering was the wedding of Louis's oldest son, Lothar. The might of the emperor was on full display. Envoys from the papacy delivered rich gifts, and representatives from victorious Frankish armies announced their triumphs. But there was more. According to the *RFA*, "the most pious emperor revealed his most singular mercy to those who had conspired with his nephew Bernard in Italy," referring to Adalhard, Wala, and others who had been banished. The emperor not only accepted their loyalty anew but restored their seized possessions to them. All had to swear (or swear again) to uphold the *Ordinatio imperii* of just a few years before. What that document had torn asunder, Louis was now trying to stitch back together.

The process of reconciliation continued into 822, when, at another assembly at Attigny in the Ardennes, Louis went even further. The *RFA* reported that there Louis had held council with both bishops and lay noblemen. The issue of Bernard's death had once more come up, so the emperor had decided to make a public confession and undergo penance so that God would forgive "what he had done to Bernard, son of his brother Pepin, and to Abbot Adalhard, and Adalhard's brother Wala." Louis also desired to be reconciled with his brothers, whom Louis had, we remember, exiled after he had taken power in 814. Note who was mentioned here. It was imperial business, but it was also—maybe more—family business. As if to emphasize the point, Louis closed the assembly by presiding over his son Pepin's wedding. Pepin and his wife were sent to their kingdom in Aquitaine and Lothar back to his kingdom in Italy, the latter this time with the newly restored Wala as adviser.

Everything from 819 on—Louis's remarriage, as well as the two councils in 821–822—was not only about the role of the ruler within the empire but also about the ruling family itself. The Astronomer (again, writing decades later) hoped to show Louis as overwhelmingly merciful—endlessly willing to take responsibility upon himself and to forgive in order to knit the empire back together. The two councils show Louis calling people back "home" to court. Adalhard and Wala were blood relations and had been in Charlemagne's inner circle, and so, too, had Louis's brothers been ever present at court before they were all banished. Louis's sisters, however, remained unmentioned, outside the emperor's grace even after his merciful forgiveness of people such as Wala and Adalhard.

In his discussion of the public penance at Attigny specifically, the Astronomer added one important editorial note to his account, suggesting that Louis had been inspired to his actions by the example of the Roman emperor Theodosius I. In 390, more than 430 years prior, Roman soldiers had massacred several thousand citizens in Thessalonica. It seems that there was some sort of a riot in which a Roman official may have been killed and the massacre had been a reprisal that had gone far beyond what was intended. There had been a great popular outcry among churchmen against the murders. As emperor, Theodosius may or may not have ordered the reprisal, but he took responsibility nonetheless and willingly underwent a public penance, forgoing his imperial robes—effectively humiliating himself—when attending Mass until formally reconciled to the bishop of his city. The memory of those events—a memory meaningful to the Carolingian elites sharing a common education rich in historical studies—was likely why the Astronomer concluded his account of the events at Attingy by saying that Louis "was concerned to return to God's grace, as if those things which each person had legally suffered had in fact been done through his own cruelty."

If, by this logic, Bernard had rebelled, the law said he was to be killed. Louis didn't want that, had tried to prevent it by commuting the sentence to blinding, but Bernard had died anyway. The buck had stopped with the emperor in the fourth century, and now it stopped with the emperor once more. All present hoped that God would reward Louis's sincere desire and look favorably upon the whole Frankish people.

Louis and his advisers looked at the events of 818–820 in dismay: disaster upon disaster. With the assembly at Attigny especially, the king and his advisers were trying to put a cap on all of it, to stem the rising tide of God's wrath upon the Franks. A recently unearthed manuscript, seemingly a record of the bishops who attended the assembly, makes clear that they thought the responsibility for penance, the attempt to fix the Franks' relationship with God, lay with everyone who attended—not just the emperor. All the nobles, all the bishops, and the emperor himself had a responsibility to the realm. They must all commit to asking for mercy and atoning for their sins. In Louis's case, it was also an opportunity to call his Carolingian family back home to court, especially as he was preparing his sons Lothar and Pepin to marry and take up their kingdoms. In one fell swoop, if the rituals worked, Louis the Pious could bring the old hands back into his circle, display his power and magnanimity to the realm, and also provide both himself and his sons with some trusted advisers.

But he could also kill two birds with one stone. Forgiving the nobles who had been implicated with Bernard was also, at the moment, an astute political maneuver. The eastern fringes of the empire had become the empire's most pressing concern, in large part because of the Slavic rebellion in Lower Pannonia. Much of Bernard's support, which in part devolved from his father (Louis's brother), was based in either Italy or Alemannia, the latter a critical region centered roughly where Switzerland and southwest Germany meet today. Though not a frontier region per se, it was close to the fighting in Pannonia and an important source of troops and supplies, as well as a foundation for further expansion eastward.

Alemannia was also critically important to Louis beginning in 819 because of his new wife. As we saw with Charlemagne (and maybe every stepfamily ever), second wives can create problems for the children of previous wives. At first, Judith seemed to integrate well into court life and be a generally benign presence; she was certainly *there* but is hardly mentioned. Her daughter with Louis, Gisela, was born in 820, and not a single narrative source mentioned it. That changed at Attigny, or at least not very long after the council there in 822, when Judith became pregnant again. Maybe the penance at Attigny, the calling home of family, had indeed set the empire on a better path.

In June 823, the empress Judith gave birth to a son. Though the fact is curiously unrecorded in both the *RFA* and Thegan, the Astronomer (writing with much hindsight) was unsubtle in his recollection of the moment. He wrote:

> At about that time strange signs and omens stirred up the emperor's spirit, especially an earthquake at the palace of Aachen, weird sounds at night, a certain girl who fasted for twelve months, virtually

abstaining from food, frequent and unusual lightning, stones falling with hail, and diseases of people and animals. On account of these remarkable occurrences, the pious emperor urged that frequent fasts and continuous prayers and generous alms be offered through the priestly office to placate God, saying on his own behalf that on account of these prodigies an enormous future catastrophe was in store for the human race. In that same year, in the month of June, Queen Judith bore him a son.

Unrecorded in that account but acknowledged in another later work, Lothar was there at the birth with his father and stepmother. He'd become co-emperor with Louis the Pious six years earlier, in 817, and had been recrowned in the months preceding the birth in Rome by Pope Paschal II. The latter event was surely an insurance policy agreed to by both Lothar and Louis the Pious, who was about to become a father once more.

Still, Lothar must have shuddered—perhaps even gasped—as his father decided to name the youngest newborn Charles. After Charlemagne, after Louis the Pious's own father, it was a name not given to any of the other sons. The child, through no fault of his own, was immediately a threat to his brothers. The omens that so "stirred up the emperor's spirit," that every reader would so clearly see as connected to the birth of Louis's new son, may have been the work not of God but of the Devil.

ACT II

Family Trouble

CHAPTER 4

Sex, Witchcraft, and Angry Nobles

828–831

𝕿he demon called itself Wiggo. In late 828, a young girl of about sixteen began behaving erratically until eventually the girl's despairing parents had no choice but to seek an exorcism. Desperate for help, they took her to a church sanctified by the recent arrival of some saintly relics from Rome. The priest there talked to the demon living in the girl's body, but the creature was initially silent. Then suddenly the child smiled and a reply came out in Latin, a language she did not know. Only then did Wiggo identify itself and freely admit what it was doing.

He was Satan's doorkeeper, Wiggo declared. He had been roaming the land of the Franks with eleven friends for the last couple of years. "Following our instructions," the demon continued, "we destroyed the grain, grapes, and all the earth's produce that is useful to mankind. We slaughtered the stock with disease and even directed plague and pestilence against human beings." "How?" asked the priest. What had given the demon such power? With a toothy grin, the demon replied, "You."

The sins of the Franks and their rulers had made the land fertile for Wiggo and his friends. This is a land without justice, Wiggo said, in which greed runs rampant. The powerful "abuse the higher place, which they received that they might justly rule their subjects, giving themselves up to pride and vainglory; hatred and malice they direct not only against those who are far off but against their neighbors and those with whom they are allied; friend mistrusts friend, brother hates brother, and father has no love for son." None, Wiggo concluded, give honor to God as they did in previous generations. His speech finished, his work apparently done, the demon left the girl, overcome by the power of the martyrs.

Medieval stories about the sacred or supernatural—demons, angels, saints, relics, miracles, visions—take place in a world where the borders between natural and supernatural are thin or nonexistent. They often have a didactic purpose: to teach or to reveal, to make an argument, especially, about how the world has become disordered. Because their mouthpieces are beyond this world, these texts can say the unsayable, a form of speaking truth to power. Sometimes it's hard to know if any individual surviving text had a wide readership, but we can say with absolute certainty that hagiography, or stories about saints, their miraculous and holy acts both before and after death, had a wide and enduring audience, permeating medieval European society through text, speech, and images.

This story of Wiggo, taken from a hagiography about the acquisition and ritual installation of the relics of Saints Marcellinus and Peter at the new church, was likely written in late 830 or early 831 by a man named Einhard, a name familiar to us. Einhard was a courtier of Charlemagne and his biographer. He was also a close associate of Louis the Pious and, in fact, so important at court that he served as the childhood tutor for Louis's eldest son, Lothar I. The demon's accusations themselves should also be somewhat familiar to us, as they echo the "Vision of the Poor Woman of Laon" from the previous chapter. That vision, too, had called out dire warnings about the state of the realm. But apparently, that text's warnings hadn't been taken seriously enough for the empire to change course, or they hadn't reached the right ears, so the supernatural warnings were repeated and scaled up from a vision of the afterlife to a visit to this world from Hell's minions.

What had seemed so promising in the early 820s had turned into disaster by the end of the decade, or so went the argument of the authors of both of those visions. Louis had learned nothing from his previous supernatural admonition and continued to surround himself with greedy men and women who plundered good Christians across the empire. The message embedded in the story of demonic possession was not just that things were very, very bad but that they'd in fact gotten worse since "Vision of the Poor Woman of Laon." In that earlier text, corruption had been contained within the court. Now demons roamed the earth. They were responsible for plagues and famines but not, we note, for the sins of men. Those sins, the pitting of fathers against sons, friends betraying friends, and brothers holding evil in their hearts for one another, were signs of human failings, not infernal subversion.

The situation in the Frankish Empire had gotten so bad that now only a poor, uneducated girl, acting as a mouthpiece for a demon, was willing to speak truth about the evils of the time. The Franks were blind to the reality of their situation; this story is a demonstration of that. Even worse, whereas in circa 820 the poor woman of Laon had been a vessel for a divine message, women had now become (unwitting) agents of the Franks' destruction. The demon was using the woman to destroy, rather than as in earlier visions, God had used a woman to convey divine truth. But why? What terrible deeds might inspire such a ghastly story of plague, famine, and death? Could it have been a rebellion? A coup? A murder? In this case, it was none of those. The world had been thrown upside down by a marriage.

"Ah for pity! Into what great miseries our times have sunk, when evil demons rather than good men are teachers, and the proponents of vice and inciters of crime admonish us for our own correction," Einhard concluded his work in a lamentation. He had seen the crisis—the behaviors of men and women that had opened the hellmouth—play out before his eyes. So he wrote to the king with a warning. The political consensus, always fragile beneath a projection of divinely appointed strength, had begun to fray, and the positions of the ruler and his queen were just as vulnerable to the machinations of the aristocracy as they had been in previous generations. They were avatars of the empire, and so if things were going poorly, Einhard and every other noble seeking to improve the kingdom (or at least his own position in it) felt that change should start at the top.

❧

In 819, Louis the Pious had married Judith of Bavaria, his second wife, and stability and prosperity seemed possible. By 828, demons such as Wiggo were roaming the earth, speaking Latin out of the mouths of little girls in order to give warnings to priests. The road from Judith to Wiggo required many different stops along the way, many different causes. But one new, critical development in the 820s that turned the Frankish world upside down was this: for the first time in living memory, Frankish warfare against outsiders started to go poorly.

When Louis had been younger, he had won important victories on behalf of Charlemagne just south of the Pyrenees. Louis had been king in Aquitaine under his father, and the so-called Spanish March centered around Catalonia was very much part of his purview. In 801, for example, he conquered Barcelona and expanded the Frankish frontier southward. A local count named Bera, part of Charlemagne's old guard, was left in charge to defend the city but seems to have been removed from power around 820, likely as part of Louis's housecleaning in the wake of his nephew Bernard's revolt. We're not quite sure what happened to the city of Barcelona in the following few years, but around 826 the city was placed into the hands of a man named (again, they were sometimes not supercreative when it came to human names, as opposed to demonic ones) Bernard of Septimania.

This other Bernard was a Carolingian, a son of the count of Toulouse, but more important a descendant of Charles Martel and hence a distant(-ish) cousin of Louis the Pious. He was also the emperor's godson. The timing of Bernard's appointment matters, because in 826, right about the time Bernard took over the city, a man named Aizo fled the court at Aachen to return to the Spanish March, gather military support from local Islamic powers, and then launch a rebellion against Louis. He was joined by several regional rulers, as well as Bera's son.

We should note two things here: First, the lines between religious traditions were (and continued to be) porous in that period. Muslims helped Christian rulers and vice versa when it suited their needs. Second, we really have no idea who Aizo was, though our best guess is that he was a Christian Goth, almost certainly from Iberia, and probably connected in some way back to the old count Bera. Aizo might even have been a hostage at Louis's court, which would explain his presence at Aachen, his flight to Iberia, and the timing of his rebellion right after Bernard's appointment. Early-medieval hostages were often sent by the defeated, or in Bera's case, the purged, to the court of the conqueror as guarantees that the conquered party would behave. The hostages were never held under lock and key but rather became part of the entourage of the ruler, who still of course could decide whether or not the hostage lived or died. In this case, if he was connected to Bera, Aizo likely saw Bernard of Septimania's appointment to the county as a betrayal and so fled south to try to claim the territory for himself. Although it was rare for a hostage to go to Barcelona to raise an army against a Carolingian ruler, if we had a nickel for every time it happened, by the end of this book we'd have two nickels. Which isn't a lot, but it's weird that it happened twice.

Aizo's revolt infuriated Louis. Those types of uprisings dotted the history of the Franks; regional nobles might well raise an army and try to seize lands or titles in the hope of eventually having them acknowledged by the emperor. Aizo's revolt was thus not a threat to Louis's actual power, but it was an act of defiance and Barcelona was Louis's personal conquest, his prize, and no one else would be allowed to control it. Or so Louis hoped.

The emperor quickly gave orders to assemble a massive army, to use overwhelming force to sweep the enemy away. But that was not what ended up happening. In 827, Louis sent two armies into the Spanish March to quell this rebellion. The first army, led by Louis's former chancellor, met with very limited success, but it did at least put the rebels on the defensive. But when the imperial army's campaign concluded, Aizo reinforced his army with one sent by the Islamic lord of Saragossa and used the breathing room to regain the ground he had lost.

Louis then sent another, even larger army, led by his son Pepin of Aquitaine, as well as the hugely influential counts Matfrid of Orléans and Hugh of Tours. But the army dithered, moving southward too slowly. Barcelona was put under pressure by Aizo, saved only, our sources reported, by the heroism of Bernard of Septimania. So by the time the second army got there, Aizo had gone to ground. The imperial army melted away having accomplished nothing.

Here's where it seemed to get personal, because Louis just wouldn't let the matter go. He sent a third army in the summer of 828, led again by Pepin of Aquitaine but accompanied by Pepin's elder brother, co-emperor Lothar I. The brothers met at Lyons before heading farther south; but they decided the threat was no longer grave, so they disbanded the force. And maybe they were right; we don't really hear more about the rebellion after that. Barcelona stayed in Bernard's hands, and thus remained part of the empire and loyal to Louis the Pious.

But right or not about the true level of threat, there was no glorious victory. When Frankish armies marched against outsiders, they were supposed to win.

Someone needed to take the fall for the failure. It couldn't be his sons, so Louis chose Matfrid and Hugh. At an assembly in Aachen in early 828, they were stripped of their positions (their *honores*), so literally dis-honored and sentenced to death. Again, showing mercy, Louis commuted the sentence—a serious miscalculation in the long run, because Matfrid and Hugh's dishonoring set off a political earthquake that would have ramifications for decades.

Hugh's daughter was Lothar I's wife, and Hugh had served Charlemagne as one of the emperor's emissaries to Constantinople. Hugh also seems to have been close to Pepin of Aquitaine, serving with him on campaigns in Brittany. Matfrid was perhaps even more powerful. He seems to have been one of Louis the Pious's made men, rising to the heights of Frankish nobility in the company of the heir to Charlemagne. Matfrid had been present at key events: the *Ordinatio imperii* in 817, the council at Attigny in 822, and in the army of Louis the German in the Breton campaign. And at least one letter described Matfrid as the man who controlled access to the emperor, using that position to create his own network of patronage and hide corruption and greed from the eyes of Louis the Pious. The two men had power, but that meant they also had enemies. And when they did go, neither went quietly.

Feeling empowered by the massive reshuffling around him, Louis quickly began to reshape the court dynamics in ways that reflected the new focal points of power: out with the old guard—Matfrid and Hugh—and in with the new—Bernard of Septimania, the hero of Barcelona. Louis elevated Bernard to the position of chamberlain both as a reward for his heroism and because Bernard was dependent upon Louis for his ascent to the highest ranks of the imperial court. Louis thought Bernard was someone he could trust. Whoops.

We don't always know exactly what court positions meant in terms of the day-to-day operations of the royal government, but the chamberlain seems to have been responsible for working with the empress to hand out gifts to courtiers and visitors. That would have given the chamberlain considerable power, with control over money and direct access to the imperial bedroom. The combination of power and specific responsibilities suggests that the chamberlain operated as a creature more of the queen than the king.

The reshuffling of high society continued outside the immediate court, but those who rose were connected by blood. Louis gave some of Matfrid's land to two of Bernard's cousins, Odo and William. Also at Worms, Bernard was charged with the care of the young Charles the Bald. This is particularly significant because at the same time, Charles was given rule over Alemannia (where his mother, we remember, had strong family support) and some lands in the region of Alsace. Lothar and Louis the German, the latter having just recently married Judith's sister (!) in 827, were present at Charles's elevation and seem to have been supportive of the move. Not all the brothers loved the idea of the reshuffling, though. Pepin of Aquitaine refused to attend, still stung by the blame for the earlier army's failure re-dounding on him, or perhaps he just realized that the elevation of Team Judith might be bad for Team Pepin.

To summarize: Louis the Pious had earlier conquered Barcelona from the Emirate of Córdoba, his greatest victory under his father. Decades later, when a rebellion led by Aizo threatened the city, Louis as emperor sent three different armies to address the problem, all of which failed to various degrees. But Bernard of Septimania, as ruler of Barcelona, successfully defended the city. In the aftermath, the emperor removed two of his most powerful, best-connected nobles and replaced them with Bernard and his allies, while also linking Bernard to his young son Charles, a prince with an imperial name from a different mother than the older princes. If the *Ordinatio imperii* organized an empire and defined a family, the elevation of Bernard, Queen Judith, and the infant prince Charles potentially reorganized and redefined both. It was an upheaval. It was a recipe for disaster.

And things quickly turned. Bernard used his new status to imme-diately reshuffle the court, establishing his own position and build-ing his own network of patronage, elevating family members, and blocking old routes of access to power and privileges. Lothar, who had been elevated to co-emperor a decade earlier, had since that time always been noted as such on imperial diplomas. After Bernard's elevation, though, diplomas began to omit Lothar's name.

Lothar was in Italy throughout all of this, viewing the turn of events from afar, and could not have been happy about it. Pepin of Aquitaine had at least in part felt the sting of the blame for the failed expedition in 827, so he was pissed off. Meanwhile, Matfrid and Hugh weren't wholly neutralized; even while exiled from court, they main-tained the political and social networks they had built over a lifetime, which included Louis the Pious's two eldest sons (Lothar as Hugh's son-in-law and Pepin as the commander of the disgraced army). As Bernard's star rose, the old guard got very, very angry.

✤

The rebellion came quickly.

Not a year after the gathering at Worms that saw Bernard's rise, the emperor gathered a Frankish army in early 830 not far from Orléans in order to campaign in Brittany—one of those border spaces against which the Carolingians had traditionally experienced so much success. Louis the Pious had ridden ahead with a small troop of soldiers to scout. It was a fateful decision.

The army, without its emperor, was hijacked. Back at the main force, Hugh and Matfrid unexpectedly showed up and took control, using their long-standing connections to the old guard, most of them not fans of Judith and Bernard, to channel their anger. Hugh and Matfrid had been joined by the highest ranks of the nobility, men who had been intimate advisers not just of Louis the Pious but of Charlemagne beforehand. Those men represented the highest echelons of Frankish power, revealing the breadth of the dissent at Bernard's rise. Instead of heading for Brittany, they marched in the other direction, toward Orléans. There, Hugh and Matfrid removed Odo, Bernard's cousin, from his new county so that Matfrid could be reinstalled and then dispatched messengers to Pepin of Aquitaine to invite him to join the party. Pepin arrived very quickly—maybe too quickly!—and joined the rebels as they then marched to Paris.

Louis was shocked when he heard about the revolt within his own army, but he didn't immediately panic. The presence of Hugh and Matfrid seemed to make clear that the conflict was over power in the court rather than necessarily a direct threat to the emperor's rule. He thought he could still cow them into submission or, failing that, stall and negotiate. To his mind, he had done just that to Bernard of Italy in 817. There was no reason to think it wouldn't work again.

Louis the Pious summoned Judith to meet him so they could intercept the rebels at the imperial palace in Compiègne, north of Paris. It must've been about that time that he heard that his eldest son, the co-emperor Lothar, was on his way north from Italy with an army of supporters, supposedly to back his brother Pepin and the disaffected nobles against their father. Louis was in trouble now, and he knew it. Had Lothar been a part of the conspiracy all along? Emboldened,

Matfrid and Hugh (and Pepin) made their plan known. It was simple: diminish the emperor (whether or not he'd be deposed or just humiliated is unclear), get rid of Judith, and kill Bernard of Septimania.

From the rebels' standpoint, the entire drama was a tragedy. Even though they seemed to have the upper hand, they believed that they had been forced into that course of action because the emperor had been led astray by bad advisers (mainly Bernard) and neglected the common good. As Frankish armies had been losing battles across the Frankish frontiers, it seemed that God had manifested his displeasure with the Franks as a whole.

The events of the world, the way they'd turned against the Franks, may have been evidence enough that God was not happy, but the Franks of the early ninth century were also a prodigiously literate culture. They read and they wrote. The rebels' supporters, knowing they had an audience, compiled a sort of dossier of sermons, stories, and other forms of communication that mostly haven't survived to show that the fault for their people's misfortunes lay with the emperor, or at least in the emperor's bed. The rebels and their backers could, perhaps ironically, use the Frankish ideology that placed the Franks as God's chosen people, recipients of His favor, as a tool to back their rebellion. That very ideology had seemed like a strong foundation on which to build the empire, especially since the Frankish leaders had justified that belief by pointing to their victories in battle and their mighty empire. But now the Franks were in retreat. The empire was in trouble.

Into the crack in the ideological foundation, the rebels drove their chisels. Why not try to confound your opponents with parchment and ink, with words and sermons, rather than with blood and fire? The rebels themselves, they thought, were the ones doing the work of the empire by speaking hard truths about its direction. They pointed to the losses in war, arguing that, yes, the emperor was partly responsible, but really only because he had been led astray by Bernard and the new queen.

And the accusations were spectacular, Wiggo level in their supernatural wildness. The historian Thegan said the charges made by the rebels were too "foul to tell or to believe," but he did report, along with the Astronomer, that Judith had supposedly used magical "tricks" to deceive Louis and bed Bernard. But Bernard was complicit, too, not just a victim of feminine witchcraft. As Bernard was Louis's godson, sex with Judith would have been considered incest as well as adultery. Archbishop Agobard of Lyons wrote that Judith's beauty had become a fun house mirror of itself, an inversion of the depravity of her bedchamber, where she regularly cuckolded the emperor.

Writing later, in the 850s, the monk Paschasius Radbertus (a monk connected to Wala, one of the first to lose power under Louis the Pious, and therefore one of many bearers of old grudges) went into salacious detail on that point. Paschasius was unrelenting against Judith, whom he referred to as "Justina." Here is a moment where we modern readers must pause and learn to read critiques with the understanding of ninth-century learned individuals. It wasn't enough to say that something was bad in the present moment, in the late 820s. Instead, one needed to locate current events within patterns set down by history, ideally sacred history. In this way, referring to Judith as "Justina" functioned, in such learned circles, as a devastating double recursive critique. The Justina to whom Paschasius was referring was a fourth-century empress who had almost led the Roman Empire to ruin, in part by persecuting Ambrose of Milan, one of the Fathers of the Church. But such a name also conjured into his contemporaries' minds the Old Testament Jezebel who had done the same to ancient Israel. Jezebel had been the wife of the Israelite king Ahab and had convinced him to worship Baal instead of the Israelites' god, even murdering many of the prophets who warned against doing so.

Through those arguments, intellectuals on the rebels' side provided the justifications for breaking their oaths of loyalty by binding Judith rhetorically to Jezebel and Justina. Not only had such women been, in that misogynistic view of history, disastrous for their realms, but Judith's supposedly sudden rise to the center of power could be attributed to the use of dark magic. Indeed, some of the rebels claimed that Judith was a witch, and Paschasius argued that Bernard, too, was a sorcerer and a tyrant who meant to rule on his own. Judith, as "Justina," was a whore who had conspired with Bernard to poison Louis the Pious, then kill his sons and the leading nobles of the realm. Bernard and Judith would then rule together among the ashes. The court itself had been turned over, said Paschasius, "to the delusions and divinations of sorcerers . . . all of which had converged on the palace from every corner of the world, as if the Antichrist had appeared with his witchcraft." It was therefore, according to that logic, not only justified but necessary, even holy, for the emperor's children and the realm's most faithful nobles to act.

The sexual innuendoes against the empress were almost certainly false and not an unusual way historically for men to discredit a queen they disliked, but buried underneath the scurrilous rumors was the real problem: Judith and Bernard had begun working together and controlled access to the emperor, access to wealth and favors. The chamberlain (according to our best source) was, along with the queen, responsible for the imperial treasury, for dispensing gifts and showing favor to visitors and those in the entourage. In a world that saw the workings of the divine everywhere, in which demons and angels could speak truths about corruption at court, the accusations of sex and witchcraft helped the Franks make sense of such a sudden change of political favor.

That was the anger that confronted Louis when he met with the rebels at the palace in Compiègne. Almost always multistory, towering structures, Carolingian palaces were constructed to display power over their surroundings. There were multiple buildings connected by covered walkways, rooms adorned with cloth and paint. An 820s poem famously described the paintings on the walls of the palace at Ingelheim, telling a history of Christian rulership (from the Franks' perspective) that began in biblical antiquity and continued through the Christian Roman emperors, culminating in Charlemagne's conquest of the Saxons. Compiègne must have been similar.

Louis surely confronted his son and the rebels in the main hall, a massive space fronted by a raised platform on which the emperor sat, surrounded by such display: the symbols of power. But Pepin and his cohort were unbowed when they strode in and leveled the accreted accusations of corruption in front of the assembled nobles. The smell of incense hung in the air; the trappings of power were now turned against the ruler, transforming his court into a kind of courtroom. The nobles and churchmen shouted their assent as Pepin stepped forward and took his father into custody, sending his men to fetch Judith and Bernard. Louis had wisely told Bernard to flee before the meeting. Bernard, no fool, was back in Barcelona by the time the confrontation went down, out of the rebels' hands. Judith was not so lucky.

Louis had left Judith safely, he thought, in a monastery about forty miles to the east. But the rebels, led by Pepin, Matfrid, and Hugh, sent some of their counts to fetch her. They found the queen in the basilica of the monastery, secured under the Church law of sanctuary that was supposed to provide refuge to even the worst criminals. Instead, with swords drawn, Pepin's men stormed into the basilica, pushing past the monks, ignoring the pleas of the abbot. The rebels thundered their own version of the charges of witchcraft and adultery. Then they seized Judith and literally dragged her out of the church. As they carried her back to her husband, they likely tortured her and threatened her life, and her agreement to immediately enter a convent (and try to convince Louis to enter a monastery) may have been all that spared her.

It seemed as though the rebels had won, had succeeded in their coup. Judith was dispatched to the Monastery of Sainte-Radegund in Poitiers, a territory under Pepin of Aquitaine's control. Judith's brothers were also seized, forced to become monks, and sent to monasteries in Aquitaine. Bernard was gone, not in custody but also not in power. The emperor had been humbled, his wife tortured and banished, his chief nobles either forcibly tonsured or driven from the land. There wasn't open warfare, but armies had gathered on the field. Pepin, Hugh, Matfrid, and their allies had used the threat of violence to get their way, taking the Frankish Empire right up to the edge of civil war. The emperor and empress were in custody, the nobles were in charge, and Louis's middle son, Pepin of Aquitaine, was along for the ride.

Then the situation changed. In May 830, Louis the Pious's eldest son, Lothar, finally arrived and took over. The rumors of his arrival, the rumor that he was connected to the rebellion, had played a major role in forcing Louis to meet his enemies in the palace. But even today we can't be sure whether Lothar intended to join the rebellion or to quell it. Perhaps the rebellion had been planned since 828, when the two brothers, Pepin and Lothar, had met on their way to the Spanish March, only to suddenly disband their army against their father's orders. This interpretation of that meeting maybe makes sense for Pepin, who had been aggrieved for some time at his father's meddling in Aquitaine and then the disgrace of Hugh and Matfrid's punishment the year before, but there's really no reason to think that Lothar was disaffected at that point. Lothar's tutor, Einhard—yes, the author of the story about Wiggo (and more famously Charlemagne's biography), someone deeply concerned with maintaining the proper order of things—wrote Lothar a letter sometime in early 830 warning him about plots against his father and urging him not to be persuaded to join them, to show proper, godly filial piety. Even the Astronomer (who showed no great love for Lothar's actions later on) was ambivalent about Lothar's role in the events, saying that when he arrived to meet the rebels, he "does not seem to have caused any disgrace to his father at that time, but he did approve what had been done." Perhaps Lothar had been plotting with Pepin, or perhaps when Lothar arrived at the palace and encountered a large and very angry army of rebels, he went along with what he found in front of him. At least for the moment.

At any rate, Lothar's presence as co-emperor shifted the direction of politics away from a total upheaval to a return to the status quo of pre-829, before the elevation of Bernard of Septimania. Matfrid was reinstated, and Bernard's brother was blinded and exiled. Lothar got his status of co-emperor back, but no one tried to push Louis the Pious out. The father and son reigned just as before, with both names appearing as signatories on imperial diplomas. The rebels were encouraged to disperse, to claim a victory, but not to seek any more change. Patience prevailed. Or was Lothar stalling, allowing or even enabling Bernard to be excised from court but otherwise protecting his father?

It does seem that way. Louis requested, and Lothar agreed, to settle the matter of the senior emperor's fate at another assembly to be held in early fall in Nijmegen (in the modern Netherlands). This was, for Louis—and presumably for Lothar as well, as he allowed it to happen—a brilliant political choice.

First and most important, it moved matters away from the strongholds of the rebels and farther to the east, allowing Louis's son Louis the German (who was still married to Empress Judith's sister and who hadn't participated in any plots as yet), to enter the fray on his father's side. Second, Louis the Pious managed to manipulate the framing of the assembly in order to limit who attended. One of the key rebels, Louis's archchaplain, for example, was sent away from the assembly by general consent because he had attended "with hostility" (likely meaning that he had brought armed retainers with him). Wala, Louis's old nemesis and one of Lothar's key advisers, was also sent away, back to his monastery, after it was judged that he had abandoned his responsibilities as abbot. Two key rebels with powerful networks of supporters were thus deftly taken off the table.

Chaos and violence still threatened to descend, though. As the assembly opened, the rebel faction very quickly realized that they had been outmaneuvered. Desperately, they went to Lothar, urging him to start a war to push his father off the throne for good. For the rebels, all hung in the balance. They needed to win, or they would hang. As Lothar deliberated—or perhaps pretended to deliberate— the assembled nobles rushed "against each other in an almost insane fury," according to the Astronomer. The main hall of the palace became a cacophony. Swords were drawn. The halls echoed with furious screaming.

But as the nobles clamored in the main hall, surrounded by all the pomp and display, Lothar went to his father in one of the many adjoining rooms to converse privately with him. We have no idea what was said, but a decision was made. Shortly thereafter, and before blood was shed, the main hall of the palace at Nijmegen was once again transformed. Bearing their regalia, the co-emperors strode together into the center of the fray, presenting themselves in all the majesty of the imperial office to the crowd. United together. The clamor quieted. Awe. With the assent of his eldest, Louis ordered the instigators to be seized, and they were. The rebellion ended with the whimpers of the nobles, cowed by the explosive display of majesty made by the emperors.

If the rebels had hoped that patience would work out well for them, they misunderstood. The title of emperor still meant something, definitely to Louis's sons but even to the rebels.

Louis immediately sought to restore order, and first on his list was rescuing his wife, the empress. He summoned Judith from her monastic confinement, and after she swore an oath that the accusations against her—sex magic and adultery—were untrue, she was restored to court. Later that year, Bernard was also allowed to clear his name, if not permitted back into court. Less than a year later, Louis revisited the sites of his near humiliation at Compiègne and Nijmegen to host new assemblies. There, the emperor sat in judgment alongside his three eldest sons (Charles the Bald is notably absent from all the accounts, though of course he was only seven).

All the conspirators—well, all except the sons themselves—were sentenced to death by the three sons, only to have those sentences quickly commuted to monastic confinement and exile by Louis the Pious, ever the Pious. What a change of events. The brothers: a rebel (Pepin), a maybe rebel (Lothar), and a nonrebel (Louis) came together to condemn their conspirators. Louis, on the other hand, got to accord mercy. In fact, by the end of 831, Louis had fully pardoned almost all the conspirators (except Wala, who remained in exile; Louis the Pious still really didn't like him) and allowed them to leave confinement.

That would later turn out to be a huge mistake.

❖

Although the council at Nijmegen resolved peacefully, a seal had been broken. The coup attempt was, of course, highly precedented, and that's the problem. Similar to what had happened in Bavaria with Pepin the Hunchback in 792, powerful nobles had centered their disaffection around an aggrieved son of the ruler. In 830 it was Pepin of Aquitaine. But unlike in 792, this time the rebels almost won, their coup attempt undetected until they had already surrounded Louis's palace with an army. Louis was detained; his wife was tortured and imprisoned. His eldest son, briefly, took over. But maybe more important, also unlike the events of 792 and perhaps more like those of 750—another coup by another Pepin, the one that had brought the Carolingians to the throne—Frankish nobles had counseled war against the ruler. Bloodless had almost turned bloody—very quickly.

Three coup attempts so far, three Pepins. And while it's a coincidence that they were all named Pepin, it's not a big coincidence. Names and symbols had power. Events, just as with the activities of Judith/Justina/Jezebel, had more power if they could be interpreted through the lens of history. By 831, every elite Frank understood that at least one son had risen in open rebellion and sought to depose his father. Further, it was now much easier to imagine the pattern happening again in the future, every taboo broken.

Louis the Pious seemed to be back in charge at Aachen, but was he really? Hugh and Matfrid were free. Wala was stewing in monastic exile at Corbie. Pepin was still very angry. Louis the German was getting tired of waiting for his reward for saving his father. Lothar's situation was unclear, but he was sent back over the Alps to Italy, far from the centers of power. Still, none of them was actively trying to kill or imprison the others at the moment. Even as the shock waves of 830 continued to ripple outward through the empire, maybe, if everyone behaved themselves, the empire might again know peace.

CHAPTER 5

Deposed

833–834

When the future emperor Louis the Pious was born in 778, he was given to a wet nurse named Himiltrud. We don't know much about her other than that she seems to have been enslaved and had originally come from somewhere in the eastern part of the empire, possibly Saxony. There's a good chance that she was enslaved during one of Charlemagne's brutal campaigns in that region. She was able to nurse the newborn prince because just a few years before, she had had a son by the name of Ebbo (born ca. 775). The enslaved Ebbo and the princeling Louis grew up together, sharing not just Himiltrud's milk in their earliest days but later schooling as well. The chronicler Flodoard of Reims, writing in the 900s, called Louis and Ebbo *"collactaneus et conscholasticus"*—"joined in mother's milk and in education."

Louis, of course, grew up to be the emperor, but Ebbo, effectively Louis's foster brother, did pretty well for himself too. Ebbo's genius and potential as a scholar were recognized relatively early and he was freed by Charlemagne, then followed Louis to Aquitaine after the latter became king, serving him as an adviser. They both returned to Aachen in 814 after Charlemagne died, and Ebbo first became Louis's palace librarian and then rose to the powerful position of archbishop of Reims. As befitted a well-educated Frank of the period, he was also renowned as a writer, as a participant in the shared elite literary culture so important to Frankish nobility, and as a patron of the arts. He took many of the palace scribes at Aachen to Reims with him, supporting them with positions in the churches in his archdiocese and commissioning works for specific audiences. One of those manuscripts from the 820s seems to have been intended for his milk brother, Emperor Louis the Pious. It contained a dire warning: disorder, mayhem, and violence can be laid at the feet of the ungodly ruler. Ebbo was telling his friend the emperor that he needed to change his ways.

This particular book is a psalter (a famous one, now known as the Utrecht Psalter after the city in which it is housed). Psalters, collections from the Book of Psalms, were common at the time. The ubiquity of psalters is due to the tremendously important role that the psalms played in the religious communities where the texts were created. The texts of the poems—thought in the period to have been written by King David of ancient Israel—were part of the fabric of medieval European life. Every figure in and around the Frankish court—indeed, every major figure in this book—would have used the Bible, and the psalms specifically, as a frame of reference with which to understand the world.

One page of this particular manuscript that Ebbo commissioned for Louis suggests that those using psalms to interpret current events might well be concerned about the dire state of the world in the Frankish Empire. Psalm 13 opens with the jarring sentences: "The fool has said in his heart: There is no God. They are corrupt, and are abominable in their ways: there is no one that does good, no not one." The remainder of the psalm is a lament about how everyone has turned away from goodness and embraced greed, deceit, and violence. But there is hope. The poem ends with a promise that God will lead his people back to the proper path.

What ties these verses, this message, to Ebbo's day are the images. The psalter is illustrated with scenes from the Christian Old Testament, but with all figures dressed as ninth-century Franks. Below an image of Jesus, women and children plead with a soldier with spear and shield on a hill as Frankish cavalry wait anxiously at their backs. We can almost hear the horses nicker and clomp. Then comes a scene of horrific violence: soldiers are fighting and dying, and two of the victors are pulling at a woman, making clear the sexual violence that will occur. Above this mayhem, a ruler sits enthroned under a domed canopy, a drawn sword upon his lap. Snakes climb the pillars around him. The ruler turns his attention to two soldiers who are presenting the decapitated heads of their victims. Behind the ruler, near an empty tomb with a body lying beside it, a crowned woman (the ruler's queen) shelters four frightened children. Just below the angels, the psalmist himself points toward the ruler and, with an open hand, seems to be imploring God to intervene.

What lesson would Louis the Pious have taken if he had been gifted this book by one of his most trusted advisers, one of his oldest friends? Was the friend comparing his king to the impious rulers of old: Pharaoh, King Saul, even Antichrist? The message to Louis the Pious is not so different from that contained within "Vision of the Poor Woman of Laon" or that was spoken by the demon Wiggo. Was Louis the ruler with the sword, with the Empress Judith sheltering his four children (Lothar, Pepin, Louis, and Charles)?

We can't be sure what Emperor Louis the Pious felt when he received this book from his former foster brother. But we can know that as we move past 830, the Frankish world seemed out of joint to everyone in the realm—loyalists and rebels alike. The emperor had tried to reorder the palace, with revolutionary consequences. How would he react in the aftermath of the failed coup? The accusations of witchcraft and adultery still hung in the air, and all the major conspirators were still in play. Louis the Pious had been warned in a dream vision by a poor woman, had been warned again by his close adviser Einhard's story of Wiggo, and was maybe being warned yet again by one of his oldest friends (via his commission of a group of monastic artists): the man who had shared a mother's milk, the man he had personally elevated to archbishop. Even Ebbo, like so many Frankish nobles, would have to decide where his loyalties ultimately lay: with the emperor or the realm?

The most important thing Louis had to confront immediately after his restoration at Nijmegen was how to deal with his sons. Who to punish and who to reward? Pepin had been involved in the conspiracy from the start, but Lothar's role was less clear. Maybe he was culpable, but he had also enabled Louis's path to restoration. Louis the German had arrived with timely support, so likely Louis the Pious hoped that he could at least trust one adult son. But in the immediate aftermath, Louis the German raised an army and moved to take Alemannia for his own, annoyed by both his younger brother Charles's claim on the area and his father's unwillingness to reward him properly for having saved the empire in 830. The younger Louis's maneuver collapsed quickly in the face of an imperial army led by his father. Yet Louis the German was, of course, for some reason forgiven (just boys being boys) and returned to Bavaria. The coup attempt in 830 was over, but the next crisis was just around the corner.

Just as Louis the Pious finally felt secure enough to confront Pepin of Aquitaine about his role in the insurrection of 830, the next coup began to take shape. Pepin, still aggrieved and now for some reason working closely with Bernard of Septimania (of all people!), had been openly defying his father even after Louis the Pious was restored. Finally fed up, Louis had his recalcitrant son seized and sent to Trier. But it was hard to keep a Carolingian in custody, it seems. With the help of some of his followers, Pepin escaped in a brazen nighttime jailbreak.

The emperor responded by stripping Pepin of his kingdom and giving it to his younger brother Charles, taking governance from one to give to another. There were echoes of Aizo all over again. But this time, it wasn't some faraway nobles who were rising up; it was his own son. Add to Pepin's grievance Louis the German's wounded feelings about his humiliation in Alemannia, and trouble was indeed brewing. Then came Lothar, ever the linchpin. Aware of the discontent among his siblings, he seems to have traveled to meet with his father, perhaps continuing to try to play peacemaker and preserve the status quo. And why not? The status quo was good for him: he had Italy, he had the title of co-emperor, and he was the eldest son.

On the other hand, Louis's (or, as Lothar suspected, Judith's) intention to favor Charles concerned him. Surely, Lothar thought, his father would need to find a realm for Charles to one day rule, so from whom would that land be taken? For example, Judith's ties were in Ale-mannia, a region with long-standing ties to Lothar. In addition, Lothar's closest confidants were among the old guard, the men behind the first coup, Charlemagne's old advisers. Even though they and Lothar had disagreed about how to handle Louis the Pious in the previous conflict, pressure began to mount as the year 833 dawned. Perhaps Lothar hoped to keep his options open indefinitely, but as Pepin and Louis the German began to marshal their armies in early 833, Lothar had to choose a side.

And he did. Returning to Italy after meeting with his father, Lothar felt that nothing had been fixed but everything decided. He hadn't got-ten the assurances he wanted and so decided to force the issue. He mobilized an army. He went north to meet with his brothers Pepin and Louis the German. Louis the Pious raised his own army and prepared to meet his sons on the field of battle, or at least make it clear that he was willing to fight if necessary. But it probably wouldn't be necessary, everyone thought, because Carolingians had always walked right to the edge of the cliff, then stopped and negotiated a way out.

Lothar raised the stakes, however, by bringing a new player to the table: Pope Gregory IV. As king of Italy, Lothar had of course the most direct connection of any living Carolingian to the papacy, especially because Louis the Pious had never been associated with the peninsula when Charlemagne was alive. We don't know precisely what inducements Lothar offered to bring Gregory along, but he may not have needed much. The empire was in disorder. The pope was one of the few figures who might plausibly wield enough influence over secular and lay Carolingian elites alike to swing the balance of power to whomever he backed.

The *casus belli* this time was much like that of the previous insur-rection, but the rhetoric had, if anything, been sharpened. When the brothers had reunited in June 833, their father's army waiting just across a broad field, the rebels had once again blamed the empress. The emperor's sons had sworn oaths to one another on holy relics, in the name of God and before the pope, that they sought only peace and the restoration of harmony to the land. They proclaimed that the sins of Judith had continued, despite her attesting to her blamelessness. They thundered that her lies had corrupted their father once more, taking him away from doing justice both to them (as his sons) and to the realm as a whole. The sons wanted guarantees for their land and influence over their father and the court. The pope, facing an empire in disarray, had no choice but to intervene and seems to have endorsed the rebellion as a just conflict.

The rebels and the emperor met just outside Colmar, in the Rhine River valley, just north of the Alps and conveniently almost at a four-way meeting point between the regions held by the three brothers and their father to the north at Aachen. It's in a flat, agriculturally rich region of Alsace that must have been verdant in late June, strewn with wildflowers. By the time they left in just a few days' time, though, their meeting place would be renamed "the Field of Lies."

To arrive at that field with armed men drawn from the four corners of the empire would have required an extraordinary series of events. Carolingian nobles all had small bands of highly trained personal soldiers who would be in their constant service, but raising an army was different. Magnates had to levy troops from their holdings, then gather them under (in this case) their chosen prince or the emperor, then march to meet their allies. There was no such thing in this period as a large army with a unified command structure from top to bottom; rather, every military force was composed of numerous semi-independent levies with a wide variety of skills and training—and a wide variety of motivations among their leaders.

What's more, mobilizing armies is a complicated, noisy venture. You have to feed them, or they pillage the land—not optimal when marching through your own country and stealing from your own subjects. And outside of attending to the army's needs, Carolingian military leaders had to coordinate the actions of numerous distinct military bands, from the better-trained and -equipped soldiers of the great magnates to the militias levied from small but free landowners and their communities. They had to find horses for cavalry and wagons, beasts of burden to haul supplies, adequate tents for shelter, and so on.

That was western Europe in the spring of 833 as nobles across the empire summoned troops from their towns and villages, gathered supplies, marched hundreds or thousands of men across the country-side to rallying points. Mobilization on that scale would be felt across the realm, from the great churches and halls of power to the small-est villages. Nearly everyone would know a soldier called to war. All those engaged in agriculture would see their stores and animals requisi-tioned. Anyone living by any road or river would see the troops march by as four major forces (one for each prince and one for Louis) made their way toward the Field of Lies. There must have been endless curi-osity, excitement, fear, violence, and hope spreading across the empire. But we can only know what our sources tell us, and even informed conjecture requires flashes of information, a frame around the edges, to allow us to sketch a fuller picture. Instead, this is another moment in which our sources go silent, leaping abruptly from tensions rising to armies suddenly on the battlefield. It's only after the armies have been gathered and stand face-to-face that we can continue our story.

❖

At either end of the large field, two armies lay encamped, tensions slowly escalating, but neither making any move to seek battle. Instead for several days, as the opponents—father and sons—stared each other down, Louis the Pious negotiated with his wayward sons, with Pope Gregory carrying messages from camp to camp. Each side claimed to be on a mission of peace. Both claimed they wanted to keep fathers from fighting sons, cousins from drawing the blood of their uncles. But the negotiation failed to find a pathway to peaceful reconciliation.

Yet if the negotiations for reconciliation failed, other messages clearly found their intended target. One night the pope crossed the field, talked with the emperor, and then returned to the sons' camp to relay what their father had said. Some part of the message struck a blow to the emperor's followers. The next morning, Louis the Pious awoke to an almost abandoned camp, fires still burning next to empty tents. Nearly the entirety of his army had broken their oaths and fled. Some of his followers simply took their fighting men home, but others were seduced by the sons' promises of lands, titles, and wealth, frightened by threats of violence toward them and their families, or simply convinced that God was indeed on the sons' side. Whatever justification the nobles told themselves as oathbreakers, they joined the rebellion, switching sides in the night, now facing their former lord down with hostility.

That must have almost broken Louis the Pious, awakening not to the sound of horses but perhaps crickets or, even worse, to the breathlessness of a panicked attendant rushing to rouse the divinely appointed emperor. Louis's options were few. He could flee. But where could he go? The fighting men of the empire were with his sons. What was left was simply to ask for mercy. That was what he did. Louis surrendered without a fight, according to Thegan, telling his few remaining men in a desperate predawn meeting, "Go to my sons. I do not wish that anyone should lose life or limb on my account."

Nearly alone and humiliated, Louis rode out to meet his sons between the lines. His only request was that Judith and their young son, Charles (the rebels' stepbrother), be left unharmed. The sons agreed and led their father back to their tents in captivity. Their stepmother and stepbrother were taken as well. This time, Judith was sent to northern Italy under Lothar's watchful eye. Charles, aged about ten, was sent to the monastery of Prüm, the same institution at which Pepin the Hunchback had ended his days, and urged to consider becoming a monk himself.

The rebellion, the second coup, had been won and best of all (from the victors' perspective) had been fought without violence. There were none of the blindings and executions and exiles of previous court politics. Rather, father and sons and their followers had shown that they still weren't willing to commit bloodshed. They had certainly postured as if they were ready—rallying entire countrysides' worth of fighters and rations to build armed encampments as a show of force—but the two armies could not bring themselves to go through with the fight.

Louis's followers abandoned the cause. Then, even after Louis's surrender, even with a long, comfortable history of violence against powerful figures who threatened the empire, neither Judith nor Charles was harmed. Once again the Franks had threatened civil war but retreated from the precipice. There was one lesson for all sides: raising armies and threatening violence might cause tensions but wouldn't threaten the integrity of the realm.

❈

Indeed, things seem to have been settled and the empire at first returned to a new, more stable status quo. It was less work to disperse levies than it was to gather them, and all the armed forces returned to their fields, towns, and cities. The princes went home. Louis the German returned to Bavaria and Pepin to Aquitaine, each secure in his hold over his respective region, in their position as nearly independent rulers—theoretically subject to the emperor but in practice able to rule unchecked by outside forces. The pope returned to Rome. Lothar took his father north under guard to the Abbey of Saint-Médard of Soissons. The only business left: to decide the fate of their father, the emperor.

Not long after Louis's surrender, Lothar must have called an assembly, because in early fall the great and powerful of the Carolingian Empire assembled at Compiègne, this time with Lothar presiding. Emissaries from the Byzantines arrived looking for Louis but instead found his son on the throne. Such an upheaval wouldn't have shocked ninth-century Byzantines, who had of course seen their fair share of such turnover in rulership. All seemed to be going to plan, not least because the man corralling the bishops around Lothar was none other than Louis's friend and milk brother, Archbishop Ebbo of Reims. Ebbo had remained staunchly supportive of Louis the Pious in 830 but had switched his loyalty to Lothar in 833, convinced that because things were going so badly for the Franks, the empire required new leadership. It was a betrayal that must have particularly stung Louis.

It was also a sign, though, that the rationale behind the second coup had not been merely a cover for a venal pursuit of power; that all the invocations of sin, of impurity, of demons stalking the land were modes through which Frankish thinkers could interpret the troubled times in which they were living. The factions were not merely divisions based on self-interest. Ebbo's self-interest would have been to support Louis. His alliance with Lothar was evidence of a much broader and genuine concern that the great story of Frankish destiny was in danger. It also meant that the solutions that might save the Frankish Empire could not be merely political or judicial; something more spiritual would be needed to right the ship.

At the assembly in Compiègne in October 833, Lothar presided in his father's place while Louis the Pious, in custody at Soissons, was besieged by churchmen and nobles telling him he would have to undergo a public penance to take ownership of the sins of the realm, and the old emperor reluctantly agreed. That was, in some ways, similar to the penance the emperor had undergone at Attigny in 822, when he had sought spiritual forgiveness for blinding Bernard of Italy. This time, however, it wasn't a ritual of Louis's own choosing but one being forced upon him.

Walking slowly from his confinement, likely contemplating a bleak future that was now out of his own hands, Louis entered the basilica of the Abbey of Saint-Médard of Soissons. The smell of incense once more hung in the air as the morning light passed through the south windows of the church. The space was filled with spectators, including Lothar (but notably not his brothers), many churchmen, and a crowd of the general populace, the composition of which symbolically represented the entirety of the Frankish people. The whole realm, or rather representatives of the whole realm, had to witness what was going to happen.

Louis, likely clad in white linen with a sword on his belt, entered the church and fell upon a hair shirt—a garment intended to irritate the wearer's skin—theatrically placed in front of the high altar. There, he "voluntarily" (it wasn't voluntary) confessed his faults to all present:

He was unworthy of office. He had neglected his duties as ruler. The Franks had fallen into disorder because of his sins. He asked the bishops if he could atone, if there was hope for his salvation. It's no surprise that Louis the Pious's confession mirrored almost precisely the charges that the rebels had made against him.

It was a ritual intended to send a message to the onlookers, to justify the rebels' actions: Louis was acknowledging and submitting to judgment for his wrongs. In that case, there must have been wrongs. The rebellion was necessary. It must have been necessary, because it seems to have won! As such, it was a tightly scripted performance, carefully prepared in advance. But it was also ad hoc. It had never happened before. Political ritual requires repetition, consistency, tradition, in order to be reliable. For actions to make meaning, everyone has to understand what that meaning is. But because it was new, just like the performances of anger and reconciliation that had happened in 830, it was unclear if the meaning would stick, even as the assembled bishops and nobles tried to make it do so.

The performance moved fluidly between what we today might call Church and state, revealing how faint the boundary between them was. Louis was the emperor, anointed by God and crowned by the bishop of Rome. He was performing the confession publicly, in front of nobles, and ultimately at the behest of his eldest son, the co-emperor who would take over in his stead. Yet he was ultimately performing a religious penance in a church for his personal sins and asking for help from the assembled bishops and other churchmen. Indeed, it was clear that the bishops—not the nobles—had taken charge of the proceedings, haranguing the emperor after his confession, arguing that Louis the Pious was not to be trusted, that he had lied both in his penance for the death of Bernard of Italy in 818 and when clearing his name in the aftermath of the first coup of 830. Louis again "voluntarily" (it wasn't voluntary) admitted his guilt and was presented with a document listing all the grave sins that had doomed his rule. Lothar remained silent, watching.

A manuscript composed afterward by the rebel bishops listed every complaint against Louis almost since the death of his father. The bishops felt that the accreted weight of almost twenty years' worth of the emperor's sins had sunk the empire. All of the dream criticisms—"Vision of the Poor Woman of Laon," the rantings of the demon Wiggo, and many more—resurfaced, but this time, instead of being buried in allegorical texts, the bishops stated them plainly, hurling them at the emperor as he stood there, humiliated and awake. The accusers, surrounding the emperor as he kneeled helplessly on the bare church floor, remembered and returned to the fact that he had murdered his nephew and committed violence against his brothers, sisters, and other kinsmen. In so doing, he had also broken a solemn, holy oath he had made to his father in 813. It wasn't that Louis's sons or his men were oathbreakers for their deeds on the Field of Lies, the indictment argued; Louis was the true violator of oaths. When he had overturned the *Ordinatio imperii* of 817 to make space for his new son, Charles, he had abused the rights of his other sons. Because of that and many other sins, Louis's current state—imprisoned, castigated, alone—was clearly the judgment of God. Or so argued the bishops.

Standing alone in the basilica of the Abbey of Saint-Médard of Soissons, Louis was stripped of his sword, the symbol of his status as a noble, and donned the hair shirt left at his feet, assuming the guise of a penitent. The bishops signed their document "under the rule of the emperor Lothar." Louis's name was nowhere to be seen. He had effectively been deposed.

But was it permanent? Penance is temporary; a penitent is supposed to be admitted back into the community after sufficient atonement. Perhaps while Louis the Pious remained under religious sanction, he couldn't reassume office, but what would happen when (or if) he was out from under it? After atonement, there was no reason to assume that the prohibition from holding office would continue. Lothar and his supporters seemed to understand that, and so Lothar took his father as hostage with him back to Aachen the next month, pressuring him to voluntarily make a monastic profession. If Louis were to become a monk, as his elder brother Pepin the Hunchback had done in 792, that commitment would be irrevocable. One couldn't unbecome a monk.

But Louis the Pious refused; he could not make such a solemn oath when he was being held against his will. He clearly understood the difference between a voluntary action as a legal fiction and actually taking a voluntary action. He had wriggled out of his previous jams, and he had faith in his own political skills. And importantly, he still wanted to be emperor—thought he still *needed* to be emperor. He was the sole surviving heir of Charlemagne, and so the only possible avatar of God's new chosen people. If Louis the Pious believed anything, it was that religion and politics in the Frankish Empire were inseparable.

Louis's consistent public refusal to take monastic vows created a pressure of its own on the alliance among the brothers. Lothar was acting as the emperor (as he was of course officially) and carting his father around. But his brothers weren't so keen on having replaced one tyrannical family member with another. By December 833, just two months after the deposition, several sources reported that Pepin of Aquitaine and Louis the German had asked their elder brother to treat their father more kindly. Lothar ignored his brothers' request—another huge mistake. From then on, according to a well-informed monastic annal, Louis the German "kept thinking over with his men how he might rescue his father from his imprisonment."

Once again the grandsons of Charlemagne decided that the best way to solve a problem was to summon an army and march. They weren't opposed to using their words, but persuasion works so much better when you have a few thousand armed Franks at your back. So Louis the German sent emissaries to his brother Pepin, and both called up the levies and marched toward Aachen to force Lothar to grant their father's release.

Lothar fled. Heading southwest from Aachen toward Paris, he stopped at the abbey of Saint-Denis just north of the city in February 834. But on the other side of the Seine, Pepin waited with an army, prevented from crossing only by heavy rains that had washed away several bridges. Louis the German approached from the east. Envoys were sent back and forth for about a week, making clear that violence was a real possibility. This time, it was Lothar who lost his courage. He fled southward, abandoning his father at Saint-Denis, and headed toward Vienne, which was safely under the control of his supporter the archbishop of Lyons. As he saw his brothers closing in, Lothar perhaps hoped to link up with more supporters who would cross the nearby Alps from Italy. Whether it was a savvy tactical retreat or a craven loss of courage, he believed that Louis the German and Pepin of Aquitaine were not just posturing and so fled.

In the meantime, Louis the Pious was reunited with Pepin and Louis the German, the two sons escorting the father back to Aachen. But the coup wasn't quite over, because, again, ritual has power and conveys meaning. The emperor had been condemned in writing by the bishops and performed public penance before the kingdom. Lothar had issued decrees as sole emperor. Louis the Pious's status was a bit in limbo. But what is done by ritual can be undone by the same.

And so on March 1, 834, Louis the Pious, along with two of his (now loyal) sons, reversed the deposition ritual. An assembly of bishops and nobles from across the realm solemnly girded Louis the Pious with his sword belt once more, placed a crown upon his head, and readmitted him to the Christian community. The young Charles was reunited with his father, perhaps taken to him personally by Louis the German. Judith was daringly rescued by loyalists in Italy and brought back to Aachen, later commemorated in an epic (and exaggerated) poem including the fording of rivers, the scaling of towers, and other feats of derring-do. Judith, the focal point of so much critique, was back at the emperor's side.

Once he returned to Aachen, Louis the Pious formally reconciled with Pepin of Aquitaine and Louis the German and thanked the two for taking up arms against Lothar, ignoring the fact that a few months before, they had taken up arms against him. The restored emperor once more forgave (almost) all the other nobles involved.

But not Ebbo. Definitely not his milk brother.

Thegan captured some of the loyalists' anger at him in a scathing, almost shocking three-page-long tirade. Ebbo, a freed slave, had betrayed his liberator. "O, how you have repaid him! He made you

free, not noble, which is impossible. After he clothed you with freedom . . . you dressed him as a penitent. . . . You wanted to expel him
from the throne of his fathers by a false judgment. O cruel man, why
didn't you understand the teaching of the Lord: 'A slave is not above
his master.'" Dripping with biblical allusions related to tyranny and
divine punishment, comparing him to the most wretched figures of
the poetry from classical antiquity, Thegan finally ended, "Even if I
had an iron tongue and bronze lips, I could neither explain nor count
your iniquities in all respects." Ebbo, according to Thegan, had upended the proper order. Louis, by stripping Ebbo of his office and
sending him to monastic confinement, was setting things right.

The only problem remaining to be solved was the biggest: Lothar.
All the sources say that Louis tried to reconcile with his eldest, though
we ought to question how happily he did so. That betrayal, like Ebbo's,
must have cut deeply, especially if Lothar had indeed helped his father
at least passively in the first coup of 830. But Louis the Pious's overture
didn't matter, because it takes two to reconcile and Lothar wasn't ready.
He still held out hope that his rebellion would not be undone, perhaps
because he had liked being the sole emperor for those few precious
months and perhaps because he genuinely believed that Louis had
sinned, that Judith had corrupted the court, and that he himself would
still need to rescue the empire. He refused to return to his father, even
though surely he could have done so safely, so long as he submitted. We
have evidence of Louis the Pious's (repeated) forgiveness of Pepin of
Aquitaine and Louis the German to guide us. But Lothar chose another
path and instead gathered strength in Burgundy.

As he waited for reconciliation, Louis decided to hasten things
along, to box Lothar into a corner by cutting away at his eldest son's
supporters. Hugh and Matfrid, the dishonored nobles who had birthed
the first coup of 830 and had taken leading roles again in 833, were
encamped near Brittany and had remained both loyal to Lothar and
sworn enemies of Louis the Pious. There they waited at the fringes of
the empire, not ready to give up, gathering forces and ready to march
toward Lothar and continue the rebellion.

Counts Odo and William, Bernard of Septimania's cousins who had been given control of much of Hugh and Matfrid's lands upon their disgrace in 829, led Louis's army toward Hugh and Matfrid while the emperor chased his son south. In early 834, Hugh and Matfrid met their counterparts Odo and William in battle. Again, the sources go, if not totally quiet, at least vague. They're covering up something embarrassing. The imperial army was large but poorly organized, perhaps not adequately scouting for its foes as it marched. And then came an ambush, a panicked retreat, the imperials cut down as they ran away. It was in the pursuit after a victory, as we will see again on an even greater scale, that much of the killing took place on early medieval battlefields. Odo and William were killed, as were the abbot of Saint-Martin of Tours (also Louis the Pious's archchancellor) and other important nobles. That wasn't good for Louis the Pious, hence our sources' reluctance to speak of it in any detail.

Heartened, Lothar headed north to meet up with his allies and press the advantage. At Chalon-sur-Saône, between Dijon and Lyons, he encountered resistance so laid siege to the city. After the city capitulated three days later, he burned it to the ground. Lothar made the leader of the garrison swear loyalty to him but singled out three prisoners for execution. Only three. Two of them were Count Gauzhelm and Count Sanilo. The cycles of violence and rebellion came full circle in these executions; Gauzhelm was the brother of Bernard of Septimania. And Sanilo was the noble who had brought charges against Count Bera of Barcelona back in 820, the incident that had led to Bernard of Septimania's ascent. Lothar executed them to exact vengeance, not just for himself but for every noble who felt disrespected by the elevation of Judith and Bernard and their usurpation of the pathways to power within the imperial court.

As if the message at the heart of that phase of the cycle of violence weren't clear enough, the last thing Lothar did at Chalon-sur-Saône was to drag a nun out of her convent: Gerberga, Bernard of Septimania's sister. Thegan suggested that she was singled out and tortured based "on the judgment of the wives of his impious advisers." That might have been true, but it was more likely a way for Thegan to deflect blame for what happened next. Regardless of who advised him, it was Lothar who made the formal accusation. It is familiar: witchcraft. Gerberga was found guilty and sentenced to death. Lothar had her put into a barrel and thrown into the Saône River. Lothar's whole army cheered as it happened.

The charges against Gerberga were, not coincidentally, the same charges leveled against the empress Judith. The rebels' single-minded pursuit of Bernard's relatives and the attack on his sister specifically suggest that the rebels really did believe the accusations—that they weren't a literary pretext or veil for some "more real" political grievance. This does nothing, of course, to mitigate the family's sudden extermination, the horror of the sentence against Gerberga, and the scenes of men gleefully shouting as she is drowned before them. But it should make us understand the gravity of the conflict in the minds of those who began both of those short-lived rebellions. Bernard of Septimania's ascent had enabled his family to rise, but in the eyes of their enemies—the old guard, including Louis the Pious's sons—Bernard's rise was precisely why the court had been turned over "to the delusions and divinations of sorcerers." Perhaps Louis really was the impious ruler who allowed the ink from the psalter to leap off the page and into the world. The new guard was perceived as an evil that had to be eradicated. Politics and religion were intertwined to horrific consequences.

That spectacular, ungodly act of holy violence was the last hurrah for the rebels. Louis the Pious and his other sons intercepted Lothar before he could meet up with Matfrid and Hugh. Lothar threatened battle again but this time conceded and asked for forgiveness, which his father granted. Lothar was banished back to Italy and told not to cross the Alps again. Thegan cheerfully reported that Matfrid died of a fever on the journey. Pepin returned to Aquitaine. Louis the German crossed back over the Rhine. Louis the Pious, his position and court restored, spent the winter at Aachen, contemplating the past few years and looking to the stars for some divine sign of what the future held. It would arrive on the tail of a comet.

CHAPTER 6

The King Is Dead, Long Live the Kings

835–840

In the middle of the Easter celebration at Aachen in 835, no more than a year after Louis the Pious's restoration as emperor of the Franks, a bright streak of light blazed through the night sky. Indeed, it must have been awesome; in a world before electric light, the heavens at night would have been a canopy of stars visible from horizon to horizon. Now a glorious traveler wound its way through the constellations.

Evidently, that spectacular event put Louis into a meditative mood. Before retiring one night, after the comet's disappearance from the night sky, the emperor summoned—as told to us by the Astronomer—"A certain person . . . namely me." Louis was worried that the comet meant "a great change in the realm, and the death of a prince." The Astronomer tried to soothe the ruler's mind, but Louis was not fooled; he knew the celestial wonder was a sign. It did not have to be a prediction of disaster but rather, Louis hoped, was a warning to "do everything we can and know how to do, so that we do not find ourselves unworthy of the mercy we have already asked for." It was time, he seemed to think, to finish putting the empire back into order and prepare for the next generation.

That night, Louis the Pious "indulged in a little wine" and stood guard on his balcony, watching the heavens for more signs. At dawn, he prayed fervently, then distributed alms to the poor and needy. He ordered that Masses be said for himself and the good of all the Franks. And things turned out well. His hunt shortly afterward was bountiful and rich, "and everything that pleased him at that time turned out to have a happy end." Not long after his hunt, he began organizing another great assembly at which he would gird his youngest son, Charles, with a sword, the weapon of a man, a sign of his adulthood, and grant that same son a large section of the empire, Neustria, in the northwest. Louis must have thought himself, in that moment, to have been a better reader of God's will than his astronomical adviser was. The emperor was beginning the work, marked by a sign from Heaven, of setting things to right.

In recording these events, the Astronomer had his dates a little muddled—not accidentally. Halley's Comet returned in 837, not 835. Charles entered adulthood in September 837. But the Astronomer wanted to place the comet at the denouement of the rebellion of 833–834, signaling a firm transition into the final half decade of Louis the Pious's life. Remember, he wrote his history only after he knew the end of the story, and he wanted to show correlation and causation. In modern historical terms, this is teleology—writing the past toward some sort of foreordained conclusion, demonstrating that things *necessarily* turned out the way they did. We know that this isn't how history actually works; the past is always messy, human, and filled with people who made choices and who could have chosen otherwise, but authors such as the Astronomer were sometimes trying to tell an entirely different kind of story. They were trying to tell a story about truth as they saw it, rather than what happened.

In his retelling of the restoration of Louis, of a well-ordered empire during 834 and 835, the Astronomer saw things hurtling toward a specific predetermined outcome. His account of those years in particular makes events move with something akin to divine vengeance visited upon those who had wronged Charlemagne's son. The Astronomer noted that a great plague struck Lothar's retinue as they moved

back south over the Alps. Over the next year or so, in fact, almost all
the troublemakers of the previous decade would be dead of various
causes; Matfrid and Hugh, Wala, and several rebellious bishops all
gone. The Astronomer smugly deemed their deaths the judgment
of God upon the wicked and a sign of the return of God's favor to
the Franks. Louis did not take pleasure in his opponents' downfall,
though. Instead he wept at the news and prayed for their souls.

The Astronomer found further evidence of God's renewed favor in the events following Louis the Pious's restoration. Instead of
Frankish armies threatening other Frankish armies, instead of defeats
near Barcelona, now when the Bretons attacked into the Frankish
Kingdom, they were quickly repulsed. On the domestic front, Louis
called great councils to investigate the upheavals of the successive
insurrections and put things back in order. Pepin was admonished to
restore the churches he and his followers had plundered during the
early 830s. Perhaps surprisingly, given the turbulent history between
father and son, he did. Then Pepin and Louis the German (Lothar,
being ill, apparently couldn't attend, but he was also, of course, not
his father's favorite at the moment) were brought in to help Louis
sort out Bernard of Septimania, who was once more causing problems in and around Barcelona. Father and sons, once again acting as
a united family, dispatched envoys to better understand the situation.
Carolingians (mostly) united. In war, in religion, in politics, in family
dynamics, the normal service of the empire seems to have mostly
been resumed.

The disorder and rebellion over the last few years had culminated in
shocking accusations of witchcraft, adultery, sin, treachery, and even
more shocking actions by the emperor's sons and the highest magnates of the realm as armies of Franks reached the brink of bloody
combat again and again. Now that the second coup was over, though,
the quick movement of the Astronomer's narrative, the compression
of years into single sentences at times, was a kind of apologia—an
explanation to show how wrong the rebels had been. Louis the Pious
remained a vigilant and upright ruler, magnanimous and just, a sen-
sitive reader of God's will via heavenly signals such as the comet,

and an appropriate enactor of God's plan for the Franks. If he was to avoid the death of a prince, he would do what God asked of him. All seemed to have ended happily.

But that happy ending wasn't *the* happy ending, nor even really an ending. The death of a prince foretold by that comet still came. In December 838, Pepin of Aquitaine, Louis's second-born son, departed this life at the age of forty-one.

That same year, Louis turned sixty. Mourning Pepin, feeling age settle heavily on his shoulders, Louis, like his own father, tried to set things in order for the future of his family and all Francia. But we'll see that his remaining sons didn't want to be managed. Old wounds were plastered over but still festered. Louis the German kept rising in revolt to secure his right, as he saw it, to rule over the eastern half of the empire and to secure what was owed to him for saving his father twice. Moreover, Louis the German was worried not only about his father but about what would happen should his brother Lothar become emperor and try to limit Louis the German's prerogatives. Lothar alternately tried to reconcile with his father and assert his authority over his brothers. He seems to have sincerely thought that he was enacting God's will when he led the second insurrection and felt the sting, he thought, of betrayal when Louis the Pious was restored. He may have wanted another bite at the apple—or the whole tree—once his father was gone. Pepin of Aquitaine's son Pepin II of Aquitaine stood to inherit his father's kingdom. And then there was Charles, who had finally come of age.

Louis the Pious may have been attuned to the will of God in the Astronomer's eyes, but to many observers, the rest of the Franks—nobles and churchmen alike—greedily positioned themselves against one another, always maneuvering—always, it seemed, on the brink of open war.

❖

During the ninth century, starting under Charlemagne but really taking off under Louis the Pious, the Franks looked to the biblical past for models of how to organize their politics. They thought themselves to be a new chosen people, so they looked to the ancient Israelites for guidance. The clerics of the period, especially during times of plague, rebellion, or armies marching across the land or as they gazed into an uncertain future as their emperor aged, took their examples from the prophet Elijah rebuking the evil King Ahab, from Jeremiah supporting the righteous King Josiah, and from Daniel speaking truth to the powerful Babylonian king Nebuchadnezzar II. That was the proper relationship between a king and his subjects. The king ruled by the grace of God, but bishops and abbots had to monitor and enforce the divine law as laid out in the biblical past. If they didn't, further disasters—God's wrath—lay ahead.

In the early 830s, one story that seemed to be on a lot of people's minds was that of King David and his son Absalom. After Absalom's sister was raped by a stepbrother and after their father refused to punish him, Absalom avenged her by murdering that stepbrother and fleeing the kingdom. Confronted with the persistent unwillingness of King David to administer proper justice, Absalom eventually rose in revolt and forced David from Jerusalem, taking the throne for himself. In a climactic battle, David's forces defeated those of Absalom, who was killed while fleeing, against David's explicit orders. David wept bitterly when he heard the news, even as he was restored to his throne.

The lesson for the Franks here was about rebellious sons but also about a father's grief, the need for forgiveness, and the need for real atonement. Absalom may have been justified in his anger, but he had gone too far. David had failed in his disposition of justice, but his behavior after his deposition had led to divine reconciliation and a promise that his line would endure forever (in the Christian understanding, culminating in Jesus). You can probably see where the Franks were going.

These biblical models could be read, heard, or seen—whether in texts, sermons, or art—and applied to the conflicts between Louis and his sons. In that intensely literate elite society, the stories of David and Absalom, Elijah and Ahab, Jeremiah and Josiah, Daniel and Nebuchadnezzar provided a sacred guide for proper behavior going forward, lessons that if not followed would have terrible implications for the Franks as a whole. And the stakes went far beyond the individual salvation of the Carolingian family. At a time when God was considered to intervene in the world and proper actions spoke much louder than words expressing faith, the rulers' behavior determined the outcome of events and demonstrated their adherence to God. If Louis didn't get it right, the entire Frankish people would suffer.

Louis's decision to elevate Bernard of Septimania and his capriciousness in removing the old guard were understood as the cause of the disasters of the 820s by rebels and loyalists alike. So, too, now. A common political, social, and religious culture circled around the emperor's court. Churchmen may have summoned ancient religious examples into their present, but everyone—nobles and churchmen alike—understood the analogy. The wrath of God loomed unless the family, and hence the realm, was put back together.

Doing so would require a lot of work.

If it wasn't clear before, the events of the early 830s had revealed that the Frankish Empire was nominally united but functionally fractured by region, under the rule of various members of the Carolingian family. All of the members were gravitational wells to which powerful nobles and men on the rise were drawn. Aquitaine gravitated toward Pepin, Bavaria to Louis the German, Italy as well as parts of the core northern Frankish lands to Lothar (he was, after all, co-emperor). Louis the Pious, as emperor, could theoretically draw from everywhere, though he, too, had his regions of relative strength. But more than that, the events of the period proved that the nobility had never lost its power to act in its own right. The nobles—elites of the court, rather than Louis and his immediate family—had been the instigators of the coup attempt of 830. They pushed the sons to try their luck again in 833. And even if the mortalities of the later 830s thinned their ranks, those failures didn't have to mean that they wouldn't try again. Indeed, they did.

Louis the Pious, especially after two coups (semisuccessful ones at that!), was fully aware of the danger that a disgruntled nobility might pose, so he pursued a dual strategy of appeasing his former rivals and challengers while surrounding his person with men and women of proven loyalty. He was circling the wagons.

It wasn't a bad strategy, necessarily, but it ran the risk of isolating the ruler without addressing the many challenges for the future of the empire. He recalled to court his half brothers Drogo and Hugh, men he had feared as potential rivals at the beginning of his reign and so had put into the Church. Now, decades later, he hoped that his brothers could be counted on. Drogo, now bishop of Metz, became Louis's archchaplain, and Hugh, now the abbot of several houses, became archchancellor. Other critical positions, such as those that had once been held by Matfrid and Hugh, then by relatives of Bernard of Septimania, were redistributed to those who had remained loyal. And because Louis had control of the appointment of bishops and because bishops at the time (as landowners) owed military service to the empire, he could fill the episcopate with carefully selected supporters, both filling the churches with men he trusted and ensuring that they would provide him with soldiers when called upon. Yet he still felt Ebbo's betrayal.

Bishops had been at the forefront of the deposition at Soissons in 833, the dramatic scene during the second coup when the emperor had publicly been accused of countless sins and forced into the role of a penitent. But most bishops' loyalties were as changeable as the wind. After Lothar fell and Louis was restored, most bishops, save Ebbo, were forgiven and returned to their sees. Even Agobard of Lyons, who possibly even on the Field of Lies itself preached a fiery sermon on the depravity and wickedness of Judith and the fecklessness of her husband, was back in the emperor's good graces and as a loyal servant, campaigning with the emperor in the late 830s.

This consistency in the episcopacy should be seen in part as a sign of how insular and closed off the highest levels of the Frankish world were; these people were extensively connected to one another and to the king. But also, the consistency demonstrates the tenacity of people to hold on to what they considered to be theirs—to look out for themselves. Louis the Pious may have thought his magnanimity toward the nobility was a model for making things right with the divine, but in many ways, it also signaled to some of them that they could walk the edge of rebellion, perhaps preach an incendiary sermon, and then retain their position regardless of whether or not they won or lost. If they won, they had been there from the beginning. If they lost (as they did in the 830s), they could claim they had been pressured and count on the emperor's forgiveness. But even though mercy was a key virtue for rulers to display, it destabilizes a society when elites attempt a coup, fail, yet suffer few consequences. That precedent would bear bitter fruit.

As we approach the end of the decade, each of Louis the Pious's sons has his own story: interlocking, interacting, but often spinning out into their distinct regions of influence, only to once again be drawn back into the family affairs at the heart of the drama.

Lothar seemed cowed after the second coup, never again coming north of the Alps, at least until 839, and then only by his father's invitation. That could have been defiance, sulking in his Italian kingdom, but it also might have been a sign that he recognized how close he had come to losing his own life—or perhaps being bundled off to a monastery—at the end of the second coup. He had pushed the boundaries of rebellion to the brink of total war but failed spectacularly and couldn't hold on to power. Moreover, Lothar had lost much of his support with the death of the old guard (Matfrid, Hugh, and Wala, among others) and so feared the wrath of the reconfigured empire now once more firmly in his father's grip. Yet Lothar knew that his father was old and that as eldest son he was still theoretically heir to the empire.

But only theoretically—indeed, only according to the 817 *Ordinatio imperii*. Louis the German had emerged from the coups as his father's clear favorite. He had stayed loyal in 830 and had rescued his father in 834. Even if he had been with his brothers on the Field of Lies, well, his backers might say, to err is human and nobody's perfect. In the mid-830s, his father seemed to be gravitating toward him, and some thought he might inherit the empire as a whole, given the current state of affairs. It isn't a coincidence that one of our major sources, Thegan's biography of Louis, the one with the thundering denunciation of Bishop Ebbo, was written in 836–837.

It was a record of events, yes, but more important, it was a guide for the future. Thegan highlighted the virtues of Louis the German, illuminating the middle child's special place in safeguarding the Franks, often reminding the reader that the father and son were namesakes. He described Louis the German as the youngest but greatest of Louis the Pious's sons (by Ermengarde), just as Louis the Pious was the youngest but greatest of Charlemagne's sons. Thegan ignored the inconvenient existence of Charles, the actual youngest son, still one year shy of adulthood in 837. For Thegan, as for many other Franks, it made sense to elevate Louis the German over his brothers in the immediate years after the younger Louis had come to his father's rescue twice and with his star on a meteoric rise. From the perspective of 837, Louis and Louis, the Pious and the German, were the glorious present and future of the Franks.

Yet no matter how much Thegan might wish otherwise, Louis the German was not his father's youngest child, nor his favored. Late in 837, Empress Judith began petitioning her husband to provide for her only son, Charles. Louis the Pious agreed, granting him some lands in the north, near the center of the empire. That was no small thing. They were rich lands, filled with mints for coinage and heavily populated counties led by powerful nobles. Pepin and Louis the German consented to the agreement, but Lothar was not happy with it. The land had been promised to him in the 817 *Ordinatio imperii*, and so he read that, rightly, as a punishment for the second coup. He wasn't foolish enough to challenge his father directly—not again—so instead he requested a meeting with Louis the German shortly after news of the grant of land to Charles reached him. Could he have simply been asking for his younger brother to put in a good word for him back at Aachen? Perhaps. Or could he have been trying to poison the well, knowing his own toxicity at that point and counting on his father's (probably justified) paranoia to cast doubt on Louis the German's loyalty? Also perhaps.

The two brothers did meet briefly, but we don't know what they discussed. Nothing came of it at the time, so our sources are silent. But if Lothar had indeed been scheming to sow division between Louis and Louis, it worked.

The younger Louis was hastily summoned to his father and made to swear an oath that he'd planned no evil in meeting his elder brother. Father and son parted amicably, and all seemed well. But it was not.

At an assembly in Nijmegen in June 838, the two Louises had a ferocious argument, though the only description from our sources tells us that "there was a great argument, quite different from what ought to have happened." By the end of the assembly at Nijmegen, Louis the German, who had been for nearly a decade the best of Ermengarde's sons in his father's eyes, perhaps even on his way to usurping Lothar as the heir apparent to the empire, had been stripped of much of his land east of the Rhine. By the end of the year, he was in open rebellion against his father. Two years later, even as the father lay dying, the sources vibrate with their mutual hostility. In this case, the real reason for his precipitous fall from grace lay not in the conflicts among brothers but how those conflicts were leveraged by the Frankish nobility, scheming in the shadows.

The June 838 assembly, the site of Louis the German's argument with his father, was almost certainly planned well in advance. It was meant to be the site of immense pageantry because the setting, as well as the timing, were critically important. That very month was Charles the Bald's fifteenth birthday, when he'd ceremonially be girded with a sword, signifying that he was now able, at least theoretically, to fight on the battlefield, to be freed from his tutor, and to lead his own court. As Louis the Pious's most faithful son, Louis the German was justifiably hoping to stand beside the young Charles at this ritual, to become his half brother's patron and protector. In an ideal world, one that didn't include two failed insurrections, Lothar would have stood next to his youngest brother, fulfilling his role as the child's godfather given him so many years before. But that wasn't possible. If Louis the German had taken his place next to his father and Charles, he would have been in the hierarchy of the brothers—the lowest of the sons raised to great heights.

It seemed that at least initially Louis the Pious agreed; his grant of lands to Charles the year before confirmed the new status quo: Charles in the Frankish heartlands, Pepin in Aquitaine, Louis the German east of the Rhine, and Lothar confined to Italy. In addition, holding the assembly at Nijmegen on Charles's birthday was certainly no accident; it was, we remember, the same palace at which Louis the German and the Frankish nobles east of the Rhine had rescued the emperor in 830. It was a place intentionally close to Louis the German and the East Franks. As the assembly opened, all signs pointed to Louis the German emerging from it as the chosen one.

But the nobility intervened, whispering in the king's ear to their own benefit, setting into motion a cascade of animosity that would drench fields with blood. The ringleaders seem to have been Archbishop Otgar of Mainz and Count Adalbert of Metz. Adalbert had been Louis the Pious's chief administrator in 816 and seems to have remained loyal through the 830s, rising fast after the end of the rebellions. Otgar had sided with Lothar in 833 and in fact had helped supervise Louis the Pious's captivity. But he was quickly back in Louis's good graces, helping condemn his former co-conspirator Ebbo in 835. Neither Adalbert or Otgar much liked Louis the German.

The problem those two had with Louis the German's rise was a simple one: Adalbert's and Otgar's bases of power sat on the western side of the Rhine, but they both held extensive lands to the east. The original division of the empire back in 817, with Lothar holding the bulk of the territory and Louis the German confined to Bavaria, would keep their lands together and so suited them perfectly. They would serve only one master. Louis the German's claiming more power across the empire complicated that. It had to be stopped.

So Otgar and Adalbert whispered through 837 and 838 and these wormtongues planted a rotten seed in the emperor's mind. As the fateful assembly at Nijmegen approached, with Louis the German ruling his kingdom in Bavaria, Otgar and Adalbert were at Aachen, plotting and scheming. They clandestinely reestablished contact with Lothar and looked for ways to diminish the younger Louis's prospects. In spring 838, they found their moment. Lothar and Louis's meeting after the grant of land to Charles was mighty suspicious, they whispered. Could it be treason? they wondered aloud. What gives Louis the German the right to undermine his father's position? they asked. Lothar should remain co-emperor. He was, after all, the eldest and Charles the Bald's godfather, they reminded the emperor.

We don't know what sparked the fight, the "great argument" that broke the bond between father and son, between Louis and Louis, but we have hints. One royal decree from the assembly, witnessed by Adalbert and Otgar, reveals a kind of proxy war at play that the conspirators had won. In a dispute about ecclesiastical land, Louis the Pious took the side of the abbot of Fulda (a supporter of Lothar) over that of the abbot of Niederaltaich (a member of Louis the German's court). Everyone at court would have understood that as a symbol, a loss of favor, that Lothar's faction—embodied at court by Adalbert, Otgar, and their cronies—was in the ascendent. The whispering had worked.

This bitterly wounded Louis the German. He had been the most loyal of the adult sons and had now been betrayed. No fool, he understood what was happening and lost his temper, made a scene. It could have been genuine shock that motivated him, but it might also have been rehearsed; a ruler's demonstration of anger was a tool in his arsenal, a way of pushing a rhetorical confrontation to the brink of violence that would then allow someone to pull the relationship back into order. That scene would therefore have been public, another ritual of humiliation that the Franks had been trying to use against Louis the Pious for a decade. Biblical parallels would have been invoked of an ungrateful father and a long-suffering son. Absalom! Absalom!

But the ritual misfired. Maybe the emperor was just sick of his ungrateful sons. Having learned the lessons of the rituals that had almost unmade him in 830 and 833, Louis the Pious would not be shown up by his son, his namesake, in front of the court. The emperor demonstrated his own anger. He abruptly postponed the ritual marking Charles's manhood; then, before dismissing the shocked nobility and churchmen, he stripped Louis the German of almost his entire kingdom and banished him back to Bavaria. At the emperor's side, Otgar and Adalbert smiled. They had won.

But Charles still needed to become a man. Hastily, a new assembly was called at the end of the summer, held within Charles's own territory in a palace in a town called Quierzy in northern France. It was a focal point of the province of Neustria and a site of immense ritual power for the Carolingians; it was where Charles Martel had died, where Pepin the Short had met Pope Stephen II, and perhaps where Charlemagne himself had been born. Pepin the Short had given Neustria to his son, the future Charlemagne. Charlemagne had given it to his own son Charles. The message—that Charles would become a man in the site where Carolingian kings were made—was not intended to be subtle.

Finally the Franks celebrated the ritual elevation of Charles to manhood. That time the ceremony went off without a hitch. Charles was girded with a sword. Louis the German was far away and Lothar was in Italy, so Pepin of Aquitaine was the only son of Ermengarde, Emperor Louis's first wife, present. The assembled bishops and nobles assented to the transfer of power more fully into Charles's hands, now that he'd reached his majority. Then, to make clear Louis the Pious's continued anger (genuine, not ritualized, at that point), Adalbert's brother was appointed Charles's guardian—right where Louis the German should have stood.

After the assembly broke up, Charles took his entourage, likely including his mother the empress, through his new kingdom, receiving the homage of his new subjects. Louis the Pious returned to Aachen and started planning how to reshuffle his empire, cutting Louis the German out and dividing what was left among Lothar, Pepin, and Charles. Louis the German wouldn't let that happen, though, and planned ways to seize back what had been taken from him. He raised an army in Bavaria and marched toward Frankfurt, once again looking to negotiate right at the brink of civil war. Weary, Louis the Pious raised his own army and marched east. But before the armies confronted each other, all of his plans fell apart. News reached him that his son Pepin had died.

The sudden death of the king of Aquitaine threw everything into disarray. But chaos also provides an opportunity for those ready to seize it. First, the rebellion had to be dealt with. Louis was holding major cities along the Rhine, using the river as a barrier to hold back his father. The prince had summoned his Bavarian nobles and their levies but had also gathered as many soldiers as he could from else-where east of the Rhine, intending to garrison all the river crossings nearby and stop his father by controlling the key passages rather than seeking direct battle. But in the midst of winter, mid-January 839, Louis the Pious found a way across, moving his men north of Frankfurt. There he was reinforced by an army of Saxons that had been raised by Adalbert of Metz. As the emperor's combined army marched on his younger son's at Frankfurt, the younger Louis's sup-porters thought better of it and fled in the night. Humiliated a second time, Louis the German retreated back into Bavaria.

Meanwhile, in May 839, Lothar was summoned back to his father's side from exile in Italy. Lothar and Louis met at a council held at Worms, on the Rhine. The last time they had seen each other, the father had been prisoner of the son. This time, however, the son was publicly humbled.

In a carefully choreographed ritual of submission and reconcil-iation, no less real for all it was scripted, Lothar threw himself at his father's feet and begged forgiveness. Perhaps a beam of sun-light came in through the windows, birdsong audible outside, as the court waited, breath held, anticipating success for the eldest prince but knowing that it was always possible for the plans to go awry. After all, less than a year before, a different ritual had been derailed by the fight between the emperor and his namesake. But this time, events proceeded according to design. Louis forgave his prodigal son. With Charles not yet sixteen, Louis the German in rebellion, and Pepin lying in his crypt, he needed Lothar. Lothar needed Louis, too, if he hoped to have a legitimate stake in whatever happened after his father died. So Lothar formally acknowledged his paternal authority, not just for Louis the Pious but as a performance in front of the whole court.

Then matters moved quickly. Louis assigned Lothar to be Charles's protector, attempting to create a tight bond of mutual support between eldest and youngest. In a different kind of performance, one bureaucratic in nature yet with immense stakes, he proposed a division of his empire into two equal parts and offered Lothar a choice of which one he would inherit. Lothar chose the east, leaving Charles with the western half, and after celebration and gift giving between father and sons, he happily made his way back to Italy.

The new division of the empire and the rapprochement between father and eldest son were possible in large part because of the machinations of Louis's advisers and Judith's continued influence on her husband. The court must have watched Lothar and his entourage head south with a feeling of immense satisfaction (even if, justifiably, Judith remained a bit wary). In the sources describing the meeting at Worms, the Franks told themselves a bedtime story with a happy ending. The ship appeared to be righting itself. They paid no attention to the massive iceberg looming ahead.

Those icebergs were the other Carolingians, Louis the German and Pepin II of Aquitaine, the deceased prince's son. At Worms, the emperor's division of the Frankish realm had excluded Bavaria, leaving it to Louis the German. Even if he was in open rebellion, the idea of fully disinheriting a son at that point was unthinkable. So Louis did the next best thing by keeping him confined to his rump kingdom. But in theory Aquitaine, following the *Ordinatio imperii* way back in 817, could have (should have) passed to Pepin's two sons, both with royal names—Pepin II and Charles—meaning that both were eligible heirs to his kingdom.

But when the emperor had split the empire in two between Lothar and Charles, he had not excluded Aquitaine the way he had Bavaria. Instead, after the reconciliation with Lothar, the father and the young Charles traveled west toward Aquitaine, informing the expectant nobles and churchmen of the region that instead of passing the reins to Pepin I's son, the emperor would hand them to Charles the Bald. Most of the Frankish nobles in the region were fine with the emperor's decision, happy to go along with the plan, since following Louis's son might be more advantageous than following Louis's grandson—and anyway, it wasn't worth it to most nobles to defy the emperor.

But that defiance was worth it for Pepin II. He was not about to meekly let his grandfather take away his birthright. More important, he, too, could draw support from the region. He was, after all, also a Carolingian by blood and had a strong claim to Aquitaine. Among others, our old friend Bernard of Septimania—constantly, it seems, on the lookout to get his vengeance on Louis the Pious—allied himself with Pepin II against Charles the Bald and provided significant military support. It was the beginning of a grudge match between Charles and Pepin II that would have consequences for decades thereafter.

From Louis's perspective, he was prioritizing his living son. From Pepin II's perspective, Louis the Pious was again an oathbreaker who, when the opportunity arose, privileged his own sons over those in his family's next generation. Aquitaine became a war zone. Louis seemed to be playing out the disaster of Bernard of Italy in 817–818 all over again. He would raise an army to repress recalcitrant younger Carolingians, only to find that repression bred resentment. Then he would show mercy, hoping to ease that resentment, but instead just leaving bitter pretenders to power fully ready and able to betray him again. But at least so far, the Carolingians had avoided pitched open warfare. If a leader could put more soldiers on the field than his opponent, convince leaders on the other side to defect, get past geographical choke points such as river crossings and mountain passes, victory could be achieved by threatening force rather than using it.

Louis the Pious, Judith, and Charles, in a mighty, united show of force, spent autumn 839 on campaign in Aquitaine. The emperor awed the local nobility with his very presence, including all the trappings of ceremony and religious ritual. Being, of course, no stranger to the region, having been assigned the kingdom of Aquitaine himself by Charlemagne, he tried to draw on those longer familial connections to the nobles of the region. And indeed, the campaign was going well for him.

The new year brought new troubles. Louis the Pious, Judith, and Charles spent Christmas at Poitiers, an important palace and the site of Judith's imprisonment in 830. Their celebrations and rest were interrupted by dire news: Louis the German had decided not to take his fall from grace calmly and had once again raised an army and was marching toward the Rhine, once again hoping to seize the kingdom—the Frankish lands on both banks of the river—that he had held for more than a decade. Adalbert of Metz was holding the western bank, but he couldn't cross without more support; he couldn't dislodge Louis the German. Achingly, Louis the Pious left Charles and Judith in Aquitaine to keep fighting Pepin II. The ailing, now sixty-one-year-old emperor was needed back in the Rhineland.

❖

The old emperor rushed northeast from Poitiers, but the empire was big, winter travel was difficult, and Louis was no longer spry. He arrived in Aachen just as spring was coming and celebrated Easter of 840 there. The mention of Easter and Christmas in our sources often matters little for military history but is almost always noted because they mark time. Those feasts were, as we've seen, large public moments for the ruler and court and so were a way for our writers to track the movement of their principals. For example, in just a few months, the aging emperor covered more than 490 miles (on foot and on horseback), moving from Poitiers (to deal with Pepin II's rebellion), where he was at Christmas, to Aachen (to deal with Louis the German's rebellion) at Easter, and all during a snowy winter.

After Easter, Louis the Pious gathered his strength again and marched out to join Adalbert. It's not clear what Louis the German thought would happen, why he thought a rebellion in 840 would go differently from his attempt in 838. Maybe he just thought that with the emperor in Aquitaine, he could seize the major river cities, fortify them, and get his father to accept a fait accompli. If so, he was sadly mistaken.

The emperor's fortitude in crossing much of western Europe in the winter demoralized the Bavarian army, which melted away into nothing. Louis the German fled again, but this time, he couldn't reach Bavaria directly and was instead forced to bribe the polytheistic Slavs to the east to allow him safe passage back to Bavaria more circuitously. It would have been dangerous for Louis the Pious to take his army into Slavic lands. And the old man who had survived two coups, multiple rebellions, the death of a son, and near-constant betrayals by two other sons needed a break, so he stopped at the border and returned to Frankfurt.

But the work of ruling an empire never ends, so no sooner was he back in Frankfurt in late May 840 than he had to take ship up the Rhine to Worms for yet another assembly, another meeting with his son Lothar, to continue the work of reintegrating his eldest son into the fabric of the Frankish Empire.

It was at this time that the sky lit up like fireworks.

Our historians tell us that the sky reddened from the southeast and from the northwest, finally meeting "in a cone and [giving] the appearance of a clot of blood in the heavens directly overhead." An eclipse followed; the day turned dark as night; there was blood in the heavens, darkness in the daytime. Our sources were writing backward from their time and drawing connections between signs in the heavens and events here on Earth, but it was easy for the Franks to interpret what the sign foreshadowed: the death of another prince; or this time, an emperor. And indeed at that time, Louis the Pious suddenly became very sick. His breathing grew labored. He was unable to eat or drink for nausea. He coughed and choked when trying to speak.

Louis didn't make it to Worms to meet up with Lothar. He and his entourage made camp on an island in the Rhine near the palace of Ingelheim and the city of Mainz, their river voyage abandoned. There they prepared for the emperor's end. The archchaplain, Bishop Drogo of Metz, who was also Louis the Pious's half brother, was by his side and heard the emperor's confession. Other courtiers and bishops swarmed around his tent. Both the signs in the heavens and those on Earth not only pointed toward the imminent death of the emperor but raised questions about the future of the Frankish world. Most likely, Lothar was already on his way to Worms from Italy, but he hadn't yet arrived. Moreover, his reconciliation with the emperor was so new that it was unclear whether or not it would endure. Charles the Bald, along with Queen Judith, was fighting Pepin II in Aquitaine. They would never arrive in time, even if they were summoned immediately. Matters with Louis the German were, to put it politely, unsettled. The anxiety of the courtiers became oppressive.

Many of the people who surrounded Louis, his inner circle after the second insurrection in 833–834, would have well remembered the transition of power that had followed Charlemagne's death in 814. Louis the Pious's archchaplain and archchancellor, sitting by the ailing emperor's bedside, for instance, were his half brothers. They'd seen the turmoil at Aachen firsthand; both had been banished from the palace for decades. Other nobles had been in the same boat. What would Lothar do when he arrived? Would the Louises reconcile just in time?

The latter question was at the forefront of Drogo's mind, at least. In his role as a priest, he apparently tried to get the dying Louis the Pious to forgive his son and namesake. Louis did so, but in a passive-aggressive kind of way. He asked his courtiers to tell Louis the German that he was forgiven but also that he "should not forget who led his father's gray hairs to death with sorrow and, in doing so, has despised the teachings and admonitions of our common father, God." You caused this, Louis the Pious told his son. Again, we have to wonder: What on earth had Louis the German said to his father in Nijmegen two years before that had caused such animosity?

The next day, June 20, 840, Louis the Pious summoned Drogo and was blessed. He turned his eyes to the left, beheld something, and whispered, "Begone!" Louis the Pious, the youngest son of Charlemagne and an improbable emperor, raised his eyes to Heaven, smiled—almost as if he were laughing—and died. His body was placed in a Christian Roman sarcophagus carved with scenes from Moses' crossing of the Red Sea and taken to the cathedral in Metz, where he was interred near his mother.

❖

The last years of Louis the Pious's life could not have been more different from the last few years of his father's. Yes, he was dealing with more sons (and grandsons) than Charlemagne had, but his disposition of the empire had been so changeable that a son might honestly be forgiven for not knowing where he stood with his father. After the second coup had ended with Louis the Pious's restoration, things had seemed settled. Lothar was confined to Italy. Pepin was happily in Aquitaine. Louis the German held the eastern part of the empire, as well as his father's favor. Charles was approaching adulthood but could take lands from Lothar in Neustria. None of that stability lasted. Louis the German and his father fell out over bitter words in 838. Judith kept pushing to ensure that Charles was favored over his brothers. Pepin I died. The emperor and his court had tried to square the infernal circle in 839 with a two-way division of the empire between Lothar and Charles. In theory, it worked within the solemn, divinely sanctioned 817 *Ordinatio imperii* that had placed Lothar above all his brothers (and to which Louis the Pious had made his nobles reswear several times in the years afterward).

At his death, maybe Louis thought it had all worked out all right. But maybe not. Charlemagne's son may have died a good death, having set some of his house in order, but the house's closets were full of skeletons.

Those skeletons came out quickly. Just before his death, bedridden on the island not far from the palace at Ingelheim, Louis took care to divide his personal effects, just as his father had done at Aachen in 814. He gave much to charity. The most important items, however, were the imperial regalia: crowns, sword, clothes, and books, among other items. They were the symbols that signaled a ruler. He left nothing for Louis the German. That was not a surprise, but it was a blow that would fuel Louis's anger for years to come. He bequeathed Charles some small items, dispatching them westward. But to Lothar he gave the best gifts he could: a golden sword encrusted with gems, as well as a crown and, some sources say, a scepter as well. But there were strings attached to those gifts, terms and conditions to which the new emperor would have to agree. The eldest son must, his dying father insisted, fulfill his oath to Charles and Judith to protect them and to ensure Charles's kingdom in Aquitaine and the west. To take up the golden sword and then not protect his youngest brother would, the dying king was trying to make clear, turn Lothar into an oathbreaker and undermine his plan for orderly succession

Fortunately for Lothar, he was already on his way north to Worms when he got news of his father's death. Within a month, in August 840, he summoned a council of his retinue—who were now jubilant—and those who had been closest to his father—who were now quite nervous. One thing was clear: Lothar was now sole emperor, restored to favor and at the center of Frankish power.

But what that meant to Charles the Bald and Louis the German was still unclear. Would Lothar continue his father's war against the rebellion of Louis? Would the oaths that bound Lothar and Charles hold? Because when Louis the Pious died, each of the three brothers sat at the head of a large army, waiting expectantly for one of the others to make the first move.

CHAPTER 7

Feints and Provocations

June 840–June 841

S ometime around 870, an unknown cleric from Mainz wrote down a prophetic dream he'd heard. It hadn't been mouthed by a poor woman or demon though, because it had originally been given to, and then interpreted by, none other than Charlemagne himself. The emperor was a prolific chronicler of his own dreams, we're told, known to place wax tablets by his bedside every night in case he received a revelation (that also, of course, gave the author a plausible backstory for how he happened to know about the emperor's dream). One night, an unknown figure had approached the great emperor with a naked sword, not to attack him but as a gift from God. On the blade were four words written in Old High German, the vernacular language spoken in late-ninth-century Mainz. Moving from hilt to point, the words were RAHT, RADOLEIBA, NASG, ENTI.

Upon waking, Charlemagne relayed his dream to his advisers, but they had trouble interpreting it. Einhard tentatively suggested that the meaning would become clear to the great emperor in time. It was a safe analysis to make in that situation. Indeed, not unlike the way his son would interpret the meaning of a comet that blazed across the sky, Charlemagne interpreted the vision himself, realizing that the sword and its inscribed words were an allusion to the Book of Daniel. In it, the Babylonian king was given a terrible vision of four words written by a ghostly hand that neither he nor his soothsayers could interpret. In the Christian Old Testament, it fell to the Israelite Daniel to help the king understand the coming ruin of Babylon.

Our author from Mainz related that Charlemagne in the dream was both king and prophet; he both saw and interpreted the spectral words and informed his advisers of the meaning. It was a story of the Carolingians, moving down through generations. RAHT meant abundance achieved through violence wielded at the behest of God; in other words, the conquest of other peoples by Charlemagne himself. RADOLEIBA signified a decline in that abundance and the losses of both material wealth and control over peoples on the fringe of the empire that would characterize his son's reign. Then it got worse. NASG referenced the world of Lothar, Pepin of Aquitaine, Louis the German, and Charles the Bald, the grandsons of Charlemagne, whose greed would lead them to oppress the people and steal ecclesiastical lands. Finally, ENTI meant "the end"—which could mean either the end of the Carolingian line or the end of the world. Both options were possible; there was no third.

The late-ninth-century visionary text then reminds us that those things came true. The Franks had already seen RAHT and RADOLEIBA, and after the death of Louis the Pious, "his sons Lothar, Pepin, and Louis began to extend NASG for themselves throughout the neglected kingdom." Pepin and Lothar robbed monasteries, stealing lands and goods from clerics and monks. The anonymous cleric from Mainz recording the text said that the bishop of Rome himself wrote to Louis the German, begging him for peace, begging him to intervene and defend the Roman Church. Failure to do so meant that ENTI, the point of the sword, the doom of the world (or at least the Franks), waited around the corner.

We don't know what the old king Louis the German made of this vision (he was in his sixties at that point), one calculated to catch his attention, push him to protect the Church more actively, and warn him of the dire consequences if he did not. In this way the vision is indeed similar to that of the Poor Woman or the demon Wiggo: a warning to a beleaguered king from the fringes of power, asking that king to—please—right the ship. What's different is that the vision evinces a more general sense of decline, a recognition that at each turn of the generations, things seemed to be getting worse. By the 870s, the Franks looked back and could only wonder where it had all gone so wrong.

❧

At the death of Louis the Pious, the empire shook. His last years, at least according to his chroniclers, were filled with celestial signs foretelling doom. The Frankish project that had coalesced in the first and second generations, under Pepin the Short and Charlemagne, began to shatter in the fourth. Although many of those who gathered around the petty Carolingian kings still hoped for resolution and reconciliation, a war that everyone saw coming but no one believed would arrive lay just upon the horizon. Would brother fight brother? Really?

Many Frankish people (and even some Carolingian royals) have, of course, died in our story thus far, but not so much on the battlefield as via execution, torture, assassination, or ambush. That would have been cold comfort to Gerberga as the waters of the Saône silenced her screams to the cheers of Lothar's army at Chalon; to Bernard of Italy, dying in agony with his eyes cut out; or to the co-conspirators of Pepin the Hunchback who were put to death. Yet it is worth noting until this point, through crisis after crisis, just how little blood was shed. Princes and magnates raised armies, marched toward each other, threatened, postured, positioned the forces, and then found peaceful solutions. Someone blinked. So far, someone had always blinked. The descendants of Charlemagne might reasonably have thought— likely did think—that it would always be that way. The Field of Lies had been a travesty, perhaps, but it was one that could potentially be endlessly repeated. When one comes to see that the stakes are rarely lethal, there's no reason not to chase power, switch sides, break oaths.

How wrong they were. Eventually, if you keep putting armies on the field, plotting targeted executions and murders, putting the pursuit of power over the common good, allowing the perpetrators of coups to carry on without serious consequences, the killing will begin.

❊

Louis the Pious died on June 20, 840. Within a year, thousands, maybe tens of thousands, of people would die at the hands of their brothers and uncles on a brisk spring morning in a field strewn with wildflowers. But as we head into that darkness, remember that historical actors made choices, sometimes constrained ones to be sure, but choices that meant outcomes were contingent and not inevitable. At any time, any of the brothers could have changed course and decided that peace was more important than maximizing his power. One of his advisers could've bent his ear a little more and pulled him back from the brink. Or in many instances, one brother or another could have been a little faster, a little more decisive, a little more brutal, and ended the looming civil war more quickly. But that wasn't Louis the Pious's way, and neither was it his sons'; in fairness, it hadn't really been the norm across the history of the Carolingians. The norm was ritual anger, exile, and managed bloodshed, not massacre.

One of the main issues that confronted the brothers as they and their followers faced off against one another was that they had all been educated together, and thus could predict the others' next moves with alarming accuracy. In military matters, all Carolingians were trained according to a Roman military manual written by Vegetius. The tactics were adapted to the Franks and worked remarkably well when the Franks led their armies against external enemies. They won victory after victory, expanding their empire to an extent not seen for centuries. But by the 830s and 840s, when Frankish armies faced off, each leader knew what the other was thinking. Therefore, it shouldn't surprise us that Frankish military traditions formed a great part of the background, the structure, that shaped the war to come. All of the leaders shared roughly the same training, drew from the same military treatises, and operated within a tripartite troop organization system that required careful management.

First: the general levy. Within the Frankish realm, any able-bodied free man could be summoned into a defensive militia at any time, but raising a general levy was wildly disruptive and was really only used in case of direct attack from the outside and never across the whole empire at once. Rather, when a threat materialized in a specific region, the general levy was called only there. Because all able-bodied men were expected to fight, levies included some better-equipped and -trained soldiers but were composed mostly of untrained, underequipped masses. By and large, those defensive levies did not play a major role in the civil war because they were unwieldy and difficult to supply over time and distance.

Second: the expeditionary levy. For offensive wars, whether campaigns in the civil war of the 840s or earlier against external enemies, Frankish leaders could summon expeditionary levies. When we've seen armies assembled so far, such as the three sent to Barcelona at the end of the 820s, for example, this is what we're talking about. Those larger armies would be made up of men of sufficient means to possess at least a minimal amount of equipment—a weapon, a shield, perhaps a bow, perhaps a little armor. As wealth increased, so, too, did the expectations of the equipment and the number of men one might bring to a levy. Having a horse, for instance, was a sign of high status. Frankish kings, including Charlemagne and his heirs, invested heavily in breeding and raising war horses. The same kings required an annual "gift" (i.e., tax) from the wealthiest clerical and secular families that was often fulfilled in the form of horses. Moreover, it was common knowledge in Frankish society that a mounted soldier could be trained only if he started young. Mounted combat was expensive in terms of both time and material and was essential to both elite Frankish identity and military practice.

Finally, every great Frankish magnate had his household guard: well-trained, well-equipped, nearly professional soldiers, not just gatekeepers. Late in the civil war, the historian Nithard wrote about the elite soldiers of Charles and Louis competing in public war games, with "teams of equal numbers [that] rushed forth from both sides and raced at full speed against each other as if they were going to attack. Then one side would turn back, pretending that they wished to escape from their pursuers to their companions under the protections of their shields. But then they would turn round again and try

Statue of Charlemagne, probably dating from the early ninth century. Monastery of St. John, Müstair, Switzerland.

Palatine chapel at Aachen, Germany. Constructed ca. 800 on Charlemagne's orders. This was only part of the larger palace complex but shows multilevel Carolingian imperial architecture. The mosaics are nineteenth-century reconstructions but approximate what would have been present in the ninth century.

Chapel of St. Nicholas in Nijmegen, Netherlands. This structure was completed in the early eleventh century, likely commissioned by Emperor Otto III in memory of his mother. The architectural style, however, is quite similar to Aachen and therefore shows the continuity of this palace architecture for several centuries after the Carolingians.

WIKIMEDIA COMMONS, FANTAGLOBEII

Small silver denier, 21 mm in diameter, minted ca. 794. On the front, it reads "Carolus rex Francorum" ("Charles, king of the Franks"). On the reverse, it reads "Fastrada regina" ("Queen Fastrada").

COURTESY OF CENTRE CHARLEMAGNE - NEUES STADTMUSEUM AACHEN. PHOTO BY HOLGER HERMANNSEN

Louis the Pious within an acrostic. The manuscript is an early copy of an original theological and philosophical treatise on the Holy Cross. This particular manuscript was created at or near Mainz in the 830s, and it's likely it was created specifically for one of Louis's loyalists—Archbishop Otgar of Mainz, who was a partisan of Lothar and caused such trouble for Louis the German after 838. Österreichische Nationalbibliothek, Cod. 652, f. 6v.

Illustration of Psalm 13, with a frightening message about impious rulers and the dangers of impiety at Louis the Pious's court, created in the late 820s at the request of Louis's foster brother, Archbishop Ebbo of Reims. Utrecht University Library, MS 32, fol. 7v.

ET SYRIAM SOBAL · ET CONVERTIT
IOAB · ET PERCVSSIT EDOM INVAL
LE SALINARVM · XII MILIA ·

Ninth-century Frankish warriors, from the "Golden Psalter" of the monastery of St-Gall. Created by a West Frankish scribe perhaps at Soissons, France (or maybe at St-Gall itself), not long after 880. The combatants at Fontenoy in 841 would have looked much like this. St. Gallen, Stiftsbibliothek, Cod. Sang. 22, p. 140.

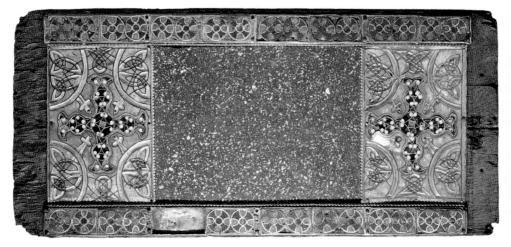

Portable altar for performing mass outside of churches. This one, inlaid with porphyry and gems, and known as the Adelhauser Altar, is Frankish and dates to the last part of the eighth century. Augustinian Museum, Adelhausenstiftung Freiburg, Germany.

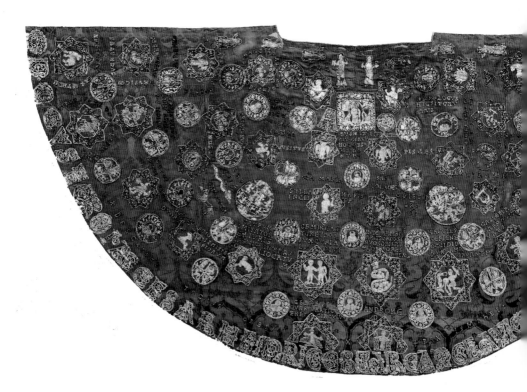

Charles the Bald, enthroned and surrounded by courtiers, soldiers, and churchmen. Note the dress of all depicted, with heavy capes, a crown for the king, circlets for the courtiers, and stylized armor for the household guard. The churchmen all sport tonsures. From the so-called "Vivian Bible," produced ca. 845 in Tours, France. Bibliothèque Nationale de France, MS lat. 1.

FACING PAGE: The so-called "Star Mantle" of the Emperor Henry II. Likely gifted to him by Ishmael of Bari in the first decade of the eleventh century. Although dating to a later period, these types of garments would be similar to what Carolingian kings would wear on special occasions, such as coronations, weddings, etc.

Monument to the Battle of Fontenoy, erected in 1860. It stands on a plateau just to the south of the modern village of Fontenoy and supposedly marks the location of Lothar's encampment. The inscription in both Latin and French can be seen.

PHOTO TAKEN MAY 2024
BY RACHEL GABRIELE

View of the Monument to the Battle of Fontenoy, looking to the north, back toward the village. The Brook of the Burgundians is among the trees on the far right of the image (to the east). Note the flatness of the landscape from this low rise of land.

PHOTO TAKEN MAY 2024 BY RACHEL GABRIELE

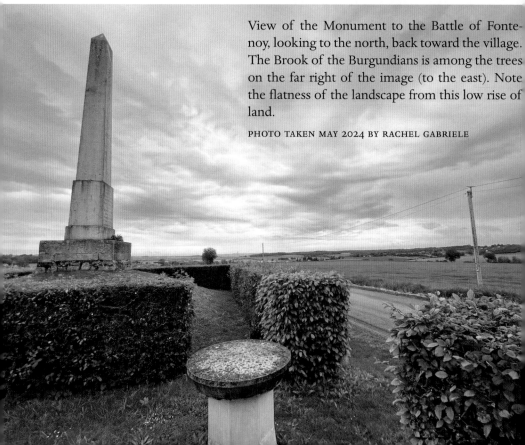

to pursue those from whom they had been fleeing until finally both kings and all the young men with immense clamor rushed forward, swinging their lances and spurring on their horses, pursuing by turns whoever took flight." The description paints a vivid picture, certainly, but Nithard was, more importantly, trying to make the point about the solidarity of the soldiers: that soldiers from across the empire, serving two different kings, could engage in mock warfare without hurting one another. That's going to be important later. But for now, we can imagine the mounted warriors, the infantry with shields, the formation work, the ordered charges and real or false retreats, all the practices that went into being a Frankish warrior. And then we must imagine the violence that those men could inflict upon one another when fighting in earnest.

Most of that violence happened to the rank and file, the infantry— groups armed, armored, and experienced at widely varying levels and of widely different sizes. Across the whole of the empire, there were perhaps 100,000 men available to fight, but such a number would never have been summoned all at once. Instead, we can imagine forces of thousands of soldiers, mostly infantry, with a core of highly trained warriors surrounding each great noble—not just the kings and emperor but their most powerful magnates as well. It was the nobles who provided the cavalry, could be deployed into battle at key moments, and would surround their principals as guards throughout a conflict. Kings and emperors themselves did not often charge directly into battle, though they were trained as fighters and wearing a sword was an important status symbol, as we saw with the removal of Louis the Pious's sword in 833, the girding of Charles with a sword in 838, and the transfer of the emperor's sword to Lothar in 840.

Armies, however, do more than fight; they also eat. Even if the biggest armies—and it was possible in 841, in the battles to come, that tens of thousands of men would face each other across a several-mile-long front line—were rarely summoned, smaller armies of several thousand men were impressive destructive forces that needed considerable logistical support to equip, move, and feed the soldiers and horses. They were difficult and expensive to keep in the field.

The presence of an army foraging for supplies, which is to say likely plundering the people, was not calculated to win the hearts and minds of a local populace. That was especially true when multiple distinct armed forces were moving through the same regions, the very territories and people their leaders sought to rule as the legitimate sovereign, avoiding battle but trying to project strength.

What's more, the geography of the empire played a crucial role in the coming of the fratricidal war, as well as in delaying the conflict's resolution. If we zoom out, we see that for much of the 830s, Lothar was in Italy, which is to say south of the Alps. The mountains made travel difficult for roughly half the year; snow-filled passes made it impossible to move troops, of course, but they also made it almost impossible to communicate with the centers of power at Aachen. That would change after the emperor's death, and Lothar, naturally enough, now north of the Alps, moved the center of his rule to Aachen to more easily control the Frankish heartland. But during that time, much of his manpower and support was still in Italy, so those same Alps that divided his base in two could make him cautious, slow to commit himself without his Italian allies. Louis and Charles, on the other hand, even at their most vulnerable, could always retreat across rivers to regions where Lothar wasn't strong enough to follow.

Both the Seine in the west and the Rhine in the east are wide, slow, and eminently crossable in normal times. They thus provided prime opportunities for ambush. Frankish generals were trained to try to catch their foes while they were crossing water or to otherwise use the element of surprise before committing their troops, rather than seeking straight-up fights. Indeed, we've seen repeatedly how during the rebellions of the early 830s, the armies stared each other down across rivers, always cautiously avoiding disaster.

The Rhine River specifically, that great north-south barrier sweeping through Europe, has played a crucial role in our story so far. When Louis the Pious decided to give his namesake control over Bavaria, to the east of the river, it provided the younger Louis with a base to retreat to, certainly not a base that a foe could march into easily. At other times, as with the campaign just before the end of the emperor's life, Bavaria became a place into which Louis the German could be driven and contained, his ambitions suppressed by the emperor. At the moment of crisis between Louis the Pious and Louis the German, the son had to retreat, in part because he had tried to hold his father on the west of the Rhine with just his household guard. But the emperor had arrived with a much larger expeditionary army, too large to be contained on the other side of the river and much too large to fight. The son quickly retreated to Bavaria (perhaps recognizing that his father was old and ill but most likely just to be able to live and fight another day). Rivers were, in other words, permeable barriers that both kept people out and kept them in. Immediately following Louis the Pious's death, these rivers kept the brothers from one another's throats.

Lothar wasn't at his father's deathbed, but he was nearby and on his way there. In addition, after the reconciliation with his father in 839 and since he had been invested with the imperial regalia and the title of emperor, he had the means to move quickly and assert his authority more broadly, to be the catalyst in the action to follow. He quickly swept up support from his father's retinue as continuator of the empire. But what to do with his brothers?

Pepin the Short, Charlemagne, and Louis the Pious had all claimed the sole place of primacy as first king and then emperor of the Franks, although all of them had delegated certain rights and responsibilities of rule to their own family and members of the other Frankish elites. Lothar understood—or claimed to understand—this as the only correct way to rule. He was almost certainly willing to leave his brothers with authority over large regions of the empire. That, too, was part of the tradition, one enshrined in the *Ordinatio imperii* of 817 that had elevated Lothar long before his father died.

Nevertheless, as that document stipulated, as his father had tried to do, even among kings, the emperor needed to be the focal point. The emperor was the one to whom everyone performed homage and the arbiter of how power would be delegated. There was a kind of inertia in the role of the emperor, so that even when tensions had previously been high, even when Lothar had rebelled against his father, power had reverted back to the imperial throne in ways that had proved irresistible (much to Lothar's discontent). With his father gone, Lothar had no reason to think it was time to do anything differently, but now he would be in charge. Seen that way, his was a reasonable position. The problem was that Lothar was not his father; he didn't have the same history with the powerful magnates who made the empire move and couldn't call upon paternal authority to rule. He was just the eldest brother, and eldest brothers aren't always known for inspiring respect among their younger siblings.

His brothers wanted independence, perhaps also a reasonable position and definitely one that they were committed to from the start. They argued that Frankish traditions mandated a fair partition among the sons and that the attempt of Lothar to elevate himself to sole ruler violated that tradition. Moreover, Louis the German (as we know) was feeling very, very aggrieved by what had happened in 838–839 and his dispossession of lands he thought he was due. It didn't help the situation that the men involved in his humiliation, Count Adalbert of Metz and Archbishop Otgar of Mainz, immediately flocked to Lothar. In that same period, Charles had also, of course, been promised extensive lands and—as a seventeen-year-old when his father died in 840—was trying to assert his independence. He must also have remembered suffering captivity (twice!) at the hands of his brothers and likely remained angry on behalf of his mother, Judith, who had been tortured, imprisoned, and condemned as a witch.

The personal feuds, the conflicting claims over the same lands, the ambitions for power, all combined to feed an irresolvable core tension: Lothar thought that power should flow through him, whereas Charles and Louis believed that they had been given independent kingdoms held within the construct of empire. With such differences of worldview and with the benefit of hindsight, a battle of brother against brother seemed inevitable.

But again, the conflicts could have gone a different way. There were moments when it seemed as though Lothar and Charles might strike a separate peace, come to a nice stable agreement, and leave Louis the German confined to Bavaria. Even in their resistance to Lothar, Louis and Charles frequently seemed unable or unwilling to coordinate their activities, each leaving the other to his own devices, but they could have worked together and boxed Lothar in from the start. Or Lothar could have committed to battle with just one of his brothers a little sooner, been a little faster, been a little cleverer. Most of all, the powerful noble Adalbert of Metz could have just done his job, kept Louis the German east of the Rhine, and not allowed his arrogance and his hatred of the would-be king to draw his army across a river and into the hills and streams above an ancient meteor crater, never to emerge again.

In late summer 840, as the chips were falling in the aftermath of their father's death, Charles stayed in the west and Louis and Lothar clashed along the Rhine. Lothar, as the new sole emperor, held an assembly near Mainz, basking in the support of the leading bishops and abbots, rendering judgments, issuing diplomas, and otherwise performing the work of the imperium. Assemblies have always been moments of public display, avenues to generate consensus and display a ruler's power. Louis the Pious certainly depended on them to do just that. Similarly, over the next few years we'll watch as Louis and Charles hold their own competing assemblies, opportunities for political performance similar to those pieces of theater from the reign of Louis the Pious, now deployed as a way of making claims against one's rivals. Battles could be won not only with levies and iron but also with rituals and proclamations, especially when the rituals convinced more nobles to give your side access to their soldiers.

Having performed the role of emperor to his satisfaction, Lothar returned to some unfinished business from the last months of his father's reign. He had to deal with his little brother Louis the German, still in rebellion and angry about his lost kingdom. Louis had left a small garrison of soldiers at the city of Worms, about thirty miles south of Mainz and also on the western shores of the Rhine. Lothar marched there, the garrison quickly fled, and then the emperor turned around and marched back the thirty or so miles north to the major river crossing at Mainz. There, he brought his army to the eastern banks of the Rhine, intending to push toward Frankfurt, which remained an important Carolingian assembly point and one critical to Louis the German's pretensions. Lothar's goal was to create a show of force and fortitude, to convert wavering nobles along the river to his side, not—at least judging with the advantage of hindsight—to invade Bavaria.

Louis the German, meanwhile, had assembled an army from his Bavarian and Saxon allies, and was, as it happened, returning west toward Mainz. Maybe he hoped to get back in force quickly enough to hold the crossing and secure the Rhine as a buffer between himself and his brother and likewise claim the allegiance of the regional nobility or at least to seize the lands and assets of Lothar's allies in the region.

With Louis the Pious not two months in the grave, his two eldest sons unexpectedly found themselves at the head of armies facing each other across the Main River, a tributary of the Rhine. The scale of the assembled forces isn't clear in the sources, but both brothers had called up expeditionary levies: Lothar from the heart of the empire, Louis from Bavaria and Saxony. Both armies were relatively fresh, well provisioned, and well equipped, but no one was ready to plunge into mayhem. Instead of battle, the two princes quickly negotiated a truce; then the two sides "pitched their camps, not exactly in brotherly love." The civil war had effectively begun, even if no one at the time fully knew it yet.

For Louis the German, it was a bit of déjà vu. Twice he'd tried to stop his father's forces at this point, and twice before he'd failed. He steeled himself to avoid the same thing happening again. He was ready to fight. He may, in fact, have felt that he needed to fight because in any conflict between just the two of them, time and resources would be on Lothar's side. For Lothar, although it seems likely that he had a stronger force, there was no reason yet for him to risk open combat, especially not when the political maneuvering seemed to be going his way. He had the imperial regalia. He had the bishops. Battle would be risky. Anything could happen. And he still had another little brother to deal with.

Instead of fighting, Lothar proposed that the two brothers go their separate ways until November 11, when they would return to the same place, try to sort out their differences peacefully, and fight things out if negotiation proved impossible. Louis, relieved, agreed. Lothar took his troops back across the Rhine and turned west. Louis got to work building up his power in the east.

No one knows what would have happened had the two armies clashed then, but it's possible that the brewing civil war might have ended right there in August 841, at the junction of two German rivers. Lothar comes off poorly in the sources, and of course his opponents portrayed him as cowardly. But our surviving narratives largely reflect the perspective of either Louis the German or Charles the Bald. Lothar was hoping that by making evident the superiority of his resources— men, armaments, treasure—eventually Louis would face up to reality and submit. From his point of view, he was acting in a way that fit the pattern of every crisis from the previous decade: summon armies, play the part of ruler, demonstrate his willingness and ability to fight, but avoid pitched combat between Franks. Why should this time be any different? Why fight? Lothar was operating within a world in which he felt he knew how things ought to work out, and he had precedents to justify his position. Battle between two Frankish armies was never desirable, even if he might have won.

Instead, he went off to deal with Charles the Bald. He used a similar playbook, seeking to convert Charles's supporters to his side, displaying his larger army for all to see, cajoling with threats and promises. Charles, in the meantime, kept being pulled farther to the west in order to address the threat of Pepin II in Aquitaine (and escape Lothar). That postponed the meeting between Charles and Lothar, his godfather and (as of the year before) sworn protector. In November 840, right when Lothar was supposed to have returned to the Main to meet Louis the German, Lothar and Charles finally met near the city of Orléans.

Lothar's army was large, but Charles's core supporters refused to abandon him. It would not be another Field of Lies, much to Lothar's disappointment. Again, Lothar chose negotiation over battle, using the leverage he had (the imperial title, control of Aachen, the larger army) to impose a truce on Charles and his supporters, requiring the younger prince to reduce his control to a limited territory and to remain in place until the next May. That last provision was important because it could theoretically stop Charles from both rallying supporters and dealing with Pepin II.

Next May, Lothar proposed, the two would meet at Attigny in northeastern France and there resolve their differences. Charles and his men agreed, swearing oaths to abide by those terms, but only so long as "Lothar would be as loyal a friend to Charles as a brother should be." Those terms, the historian (and noble in Charles's company) Nithard tells us, were immediately violated as "those who had sworn this had not yet left the house when Lothar tried to seduce some of them . . . [and] immediately sent into the lands which he had assigned to his brother to stir up trouble." In other words, according to Nithard, Charles's supporters did break their oaths, but they weren't oathbreakers because Lothar had broken his first. That might have been a case of protesting too much.

Then winter intervened, as cold as the current relationship among the brothers. All three of them and their armies hunkered down until the spring. As flowers bloom, we'll pause here and take stock.

The few months after the death of Louis the Pious had effectively seen the restoration of the status quo. Lothar had slotted himself comfortably (it seems) onto the imperial throne, and nothing much seemed to have changed for the vast majority of Carolingians. Even the conflicts were old hat by that point. Louis the German was still trying (unsuccessfully) to expand his power outside Bavaria and onto the western bank of the Rhine. Charles the Bald was still with his mother, trying desperately to pacify Aquitaine.

What Charles needed was a new ally, someone with an army of his own, a reputation in the region, someone he could trust. Instead of making a good decision, he turned his attention to Bernard of Septimania, who at least had two out of the three required credentials (army and reputation; like a bad penny, he continued to turn up). Bernard had sided with Pepin II against Louis the Pious and Charles, despite having been appointed Charles's "protector" at the fateful assembly in Worms in 829.

Charles decided, as Lothar gained power, that perhaps he could finish off Pepin II by stealing back one of his most powerful allies. Bernard had changed sides before, so why not again? And Charles wasn't totally wrong. Bernard did suggest that he was open to helping his former ward, but in the end he wouldn't be nailed down, continuously making promises, breaking them, attacking Charles's supporters, then apologizing and reconciling. What Charles did accomplish was breaking across the Seine and reconnecting with his mother, Judith, then using that opportunity to take control of Paris so that he could call a general assembly of his own in March 841 to accuse Lothar of breaking his oaths (as above). Demonstrating his magnanimity, Charles promised to go to Attigny to meet the emperor there anyway. That was, however, more posturing, with Charles and his supporters trying to portray themselves as seekers only of peace and justice, even in the face of continued and unwarranted hostility on the part of the emperor.

Lothar, meanwhile, turned back to deal with Louis, assembling an "immense army," according to Nithard, and crossing the Rhine in April 841. Louis hadn't been wasting his time, though. After Lothar had chosen not to return to Mainz the previous November, Louis had once again shored up his support in Bavaria and Saxony. Like Charles, Louis the German held a big assembly of his own in Paderborn in Saxony, the site of Pope Leo III's visit to Charlemagne in 798 and thus a site loaded with symbolic meaning. In fact, it was the first assembly by a Carolingian leader in Saxony in at least twenty-five years. Louis took full advantage of his presence, making land grants, securing the support of leading secular and religious officials, and publicly justifying his claims to power. He asserted that he was a defender of the Church; God had chosen him to be king. And his father, Louis the Pious, had named him as an heir. There was the inconvenient detail that as recently as 838, Louis the Pious had disinherited his namesake and, as we saw, driven him into Bavaria to take refuge. But Louis the German blamed that whole process not on his father but on bad advisers, the same way he and his brothers had attacked Bernard and Judith instead of the emperor in the previous crises. This time, Louis said, it was Otgar and Adalbert who had poisoned the emperor's mind against his son.

In fairness, Louis the German wasn't wrong. And conveniently enough, he'd soon have a chance for revenge.

❧

But not quite yet. Whereas when they had first met the previous year, it had been Louis who had proposed battle and Lothar who had avoided it, this time the momentum swung Lothar's way. As soon as Lothar arrived with his forces, some of Louis's allies abandoned him and joined Lothar on the other side, persuaded that his bigger army and access to resources would carry the day. Others fled, leaving Louis with a small core force of soldiers, presumably not much larger than his household guard. This time it seemed as though the Field of Lies that had almost doomed Louis the Pious in 833 would play out again. But the younger Louis wasn't captured; instead, he fled back to Bavaria a third time.

Lothar's strategy of avoiding battle, deploying overwhelming force, and continually offering clemency and privilege to his brothers' allies seemed to have worked. Lothar left Adalbert of Metz behind to guard the river crossings and keep Louis the German penned up. Adalbert had done that before, in 839, for Louis the Pious. For his service, Lothar gave Adalbert the new title duke of the Austrasians, declared victory, and turned back to the west, to Charles, to finish the civil war.

It's clear that Adalbert had one job: to keep the humiliated Louis contained in Bavaria. It's also clear that Louis the German hated Adalbert and that the feeling was mutual. Sometimes the personal is political. Sometimes history can turn on personal grudges and grievances, and this seems as though it was one of those times.

As quickly as armies can flee, they can reform. Fortunes can turn on a dime. Just when all seemed lost for Louis, months of diplomacy between his camp and Charles's suddenly began to bear fruit. We don't know who reached out first—the supporters of each brother claimed that the other had—and it doesn't really matter. What's important is that Charles and Louis reached an understanding that their fight to force Lothar to recognize their independence was one battle with two clear sides: Lothar on one, Charles and Louis together on the other. Lothar had been delaying for a year, true, but he was growing stronger and stronger, acting as emperor and picking off the younger brothers' supporters by threats and promises whenever possible. Now the brothers agreed that if they could meet, they would join forces and go at Lothar as one, forcing the elder brother to recognize their independent status. Charles was sure he could maneuver around Lothar to his north. But two (related) things stood between Louis the German and his younger brother: the Rhine River and Adalbert of Metz.

Louis had pulled together one last expeditionary force out of Bavaria. Adalbert no doubt expected him to travel along the old Roman road that ran along the southern bank of the Danube River, so most likely set up his own camp on a tributary river, the Lech, on the southern side of the Danube. Louis would march right by, Adalbert would attack, and Louis would either have to run away again or fight and lose, finishing the civil war on the eastern front. But at some point, Louis realized what was waiting for him and took a detour, using Vegetius's maxims to his advantage and taking his enemy by surprise. Just as Adalbert had surprised Louis with an unexpected river crossing a few years before, Louis the German now did something similar.

Louis made his way north of the Danube, using a rarely traveled route that he likely thought might allow him to slip his forces across the river in secret. It didn't work out exactly as planned, as Adalbert saw what was happening and reacted quickly. There was no reason for Adalbert to panic. With a large army in good order and supply, he could have played it safe, mirroring Louis's progress, ensuring that whenever his foe turned west to cross the Rhine and find Charles, Adalbert would be ready. He didn't have to fight; he just had to keep Louis out of the way. He sent out his scouts to track Louis's movements, individual or small groups of soldiers, lightly armed and armored, to creep through the countryside and track the path of

armies. So as Louis moved, Adalbert marched north as well. Here another river comes into play, this time the Wörnitz, gathering waters
from the mountains in the north, carrying them to the south, and
draining into the Danube. Adalbert marched up the west side, Louis
up the east. Adalbert was doing his job.

Then both armies made their way into the Ries in western Bavaria,
a place unlike any other on this planet, and not just because it's the
site of a turning point in our story. Around 14.8 million years ago, a

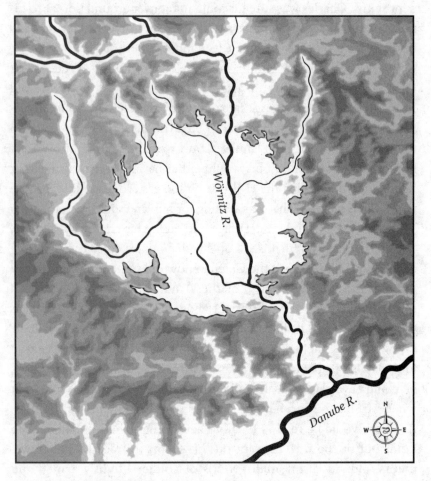

Nördlinger Ries, western Bavaria, modern Germany

huge meteor struck that spot in what would become Germany, spraying ejecta high into the air. Modern scientists have identified "shocked quartz," that is to say quartz with a distinct microscopic structure formed by intense pressure, more than a hundred miles away in Switzerland. The huge impact left behind a crater ringed by low hills, streams, and rivers. The Wörnitz and countless smaller streams and rivers flow through the topographically complex area, making transit difficult for large groups. In the ninth century, the land was verdant but the landscape complex with a large flat plain surrounded by heavily wooded hills: plenty of cover to mask the movement of troops.

Louis likely knew the region well or at least had scouts and advisers who did. He remained on the eastern edge of the crater, masking his formal movements. It was his territory, and he used it to his advantage. Adalbert should probably have been familiar with the region as well, but as the armies made their way up the rampart crater's edge, he made the first catastrophic error of the civil war: on Friday, May 13, 841, he decided to cross the Wörnitz.

Why? We don't know. He had more men than Louis did, and maybe he thought he could, yet again, use his superior power to force another retreat. He'd humiliated Louis repeatedly in just such a matter, and the time was long since past when Louis could characterize yet another retreat as strategic. If Louis didn't flee, so much the better. Adalbert might have finally seen a chance to rid himself of that meddlesome prince and once and for all assert his position as the most powerful magnate in the central Rhine Valley, perhaps the most powerful in the empire. Or maybe he just hated Louis enough to make that error.

Adalbert marched east and made to cross the river. He was crossing a plain, over a river, and toward an army waiting for him on the high ground overlooking the ford. Maybe Louis attacked while Adalbert's army was in midriver or just across or wrangling its way across one of the other small streams in the region. We don't know, and it doesn't matter. Louis's archers let fly. They charged the confused army. With the river at their backs, Adalbert's forces couldn't even retreat and try to reform. The rout was on.

We don't know who killed Adalbert of Metz. We don't know if

the soldier who cut him down even knew that the blood on his sword came from one of the empire's greatest nobles. Was Louis the German there to see off his mortal enemy? Or was it that in the mud, blood, and water, Adalbert was just another dismounted combatant struggling to escape from the onslaught? Would Louis have preferred to take him prisoner? There's no reason to think that he had any regrets. Adalbert had been his foe for years, personally stifling his ambitions and threatening first his position, then his life.

But it could have gone another way. Adalbert could have been careful. He could have done his job. Instead, he made a decision and died for it, marking the first time that the Frankish armies of the civil war met and fought. It was the first time they slaughtered each other.

It wouldn't be the last.

ACT III

Civil War

CHAPTER 8

Fontenoy

Saturday, June 25, 841

By the time the sun rose on Saturday morning, June 25, 841, the three sons of Louis the Pious had agreed on one thing: they were ready to fight. The time for posturing was over; only violence would settle the fate of the Frankish Empire. By the time the sun set, Lothar had fled, and his younger brothers were victorious. But the "victory" of Charles the Bald and Louis the German had come at terrible cost. Thousands of Frankish warriors lay dead on the fields of Fontenoy, and nothing had really been decided. Lothar may have been functionally defeated, but he and his army had escaped, still strong enough to muster a defense, too strong still for Charles and Louis to continue their pursuit, and still united with his nephew and ally, Pepin II of Aquitaine. The civil war that everyone had seen coming but no one had thought would happen had finally arrived. A seal had been broken and had unleashed what would be a recurring cycle of vengeance that would litter Europe with the bodies of Franks for centuries.

For more than a decade, both sides had studiously avoided conflict; the Franks had always stepped back from the brink of large-scale warfare. They had perpetrated atrocities and executed conspirators (real or imagined), and armies had stared each other down across rapeseed-filled yellow fields, but every time before, someone had chosen surrender or retreat over war. After Adalbert of Metz crossed the Wörnitz River only to be slaughtered by the blades and arrows of Louis the German's forces, the game had changed. Louis the German's victory, his massacre in the Ries crater, opened a door, and made clear that more blood was on the horizon.

Lothar knew that his attempts at intimidation would no longer work. But he still had a large, well-equipped army. Louis the German and Charles the Bald felt emboldened, hopeful that one massive pitched battle might settle the succession dispute once and for all. The nobles on both sides were eager for spoils, ready to prove their manhood, even if wondering—quietly—if they would be plundering the bodies of old friends. Both sides had to fight to maintain their support among the ever-shifting alliances of the great and powerful. Both sides thought they might be able to win.

Charles and Lothar had come close to direct conflict in May and June, but neither had been quite willing to fight. Charles, in particular, had made good use of swamps and forests to delay and keep Lothar at bay. By June, though, as Lothar moved east and relieved some of the pressure on western Francia, Charles had managed to reconnect with his mother, the empress Judith, and her forces. Most of the army with the former empress was drawn from Aquitaine, but certainly not all. She had, of course, been at the center of Louis the Pious's court, and Charles had been with his father constantly until 838 or so. They could therefore also count on significant support from in and around Louis the Pious's court.

Louis the German, meanwhile, celebrated his stunning victory over Count Adalbert of Metz by force-marching his battle-hardened but relatively small army more than 430 miles in three weeks to join up with his younger brother, Charles, in order to even the odds in the looming confrontation with Lothar. They arrived exhausted and without many horses. On the other hand, every soldier with Louis from elite rider to common levy benefited from having stripped Adalbert's fallen soldiers of their arms and armor and ransacked their baggage train. It was a war-weary but experienced and frighteningly well-equipped force, whose morale was high and that was spoiling for another fight.

But Lothar also had a plan. He had taken advantage of the confusion of the spring to build a sizable force of his own. It was clear to
Lothar from Charles's actions leading up to their planned meeting
in May that he wasn't going to lie down for his elder brother, godfather, and protector. And by early June, if not before, reports must
have reached Lothar from the Ries of Louis's movement to cross
the Rhine. Lothar knew another confrontation was coming, but he
would also have been at least a bit confident, with a well-rested army
and major reinforcements on the way.

When it had become clear that Charles wouldn't capitulate, Lothar
had reached out to his nephew Pepin II of Aquitaine with promises
to support Pepin's claims to his father's kingdom. Pepin II already
had an army in the field and was all too willing to help, seeing the
situation as likely his best chance against the much more powerful
force led by Charles and Judith. The strategy for both made a lot
of sense. Lothar just had to do what he'd been doing so far: keep
his brothers occupied and under surveillance, avoid a pitched battle
before Pepin arrived, and then send them scurrying back to their
provinces before the awesome might of the Carolingian emperor.
He hoped he could cow his brothers as he'd done several times
before, but after hearing about the loss of Adalbert of Metz, he, too,
was prepared to fight.

Betting men would likely have placed their wagers on Lothar. The
day before the battle, Archbishop George of Ravenna was so confident in the outcome that he told Lothar that Charles would be
tonsured and forced to become a monk by the end of the next day.
Archbishop George, like his audience, clearly remembered the fate
of other would-be Carolingian kings such as Pepin the Hunchback,
and there was no reason to doubt that events would be repeated in
substance, if not specifics. The emperor might be knocked down, but
he gets up again. The Franks would rally to Lothar, and God would
grant victory to the emperor, as he had to his father so many times
before.

The area around the village of Fontenoy was, and remains, verdant grassland, dotted with low rises of land and wildflowers speckling the countryside. A small stream meanders northward just to the east. There's nothing particularly important or strategic about Fontenoy itself. There's no palace there, no large towns or churches nearby. It's a place between two old Roman roads running north-south, both connecting Paris to Lyons, but also a place between the core lands of the three brothers. The site of the battle could have possibly been Lothar's doing, with him maneuvering to keep Charles and Louis apart. Lothar would have been able to use the easternmost of the two roads to bring his armies north from Italy via Lyons, as well as count on support from the Frankish heartlands to the northeast via Auxerre, a bishopric only twenty miles away controlled by a staunch ally who had supported him since the second insurrection of 833. Plus, in theory, he could put himself between Charles and Louis, preventing them from uniting their armies against him.

If that was the case, Lothar's gamble failed. Charles and Louis had already connected, stationing part of their forces on a small hill nearby, to the south. Lothar similarly positioned his forces a few miles away on another low rise, though specifically where is a bit unclear. We do know that the two armies were separated by swampy terrain. We also know that both sides negotiated but were unable to resolve their differences. Sources close to Charles the Bald and Louis the German say that they only reluctantly resigned themselves to battle.

On the one hand, it was posturing and apologetics. All three brothers needed to demonstrate to their supporters, their foes, and anyone who might be wavering among the claimants that they did not wish to fight. On the other hand, as we've seen time and again, the descendants of Charlemagne had always walked to the edge of carnage with one another but then negotiated and found a way out of battle. But bad blood compounds, and repeated threats eventually become reality.

And so it was with the sons of Louis the Pious. They agreed to fight the following day at the second hour (eight o'clock in the morning), and that was just what happened. As dawn broke on that crisp

June morning, as campfires were rekindled and horses fed, the Franks emerged from their tents. The fate of an empire was about to be decided. Neither side had, to the best of our knowledge, a grand strategy that differed from the other's. The dewy fog that hung just above the fields obscured their opponents' camp, yet they knew what awaited them. They'd fought alongside one another for so long. As they mounted their horses, as they cinched the leather straps of their shields and inspected the keen edge of their spears, they knew they were fighting once more for the good of the empire. This time, however, they could only hope—rather than know—that God would grant them victory.

How do you tell the story of a single battle, even a single day, when no sources reliably describe the ebb and flow of foot soldiers and cavalry, their positioning on hill or valley, the depth of the stream around which they fought, or the other details that must have had an impact? It's not easy. We're lucky that at least two eyewitness accounts survive and two other writers who had easy access to eyewitnesses are known to us. But this is where our luck ends. Those four sources, alongside all those we've heard from up to this point, were deeply partisan and more concerned with revealing greater "truths" in a cosmological or theological sense than recording facts. But we'll read through those sources together and extract what we can so as not to fall easy prey to the agendas of courtiers and claimants.

The narrative sources we do have come from East and West Francia, Italy, and the court of Lothar, but none of them—not even all of them together—are enough to place the armies onto a map, to depict the minutiae of maneuver, charge, and countercharge. But we do know how war was generally waged at the time, and we know that those armies were large, each of them in the many thousands of soldiers. Our only hard number is 40,000, and it refers to the number of dead on Lothar's side alone, but given the constraints of the time (that at best the entire empire could maybe muster about 100,000 fighting men total and that number was never in fact summoned to one place at any one time), that number is outside the realm of possibility, given the structures and sizes of levies across the empire, and so more suggestive of "many dead." In fact, because all of the nobles named in the sources survived, we cannot name a single casualty of that bloody battle with any confidence. This may seem odd, but then we remember Angelbert's anguished poem, his attempt to forget, and the trauma that had caused it. We know only the survivors, those who had to live in the aftermath; those who told their stories to others.

The consequences of the Battle of Fontenoy are clear enough, even if what happened on the ground that Saturday morning in June was not. Let us offer one version, pieced together from the sources themselves and centuries of subsequent scholarship.

In May, Charles had connected with his mother, Judith, and her army at Chalons-sur-Marne, and it was also likely there or nearby that he waited for Louis the German's tired but battle-hardened men to arrive. They were moving northwest when, according to Nithard, they unexpectedly encountered Lothar's host on Tuesday, June 21. Both sides readied themselves for battle, but night came quickly and a truce was arranged.

The next day, both armies maneuvered north. Lothar headed toward the village of Fontenoy, with Pepin II and his men on their way to assist but not yet arrived. Charles the Bald and Louis the German camped at Thury, a village about five miles to the south. The brothers exchanged their first emissaries that day and the next, Thursday, June 23. Those trusted advisers haltingly moved through a forest and swamp between the two forces. Both sides again claimed that they wanted only peace. Charles and Louis supposedly offered great concessions of land if Lothar would respect his (and their father's) earlier promises of their functional independence. But again, our sources for this piece of the story were all partisans of Charles and Louis and were writing with hindsight, emphasizing their side's reasonableness and Lothar's intransigence. All agree, however, that nothing was accomplished in the negotiations except delay—a delay that certainly helped Lothar, at the very least, because Pepin II of Aquitaine and his army arrived that evening.

Envoys were sent back and forth the next day, June 24, as well. But we must wonder if the intention was to talk or, once more, simply to delay as both sides prepared for an inevitable clash of arms. Charles and Louis repositioned their camp, moving closer to Lothar and occupying one of the small hills on the plain that separated the brothers' armies. By the end of that day, both sides were done talking and agreed to fight on Saturday morning if no peace could be reached. That same day, the Feast of the Nativity of John the Baptist, saw both armies celebrating Mass, each hoping that that day of sacred foreshadowing—the Baptist predicting the coming of Jesus—also foreshadowed a good outcome for its side in battle.

God was thought to determine the outcome of battles, having, it was thought, guided the Franks to victory after victory for generations. But that was before, when the chosen people had fought external enemies. What would happen when the new Israelites fought one another? Which brother's prayers would God honor in that case? Both brothers were certain (well, fairly certain) that it was his. Charles and Louis were at various points promised kingdoms in sacralized assemblies, blessed by bishops and the whole Frankish nobility. Lothar was the divinely appointed emperor. He had terrified his father's army on the Field of Lies. The majesty of his position had humbled his brothers separately through much of the previous year. Surely, even now, the battle might not happen. God would intervene on behalf of his chosen ruler, and the other side would surrender or retreat.

It's strange to think of an orderly start to a premodern battle, an event that becomes chaotic as soon as it begins. In the few skirmishes and battles we've seen so far, a conflict would tend to emerge unexpectedly when one side surprised the other force, usually leading to a quick retreat (as with Lothar chasing Charles repeatedly in the months leading up to the battle). Alternately, the pomp and ceremony of two large armies assembling wasn't really about battle at all but about making an argument about who would win a battle if one were joined. The Field of Lies and Louis the Pious's surrender in the face of desertion and overwhelming odds are the quintessential example for us, but far from the only one. But at Fontenoy, battle was joined. Nobody flinched.

Both sides gathered their forces. It could seem, from afar, a motley assemblage of men and beasts because a Carolingian army consisted of both foot and horse soldiers. The latter were drawn from the retinues and servants of the highest ranks of the nobility; horses were very expensive to get and to keep. The former, the bulk of any force, consisted of both the high and the low. Our sources frequently reference poor but free Franks—sometimes called *plebs* in our sources and other times *pauperi*—who were drafted into military service as part of routine levies in support of expeditions. In typical armies, these levies were lightly armored and armed at best, but with victory could come a change of forces. Defeat an army, as Louis had Adalbert's, and suddenly every man might have a fine weapon. Some might even get a horse.

What's more, size mattered, and those armies could each have easily numbered more than 10,000 troops, perhaps twice that. The brothers were a year into the conflict, meaning that whatever troops could be mobilized had, in fact, been. June was late enough in the summer for troops to get to the site from any part of the empire. If there were around 100,000 available troops who could be levied throughout the empire, it's not hard to imagine that up to half that number made it to Fontenoy in good fighting trim.

And the brothers were motivated to assemble as many soldiers as possible, at least for that one encounter (because big armies are hard to move and feed, it wasn't always practical to max out their size). One way to win a war, as we saw at the Field of Lies, was to show that your army was bigger, that death was certain if you were opposed. In other words, merely appearing like the one who would win often meant victory. Arriving to battle looking like the loser was often a self-fulfilling prophecy.

As both sides slouched toward June 841, they mustered the maximum number of troops they could into the field. We can imagine them just before dawn on that dew-drenched June morning, stretching out their lines. Six divisions, three from each army, moved out to fight. The terrain around Fontenoy is mostly flat, light woods and fields, with slight slopes here and there and a stream that is deep enough to water horses but shallow and offering little challenge to either side. From their respective small hills, the brothers and a

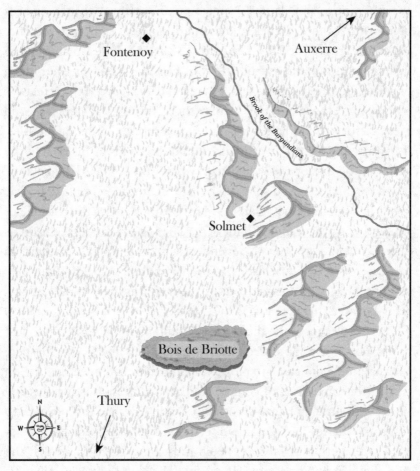

Fontenoy, Burgundy, modern France

nephew could see the whole battlefield, track its ebb and flow. Wild-flowers, abundant in May and June, blanketed the field and shimmered at the dawn. They were soon trampled.

Louis's hardened forces met Lothar's vanguard first, south of where Lothar was camped and near a small wood now called Bois de Briotte. We imagine a charge, the sweat and screaming of men and horses, the sound of collisions, metal on metal, spears flying through the air, and then the close brutal combat that followed. We might see a tight phalanx of men, the poet and Lothar's supporter Angelbert among them, forming a frontline to receive the enemy. Weapons ring, shields flash, men scream, arrows whistle, swords plunge into others' bodies, and then Lothar rides right into the middle of the fray. Gradually, he seems to have become isolated in the throng, at risk of being cut off from his supporters or even taken prisoner. But he fights his way out, even if he's forced to retreat.

We can picture Louis the German there, trying to achieve a second great victory to follow his triumph just a month earlier at the Ries. If his surprise victory over Adalbert and the death of his rival in the east, a battle that opened the pathways over the Rhine to the fields of Fontenoy, had achieved so much, what might it mean to take Lothar in battle? Would he try? Did he see his brother across the battlefield? Could the war have ended right here? The fog of war descends on us here, Lothar's supporters independently relating the tale of their patron's heroism. Military historians argue that kings never fought, they just observed, staying safely out of the fray. But either way, Lothar's army began to break apart. Why?

One answer might be the force of Aquitanians under Pepin II. Just to the east of the spot in Fontenoy where Louis and Lothar clashed, Charles and Pepin came to blows. Their armies had been fighting on and off for some time, of course, but that had been mostly feints and sieges with little direct confrontation. Pepin II wasn't in a position to confront Charles in Aquitaine directly on his own but was emboldened with Lothar at his side. Pepin must have been elated that the cold civil war had gone hot. He relished the chance to seize what his father had promised to him but his grandfather and uncle had denied him. Control of Aquitaine was on the line, but so, too, was the fate of an empire.

Charles had about half of his army with him, including other Aquitanian forces brought by his mother, Judith. It was an internecine battle and a brutal one, not just for the Franks but also for their affiliated kingdoms. But the forces had barely come together when Pepin's force fell back. Charles's men cheered and pursued, sure they had won. But instead of taking flight, Pepin II rallied his men to Lothar, reinforcing the vanguard and then launching a swift counterattack on the prematurely celebrating enemy. In fact, Pepin might have planned the maneuver as a fake retreat all along, trying a favored strategy of Frankish generals: pretend to fall back in terror, then swoop in as the enemy lines lose discipline in their pursuit. Charles the Bald's overconfident forces began to crumble. The tide was starting to turn.

Just a little farther to the north, near the tiny hamlet of Solmet, a third wing of the battle had begun with nary a would-be king to be found. Instead, Charles had deployed a powerful supporter, his father's seneschal and his future uncle-in-law, Adalard, to command the army. Charlemagne's grandson, Charles the Bald's faithful man Nithard, said that he himself had fought there. We don't know who Lothar had in command, but he had no shortage of great magnates in his company—veterans of many foreign campaigns. The battle was indecisive, the two armies coming together into close, long, brutal conflict, ultimately fought to a draw with neither gaining any significant advantage.

There was one other army in play, and it could have made all the difference. Bernard of Septimania, ever present, ever a problem for those around him, was no more than a few miles away with his army, waiting. As we've seen, he was allied at the moment with Pepin II and Lothar against Charles the Bald, causing Charles no end of grief in and around Barcelona and throughout Aquitaine. But just before the battle, Bernard dithered intentionally. He heard the clash of arms from a distance and almost certainly had scouts traveling back and forth to give him updates. Lothar and Pepin waited and waited, probably even during the battle itself, for help that never arrived.

Meanwhile, back in the main melee, the battle finally turned decisively. Pepin and Lothar seem to have fought heroically, but individual heroism is rarely enough. Pepin may have tried to rescue Lothar's vanguard and may even have wreaked considerable damage on their enemies, who thought they had already won the day. But the confusion, though dangerous for Charles's men, who had let their guard down, was brief. Louis, Charles, and the other commanders rallied their men, reformed the line, and pressed their hard-won advantage. Lothar's men had already been running before Pepin came to help, and once routed, they couldn't be reassembled. Pepin's forces, moreover, had been forced to disengage with a foe at great cost and quickly march more than a mile to the north; not such a great distance but difficult in midbattle and more difficult in armor and with enemies around. They were unable to stem the tide. Perhaps they saw Lothar's men fleeing, the emperor beset. Soon their courage broke as well. All seemed lost. Eventually, whether through the screaming of soldiers running away, messengers, or rumor carried on ill winds, the third wing of Lothar's army, the only force that had held its own, also broke.

The pursuit was on.

Modern visions of medieval battles are too often colored by action-horror movie tropes of prolific gore and mass deaths. But battles in early-medieval Europe were less lethal than one might imagine. Soldiers might feint at each other. Armor could turn killing blows into survivable wounds. Horses made it easier to escape from danger. That said, even if individual combatants did take lethal blows or sustain injuries in a world without antibiotics, mass casualties in battle were very rare in that period. More often than not, the propaganda boost of both victory and subsequent mercy was sufficiently great that the enemy didn't need to be slaughtered. Moreover, the propaganda demerit of brutality might undermine the whole justification for war.

But at Fontenoy, the norms of mercy or taking prisoners, of allowing one's enemy to retreat, fell away. The forces of Louis and Charles
swarmed after their enemies, striking down anyone they could catch,
giving no quarter and no mercy and taking few prisoners. It was only
as Charles's army reached Lothar's camp, rich with plunder but also
filled with noncombatants, that the commanders somehow reas-
serted control over the situation and turned the day from slaughter
to capture. Behind them, the fields, woods, and hills of Fontenoy lay
strewn with the fallen and dying. The Brook of the Burgundians ran
red with blood.

How do we know the story of the violence of Fontenoy? Disappoint-
ingly, it's not because there's one authoritative account that lays out
the minutiae of the conflict point by point, allowing historians to reconstruct it. Instead, we have multiple narratives that explain what
happened from a variety of perspectives. This allows us to build our
composite, but again, what we can reconstruct is an educated guess,
thanks to the labor of generations of scholars and the survival of
those sources. So let's pick the sources apart.

The most important source for the battle is our old friend Nithard,
Charlemagne's illegitimate grandson and Charles the Bald's loyalist
and cousin. As was the case in the lead-up to the war, it's Nithard's
history that provides the most critical illumination of Fontenoy, in
no small part because he was there. He wrote, "The part of our
army at Solmet, to which I gave vigorous assistance with God's help,
fought bitterly. The fight was a draw." We have no reason to doubt
that Nithard was there in battle, in the third wing of Charles's army.
His account drips with trauma. The text is more scattered in its organization, and tellingly, almost in the middle of his description of the
battle and with virtually no fanfare or explanation, Nithard declared
his history to be over. He ended Book II and seemed prepared never
to write again.

Yet we do have a third book. Still processing the trauma of the battle, Nithard opened Book III, "Although I am ashamed to hear of anything bad in my people, it especially pains me when I have to report it. Therefore, I was inclined . . . to consider my work complete with the longed-for end of the second book. But I have agreed to add a third book of the events in which I myself took part, lest some misguided man dare to record them inaccurately."

This was an incredibly personal, human admission. It's highly unlikely that the man tasked personally by Charles the Bald with writing the story of his reign might have just stopped, for no particular reason, after Fontenoy. We'll get into the postbattle propaganda wars in the next chapter, but for now we can imagine Nithard sitting in Charles's camp months later, hearing people criticizing his army specifically for its actions in the pursuit of the enemy. So he tried to put the best possible spin on the violence that followed the battle, writing:

> Louis and Charles deliberated on the battlefield what should be done about their scattered opponents. Some were filled with rage and advised pursuing the enemy, but some, especially the kings themselves, took mercy on their brother and the people. As always, Charles and Louis wished piously that their opponents would turn away from evil greed and with God's grace join them and be of one mind in true justice, now that they had been smitten with God's judgment in this defeat. They suggested things to be left to the mercy of Almighty God. Since everyone agreed to this they ceased fighting and plundering and returned to camp about the middle of the day to talk over what they ought to do next. The booty and slaughter were immense and truly astonishing, but the mercy of the kings and the entire people was equally remarkable.

Whatever Louis and Charles may or may not have said, rage carried the day. The mercy of kings was not much in evidence, at least in that initial chase. This reading is actually corroborated by another contemporary source, also sympathetic to Charles the Bald, called the *Annals of St-Bertin* (*ASB*), which reported that "the slaughter of the fugitives continued on all sides, until Louis and Charles, afire with generous feelings, ordered an end to the carnage."

Nithard and the *ASB* may well be hiding something even in their admission that killings happened during the pursuit of Lothar's retreating army. We think this may be one of those moments when a source reluctantly revealed something, when a truth forced its way onto vellum. Things must have been really bad as Lothar and Pepin's armies fled. A red mist descended along with all the frustrations, the humiliations that the supporters of Charles the Bald and Louis the German had felt over the past several years, perhaps all the way back to that fateful 838 assembly in Nijmegen when Louis the German had said something to his father that had lost him an empire, perhaps even farther back, to the humiliations of the Field of Lies in 833 or Matfrid and Hugh's rebellion in 830. Perhaps the massacre that followed the Battle of Fontenoy was simply revenge.

Nithard was therefore forced to pick his pen back up some months later to rescue a narrative that was threatening to get out of hand. What this means is that Nithard may be useful for information on the levying of troops, the movement of armies across distances, the Frankish culture of war, and the grand strategy used by Charles the Bald. But he was clearly—and explicitly—writing to ensure his and his king's reputation in the aftermath of that battle. This fact, at the very least, shows that their reputations may have needed some rescuing because of their conduct on that day.

The author of the *Annals of St-Bertin* is generally less detailed than Nithard on the battle itself, probably because he was a monk and was back in camp (perhaps at Thury) during the fighting, not on the field at all. But, like Nithard, he focused on Louis the German's arrival in the days before the battle. Louis and Charles the Bald "were bound by brotherly love," the *ASB* recorded, "and they even pitched camp together, sharing each other's company and counsels." The two brothers tried to reason with Lothar for "peace and harmony and the government of the whole people and realm," but all Lothar did was pretend to be interested in peace while really waiting for Pepin II's reinforcements to arrive.

In the *ASB*, Lothar seeks battle (agreeing with, unsurprisingly, Nithard). Only reluctantly, when all else had failed, did Louis and

Charles give Lothar what he wanted and attack. The *ASB* noted that "many were slain on both sides; still more were wounded. Lothar suffered a shameful defeat and fled." The text credited the victorious Carolingian brothers with eventually stopping the killing and then "To uphold the standards of Christianity, they refrained from pursuing the fugitives any further from their camp." Again unsurprisingly, that account squares well with Nithard's; Charles the Bald's partisans had their stories straight, even if both authors revealed that the pursuit had gotten out of hand, that that was when much of the slaughter happened, and that it had taken a while for the kings to put a stop to the killing and start taking prisoners.

One of the captives was George, archbishop of Ravenna. This is the same George who supposedly boasted to Lothar that Charles the Bald would be turned into a monk, the top of his head shaved into a tonsure, before day's end. Oh, how the tables had turned. And George was a symbolically valuable captive indeed. The archbishop of Ravenna was a core figure in the hierarchy of the Church, a regular correspondent and collaborator not only of the pope but of the Byzantine emperor as well. George was a symbol of Rome, of Byzantium, of the broader world into which Lothar sought to enter as not just an equal but a global power. But George's story also opens up a different window into Fontenoy and its aftermath, because his presence on the battlefield allowed a chronicler from Ravenna to offer his thoughts on the conflict. And that chronicler, named Agnellus, really didn't like George.

We need to understand the archbishop as essentially the same as any other great magnate involved in the conflict, trying to calculate which side to join, if and when to switch sides, and whether or not to just try to stay out of the way. At the same time, we need to see how, owing to his clerical status and specific role in Italian Church politics, he could provide Lothar key support by making the argument that the elder son's cause was just. That was something Lothar would have been keenly aware of, having himself convinced Pope Gregory IV to help him at the Field of Lies. Perhaps a blessing by the bishop of Rome—or even the bishop of Ravenna directly on the battlefield—would give his brothers ample reason to submit peacefully. Perhaps it would even help Lothar make the argument that God was on his side. But of course every cleric attached to any court would make such a statement, which functioned not so much as dogma as a political and theological maneuver.

George would have had a motive to side with the emperor. By the time Agnellus's narrative reaches the buildup to Fontenoy, George had convinced Pope Gregory to send him to Lothar as a peace mission. George's plan was not to avert the war, however, but rather to bribe Lothar into supporting Ravenna's claim of functional independence from the papacy (that was an old rivalry between the bishops of the two cities, dating back centuries). Bolstered by his aspirations and hopes, George traveled north laden with riches stolen from churches under his care. That was not a good investment. It was, in hindsight, probably a bad idea to carry so much wealth into a war zone. And Agnellus wrote about it as such.

George apparently arrived just before the battle, and Agnellus's description of the fighting here was vivid, based most likely on Agnellus's postaction interviews with combatants (or at least the Ravennese who were in Lothar's camp at the time) and classical descriptions of great battles. Agnellus described the armies as becoming tangled, like shining threads on a loom. He also gave us the heroic depiction of Lothar plunging into the enemy's lines by himself, slaying those around him with a spear, trying unsuccessfully to rally his men against their flight. The doomed Lothar "fought alone like ten men so that the empire would not be divided." Those actions, according to Agnellus, did, however, have an effect on one group; he described Pepin coming to Lothar's side and restarting the battle, briefly regaining some momentum while Charles's men were confused by their enemy's apparent retreat.

Our sources so far all experienced the battle at first or second hand; Nithard himself fought, while the author of the *ASB* and Agnellus would have spoken with a plethora of angry clerics and soldiers returning from the war. Each left scraps of narrative behind that we can seize, assess, and then use to weave the best tapestry, the best story, that we can.

But before we leave the historical loom and see the full picture emerge, we need to consider one more source, also authored by someone who was there: Angelbert's poem, perhaps drafted in a tent not long after Lothar's army left the field, with the smell of death, blood, and muck surrounding him. The author's pain rings out across the centuries, and the story he wanted to tell is a key to understanding both what happened and why it matters. But here, our question isn't about emotional content but rather about how we might make use of the poem to decide the question of what happened on the battlefield.

As we've seen with so many other sources, all of our authors have their biases. The *Royal Frankish Annals* (*RFA*) was a court product, created around Charlemagne to justify the Carolingians' and Franks' right to conquest. Thegan wrote to bolster Louis the German and defend Louis the Pious. The Astronomer wanted to keep a ledger of loyalties in the wake of Louis the Pious's death, possibly skeptical of Lothar's assumption of the role of sole emperor. Angelbert was no different. The only thing different is the form of his history—in poetry rather than prose. We need to be very careful that we don't dismiss this source just because its format reads to us as more literature than history—a distinction that meant little to people in ninth-century Francia.

We don't know who Angelbert was other than a warrior in Lothar's army. He wrote in learned Latin suggestive of the widespread literacy and education of the Carolingian elite, both lay and secular. He was surely not the only one to put ink to parchment and pour out his emotions at that moment, but his is what came down to us through the fires and incessant wars through Europe's history that destroyed libraries and archives. In other words, he was well educated, partisan but present, and his poem both confirms some of our other details and expands our sense of the terrain of the battle.

Angelbert placed himself on the field of battle. We can hear the thunder of hooves, taste the pollen on our tongues, sense the anticipation and fear of the armies. He wrote:

I, Angelbert, fighting alongside the others, saw
This crime unfold, which I have described in verse;
I alone of many from the first line of the army remained.
I looked down into the deeps of the valley and along the peak of a
  ridge,
Where brave King Lothar was battling against his enemies,
Who were fleeing to the open side of a brook.

The slaughter wasn't because of Lothar's failings, though. Angelbert corroborates Agnellus's claim that Lothar fought like ten men and that if more people had shared the emperor's bravery and skill, the outcome could have been very different. It's why despite the general wisdom of historians that kings didn't fight, our best evidence suggests that Lothar may well have directly entered the fray. It's clear that the memory of him as a warrior, as a wielder of sword and spear, was important to his followers. Even if he didn't think it was Lothar's fault, Angelbert had plenty of blame to go around. The emperor had been betrayed by his nobles, a treason akin to Judas's betrayal of Jesus, he said. One likely traitor: Bernard of Septimania, who was theoretically allied with Pepin II and Lothar and could have gone to the rescue, but encamped his army and sat idle just a few miles away. Over in Charles's camp, Nithard also wondered at Bernard's being a spectator. What's more, Lothar's supporters had good reason to call Bernard a Judas because the lord of Septimania sent his son William to do homage to Charles the Bald once it was clear that Charles and Louis had won. Charles accepted William and Bernard's loyalty, perhaps feeling overcome with magnanimity in the wake of his victory.

Louis the Pious died on June 20, 840. Almost precisely a year later, his sons were trying to kill one another. Everything he had tried to set in place had been undone, and crows and wolves feasted well on the bodies of the Franks.

Beginning in early June 841, Lothar and Charles chased each other about the region, with Charles relying heavily on swamps and woods to avoid battle when it wasn't to his advantage. Throughout, both sides sent messengers back and forth, not only as a sign of a persistent need to project one's desire for peace but also as a sign that there would be no surprises. Everyone knew where everyone else was, about how many soldiers they had, and about how well they were equipped. When Louis arrived, he locked the two younger brothers into a tight alliance and provided their side with a veteran, well-equipped core of fighters. At that moment, Louis and Charles had the upper hand, but they knew that Pepin was coming. Lothar, meanwhile, must have felt his forces, once reinforced from Aquitaine, up to the challenge. Confidently, the brothers agreed to join battle on a Saturday morning in June. Neither side's confidence was necessarily misplaced. Both almost certainly thought that dawn would break with the other side having abandoned camp and left the field. But this time that didn't happen.

In the battle itself, Louis drove Lothar's vanguard into flight, despite the emperor's personal bravery. We think Pepin tried to rescue the situation but failed, even if that wasn't how Charles's partisans would remember it. In the general pursuit that followed, Franks chased down other Franks, slaying them and taking few if any prisoners. When the pursuit was finally halted, the carnage staggered the observers, leaving a bloodstain on the fields of Fontenoy that the Carolingians never washed away.

It's easy to imagine this as the end of a story. It certainly was a turning point in multiple ways. The skeletons in the Carolingian closet, arguably dating back to the coup that had served as an almost original sin in the founding of the dynasty, finally came tumbling out. Everyone, even at the time, knew the fault lines were there but were horrified nonetheless. One source writing a bit later noted, chillingly, that at Fontenoy the Christians had "fought each other like madmen," while another flatly said that "there was such a slaughter on both sides that no one can recall a greater loss among the Frankish people in the present age."

The horror, then, spawned debate and propaganda and the writing of history far into the future, after everyone who fought at Fontenoy was long dead. That battle could have been the end of our story had Lothar fallen in battle or been captured, tonsured, and removed from the field of play. Or it could have been the end if Pepin II of Aquitaine's desperate rescue attempt had succeeded or if Bernard of Septimania hadn't broken his oath to Lothar and Pepin. Any of the Carolingians themselves could have died. But we'll see them all again.

Perhaps that 870 vision of Louis the German, in which Charlemagne had been warned about the movement of history toward some sort of disaster, wasn't a prophecy so much as a history. The Franks had moved through their age of abundance (RAHT) with Charlemagne, had seen a decline in their fortunes (RADOLEIBA) under Louis the Pious, a further descent (NASG) in the early reigns of the three brothers, and finally, approached the ENTI, the final stage. The Battle of Fontenoy signified the birth of a new world, the beginning of an endemic warfare that would last for centuries. Perhaps the Franks themselves looked at the corpses of their friends and families, heard the wailing of their sisters and daughters, and understood that the Carolingians were now approaching their end.

CHAPTER 9

The Earth Recoils in Horror

June 841–February 842

I t was a good day to be a vulture. Bodies lay strewn across miles of countryside, stripped of anything of value, no metal armor to interfere with the rending of flesh from bone. The victors had chased the enemy across field and stream, through woods, and up and down ridges and struck their enemies down as they ran. Now they had to reckon with the carnage, the screaming of birds, the howling of wolves, the groans of the dying, and were made to watch as hordes of flies began to descend on the carcasses. Was Angelbert, from the losing side, looking back on the field as he wrote:

> O what grief and wailing! The dead lie there naked
> While vultures, crows, and wolves savagely devour their flesh.
> They shake since they lack graves and their corpses lie there to
>   no end.

The victors, too, would have seen the beasts and birds picking at the bones of the fallen, some their comrades, some their foes, but all fellow Christians. Just a few years before, all had been participants in the great project of the Frankish Empire.

Saturday, June 25, 841, had been occupied first with battle, then with looting, the stripping of corpses, seizing the camps of the rival armies, and taking prisoner those left alive. Surely Louis the German's and Charles the Bald's armies were also celebrating, maybe long into the evening. Maybe it wasn't until the following morning, when the carrion eaters arrived, when the soft rolling hills and plains turned gray and black with feathers and fur, that the scope of the horror became clear. By that morning, the leaders of the victorious army must have begun to realize that the aftermath, what they thought would be a smooth path to power, was all already starting to go wrong.

But why? Louis and Charles had finally brought the enemy into a pitched battle and won. They had done so openly, without deceit or trickery, fortified by a sacred Mass, inspiring sermons, and confession. God was surely on their side, made manifest in the results of the battle.

So why didn't it feel more like victory? Perhaps it was waking up the next morning to confront the horrors of the night before, of the bodies of friends and family amassed on a stinking battlefield. But maybe more, it was waking up to the realization that the battle hadn't ended a war but rather begun one. Lothar was free, at the head of his army, still the emperor, and rushing toward Aachen to regroup. In the immediate aftermath, Charles, Louis, and their propagandists needed to find a story to tell themselves (and others) that would bind the Battle of Fontenoy to what they understood as the sacred purpose of the Franks as God's new chosen people. The problem wasn't just the scope of the death. No matter how bloody, battles against pagans or even non-Frankish Christians served the story that the Franks liked to tell about themselves perfectly fine: that they were in the right, that God was on their side. God had made His will manifest in the result. If God had been angry, the Franks thought, victory wouldn't have come.

Wars are never won in a moment. Perhaps the assembled Frankish hosts who stared each other down, then committed fratricide, thought that that battle would end things. They certainly had reason for thinking so; that was how Franks had conquered their enemies for two generations. But that clarity about outcomes didn't appear in the immediate aftermath. God's will in the world was obscured for the Franks, the divine message harder to hear when, again from Angelbert, "Brother readies death for brother, an uncle for his nephew / Some refuse to give fathers what they deserve." Franks had of course killed Franks in the past, it was true, but on a much smaller scale—in skirmishes at most. This was different. Large armies had been mustered, they had stared down their adversaries across a field, then dispersed. Conflicts had been about achieving ideological victories sufficient to keep actual battle from breaking out. But now brother had fought against brother, and bodies lay strewn across the fields to a degree unprecedented in the memory of those descendants of Charlemagne. By the next morning, even the Franks who had "won" the battle began to sense that their victory was tainted, that the path ahead would be very long indeed.

On Sunday morning, June 26, 841, the day after the battle and as Lothar's army hurried toward Aachen, the early-summer sun rose over the charnel house. Churchmen—mostly bishops—came to the battlefield, followed in somber procession by kings and magnates, Empress Judith and other women of the court, courtiers and officials, and likely a great train of freemen of no remarkable wealth, levied militias who had fought on foot with pike and sword on behalf of their rulers. We imagine the leaders in their finery after having taken the evening to wash and rest, leaving aside a few moments to drink to their victory and their survival. But now they step over corpses, each footfall echoing across the fields. The beating wings of crows and ravens reluctantly give way, if only for a moment. Wolves and other earthbound scavengers keep a wary distance. But they watch.

Those churchmen finish their procession and find a suitable spot on the battlefield, likely upwind but certainly within sight of the bodies still lying scattered around, waiting for Christian burial. The priests erect a portable altar; Mass will need to be sung, prayers recited, and offerings made. They wrap a piece of wood in richly dyed silks imported from the East, ornate and exquisite and colorful. Onto that, they carefully place a slab of stone—porphyry, a rare and precious purple stone quarried originally in Egypt—surrounded by delicate, colorful enamelwork and richly patterned silver showing a Greek cross and scrollwork inlaid with precious gems. Reverently, as incense hangs in the air, priests chant, and dignitaries with battle wounds still fresh look on, the altar is unveiled.

Religious rituals had long been central to Carolingian military practice. Soldiers confessed their sins prior to battle. Priests heard confessions and said Mass on battlefields on such altars, but over time those altars were lost or broken, and relatively few survive from the European Middle Ages, though we do know that every major army in the period had some kind of altar ready to go. For the grandsons of Charlemagne, for Charles the Bald and Louis the German, surely their altar was precious. Priests preached sermons about the justifications for coming conflicts. Archbishop Agobard of Lyons had done just that for the then-united sons on the Field of Lies in 833. Similarly, after victory, celebrations were always at least quasi-religious in nature. Charlemagne and Louis the Pious had incorporated prayers for the army, both before battle and after victory, into the prayers at imperial monasteries and cathedrals across Europe. But after Fontenoy, the assembled clerics and their secular patrons clearly felt a need to develop a new, more powerful ritual response.

First, after the smoke had cleared, they celebrated Mass and prayed around the altar. Then the survivors buried the dead, friend and foe alike, treating them with reverence, for among the enemy dead were their own brothers and friends, their own uncles and nephews, fathers and sons, former compatriots in a great empire. The members of that class of people knew one another intimately and mourned the deaths of their friends and acquaintances even at the best of times. But killing them; it was the worst of times.

We shouldn't imagine that premodern Europeans were simply more savage, more able to kill than we today are. We have abundant evidence from modern warfare about how battle can overwhelm fighters' sensibilities in the heat of the moment and lead to almost revelry in combat. We've always argued that medieval people were, first and foremost, people not so different from moderns, sometimes for good when it came to kindness and sophistication but, in this case, for ill. In the aftermath, when the blood had cooled, the realization of what had happened began to dawn on them. They may have comforted the wounded but, after the battle, they were different men than they had been before. And while common soldiers toiled digging graves in blood-soaked earth, the kings turned to their bishops to ask why: Why had that battle happened? What was the meaning in the horror they had just endured? How could they make the deaths of brothers and friends make sense?

The bishops tried to answer that question by gathering in council, assembling in the great deliberative body in which medieval Christian prelates examined the world and made pronouncements about proper conduct, proper belief, and proper interpretation. That was done not by fiat but by discussion and argument. After some deliberation, they proclaimed that the two kings—the half brothers Louis the German and Charles the Bald—had fought only for justice and equity. God had made clear, by their victory, that they were in the right. Their treacherous brother, the emperor Lothar, had been consumed by greed, had broken the oaths he'd made to his father and brothers to be their advocate and protector, and so God had forced his retreat from the field.

Therefore, they said, the violence of the battle was justified. If any combatants had fought out of anger, hate, or a desire for glory, though, those men were to confess their sins and seek redemption. The bishops concluded by calling for a three-day fast on behalf of their fallen brothers on both sides of the conflict; the dead could not confess, but through common penance, the living could entreat God to forgive the dead their trespasses and thus both save their brothers and ensure that God would continue to help the cause of Louis and Charles.

It was a powerful message they gave that day, but it was almost desperate. The bishops made use of existing liturgical forms to make it feel familiar and proper, but they did so on a battlefield, after Franks had massacred their own people, so that the familiar was adapted to the unique circumstances of that Sunday in late June. It was very clever, really. This council and its decrees through its ritual setting were meant, not unlike the rituals performed during Louis the Pious's deposition in 833, to settle matters. And also like Louis the Pious's deposition in 833, the ritual failed.

❖

No one really knew what would happen after the Battle of Fontenoy because no one had thought that the battle would actually happen. If there had been any expectations, they were upended by the result. Surely, Lothar had been expecting his brothers to flee or, if there were a battle, for it to be over quickly and end with his brothers' submitting to his rightful overlordship. But that hadn't happened, because Lothar had lost the battle. Before the battle, Charles and Louis, at best, had hoped for concessions from Lothar that would have upheld the broad outlines of the *Ordinatio imperii* (with Charles taking the place of his now-deceased brother in the West). But that hadn't happened because they'd won the battle and could instead go on the offensive, could dream of expanding their kingdoms back toward the core, squeezing the eldest brother back into Italy and keeping him there. In the immediate aftermath, a new world, undreamt of just a few days previously, was being born.

The Mass held on the battlefield in the hours following the slaughter can be read in two ways, both arguably true. On the one hand, it was another deliberate act by the younger brothers to demonstrate that theirs was the side of justice, of Providence, of the continuation of the sacred status of the Franks and their kings. But the intractable problem that Louis, Charles, and their supporters confronted was that the usual Frankish arguments for fighting—that the enemy had acted in bad faith, that God was on their side—may have been sufficient to justify heading into battle but weren't enough to explain away the carnage, weren't enough to justify chasing down your brothers as they ran, weren't enough to say "Slaughter them, kill at will." Nithard kept silence on that part of the engagement, abruptly ending his history after his second book, with Lothar in flight on Saturday but no one in pursuit.

But then the rumors started. Likely later, just some months after Fontenoy, Nithard felt compelled to continue his story and set the record straight. Tellingly, his account resumes on the day after the battle and talks about the Mass, the burying of the dead, the bishops' council. His anxiety rings loudly. He needed to show that his side had cared for the dead, that it had been justified in its actions, that God had indeed been on its side. He skirted the issue of the pursuit of fleeing enemies, never mentioning prisoners or the lack thereof. And those silences also ring loudly.

There were at least some prisoners taken. As Charles's army overran Lothar's camp, some distance from the battlefield, likely on a hill overlooking the Bois de Briotte to the south and the village of Fontenoy to the north, they seized Archbishop George of Ravenna. They stripped him of his clerical vestments, mocked him, beat him with a lance to make him walk, then threw him over a deformed and disabled pack animal like so much baggage. Ransoming prisoners of war was uncommon in that period, though not unheard of. Regardless, Charles the Bald quickly made it clear that he didn't want money from the archbishop; he wanted justice. Charles was going to send George off into exile, but calmer heads—which is to say Charles's mother, Judith—prevailed. The king confronted George dressed in "a purple robe girded with gold brooches, on his left side were hanging gold amulets set with emeralds and gleaming with jacinths, his arm protected with a shield, wearing a breastplate, holding a spear in his hands and an attached lance of iron, standing fierce in arms, head crested for the battle-line." The now-victorious king demanded to know why George had abandoned his bishopric to support Lothar on the battlefield.

George protested that he had just been seeking peace, but Charles decried that as a lie, having somehow heard about the prelate's pre-battle boasting about tonsuring the Frankish king who now stood before him, resplendent and victorious. Charles thundered at the cowering archbishop, chastising him for dishonoring God with his perfidy but ultimately allowing him to return to Ravenna in shame. But before he left, another Mass was held on the battlefield, performed by George for Charles at the king's order, a way of acknowledging the authority of the secular power. Then, his cassock between his legs, George went home—almost empty-handed. Charles did restore some tiny fraction of the Church's wealth that he had seized, but the baggage train of gems intended for Lothar found their way into Charles the Bald's camp. The party of priests, who had ridden across the Alps in fine clothing, had to walk home as beggars.

Or at least that was the story told by Agnellus, who seemed to take delight in the humiliation and failure of his superior in Ravenna. Was George really captured, plundered, and humiliated? Probably. Did anyone present take notes and relay them to Agnellus? That's possible but not likely. What we can say with some confidence is that noncombatants aligned with Lothar were at risk of capture and that the plunder certainly helped supply Charles and Louis not only with arms and armor but with considerable wealth.

On the other hand, Judith was ever the wise politician, tempering her son's wrath. It was not unusual for queens, whether mothers or wives, to fill that role at court. There were situations in which kings needed to perform ruthlessness but in fact not be so violent that they made reconciliation impossible. In such a case, the public intercession of a mother, wife, sister, or daughter could create a space for forgiveness and mercy. Louis the Pious had demonstrated both facets on repeated occasions, in some cases much to his own long-term detriment. Judith's role, therefore, might be especially important in the wake of the Battle of Fontenoy, when other norms seem to have been shattered. But then again, on a more practical level, it's worth remembering that Charles was only eighteen years old, therefore much younger than either of his brothers. He may have been a fine fighter and charismatic leader, but he was a teenager. And, importantly, he wasn't married. That made Judith's role here as portrayed by Agnellus all the more important: his mother as the polished stateswoman, especially in the absence of Charles's queen to perform that same role, rings true both in this incident and throughout the campaign.

After George's departure south, the victorious younger brothers separated. Ironically, there is somewhat more of a fog around the few weeks following the Battle of Fontenoy, from late June into early July 841, than there was in the buildup to the battle. With Lothar, on the run at least for now, there were other problems Louis and Charles had back home, so Louis went back east and Charles went west to try to deal with Pepin II and finally settle his claim to Aquitaine. Neither Louis nor Charles decided to pursue Lothar. That may seem shocking—a missed opportunity for Charles and Louis to finish their brother off. But the decision reveals two things: First, pursuit of that type wasn't in the Carolingian repertoire in the 840s; Louis the German, for example, had many times been allowed to flee across the Rhine to lick his wounds and regather his forces after they had (repeatedly) been scattered by his father's. Second, and maybe more important, Lothar was still the emperor and still their brother, a Carolingian. The debate, consecrated in blood on June 25, was between different visions of what a unified empire might be. Louis and Charles wanted functional independence. Lothar wanted hegemonic power, and he hadn't lost that debate yet.

The emperor quickly went into damage control mode to cover up his loss. He and his supporters first tried to achieve with rumor and politics what they had failed to do on the battlefield. At the very least, he seemed to hope that he could muddy the waters sufficiently to remain a viable emperor and continue to press his case despite his defeat. One of his first moves: spreading the rumor far and wide that his brother Louis had been killed in action and his brother Charles grievously injured. It's possible, of course, that he actually believed this and was operating under bad information (fake news was a thing even in the ninth century), but it's more likely that he was still looking for a way to take control of the empire as his father and grandfather had. He was, after all, moving toward Louis's territory, and if he could pry some wavering support from his brother in those regions with innuendo and lies, so be it. At the very least, he might hope that such tactics would sever the alliance between Louis and Charles or that a new army could be raised to keep the brothers apart, thus reverting to the status quo prior to Fontenoy and beginning a new phase of the conflict in which victory would be possible.

It's not clear whether Lothar's rumormongering was in any way to blame for the widespread shock among the Frankish nobility in the aftermath of Fontenoy. Whereas the rumors of the injury and death of his rivals were both false and clearly politically motivated, the butchery on the field was lamentably true and well known to anyone who was there and survived. But the reputation of the battle as a slaughter also served Lothar's attempt to cast his brothers as unlawful and untrustworthy usurpers. It was, as we've seen, pretty normal for the heirs of Charlemagne to squabble over power. The deciding factor in those contests, though, was rarely armed conflict; more commonly, it was the ability to claim and hold the loyalty of the great lords of the realm, all the while threatening armed conflict. The great lords, meanwhile, could change their allegiance as it suited them. As long as a magnate maintained a core of power and troops, he could shift back and forth as the wind blew. A Carolingian could often be knocked down but was almost never knocked out.

The rumors and truths that circulated after Fontenoy were genuine threats to Louis and Charles, ones they would have to address if they wanted to keep their kingdoms. Magnates, as we've seen, could be swayed to join one brother over another so as not to end up on the losing side. It was a risk to change sides, but one with surprisingly few consequences. After the insurrections against Louis the Pious in 830 and 833–834, few nobles suffered permanently for having risen in rebellion. There were a few executions; some folks were sent to monasteries and then never heard from again; but most of those who opposed a given ruler were offered a pathway to redemption and restoration to their community.

And again, even though he'd lost the battle, Lothar still had a lot of things going for him. It became clear very quickly that Fontenoy had simply been the beginning of the civil war, not its conclusion. He was the emperor, and that mattered. His father and grandfather had made sure that mattered. It was a title inherited by blood that couldn't really be stripped by defeat in battle or ad hoc religious ritual (as Lothar himself had found out when he had tried to depose his father in 833). Lothar also had the wealth of the palace at Aachen to support his war effort, which he now deployed. He began to raise a new army to try to keep Louis and Charles apart while still performing the work of the emperor—using the public display of his office to remind wavering magnates, worried by either the bloodshed they saw perpetrated against their colleagues or the rumors they'd heard about Charles and Louis's demise, that Lothar was still in the fight.

To do so, Lothar issued charter after charter to his supporters and potential supporters, granting land to monasteries (and often invoking the loving memory of Louis the Pious, touting the connection of emperor to emperor). Such documents were performative, not simply minor administrative matters. An imperial diploma was an act that had to be witnessed, a demonstration of favor to a group of nobles and powerful churchmen who either had initiated the gift themselves or were allowed access to the emperor to witness (and sign) the creation of the document. Just such a donation to one monastery over another had been part of the irreparable rift between Louis the German and his father in 838. So although many of Lothar's diplomas were directed to Italian churches and monasteries, which were still his base of power south of the Alps, those religious houses usually had long-standing connections to elite secular families and held lands across the empire. Such a privilege offered by the emperor was always a reminder that it remained worth sending support north of the Alps. In the lands he was contesting with Charles, the grants were more significantly an assertion of authority, even if they were also a plea for continued support. The hot war of the military campaign would continue but would now be accompanied by another cold war of politics, gift, commemoration, and ritual.

It helped Lothar that the younger brothers had work to do in their own kingdoms, work that pulled them apart geographically, if not politically. They split up, promising to meet in September, a rendezvous they would end up missing. Charles and his entourage moved constantly, traversing most of France between July and October 841. It was an itinerary of hundreds of miles with three main goals: to shore up support with his backers to ensure that they didn't desert him and switch sides to the emperor; to do the opposite to supporters of Lothar by trying to recruit nobles who were on the fence or had decided not to fight at Fontenoy for either side; and to handle Pepin II of Aquitaine once and for all, ideally by forcing him to give homage to Charles and acknowledge him as his lord.

For the last goal, Charles thought he had an ace in the hole. Bernard of Septimania, having held his troops back to the irritation of both sides, chose to reenter play. Just after Fontenoy had been decided, he had sent his elder son, William, to join Charles's army. William carried with him a tempting offer. First, if Charles confirmed William's possession of lands in Burgundy (lands William already had from previous grants but not approved by Charles), William would pledge his loyalty to Charles the Bald. Second, once William's lands were confirmed by Charles, Bernard promised to use his military to force Pepin II's surrender, ending the contest over Aquitaine. But a lesson Carolingian rulers never seemed to learn was that you shouldn't trust Septimanians bearing gifts.

The first part did happen; William joined Charles's court as a hostage for Bernard's good behavior. But status as a noble hostage at court wasn't about confinement so much as joining the king as a member of his court—even if a sword always hung just over his head, ready to fall on William if Bernard went back on his word. Charles and his new allies then marched to Aquitaine. But it's hard to keep an army together, especially when the goal isn't to conquer and plunder. Nithard said that slowly, everyone just "carelessly wandered off," and Charles's army was too small to compel Pepin II's submission. It's possible that the shrinking of the army wasn't malevolent but rather that campaign season was ending and the army had to return home for the harvest.

Perhaps Charles the Bald counted on his recent victory to overturn that precedent, or maybe he was just an inexperienced, headstrong eighteen-year-old, but the end result was that he perambulated about West Francia with a small army, large enough to require the complexities of provisioning (surely much to the anger of locals whose stores might be requisitioned or plundered) but not large enough to assert any kind of authority. Even Bernard, who continued to travel with Charles, kept apologizing and postponing his submission, never formally offering it to the king, surely much to Charles's irritation. And with Charles's having marched off to the southwest, the rumors of his debilitation in battle at Fontenoy began to weaken his grip on the nobles of the north, who understandably asked—but really insisted—that he come show himself. When he finally did, he was still accompanied by a small army, and only a few key nobles rallied to his side. One of those nobles was his uncle, an illegitimate son of Charlemagne and close adviser to Louis the Pious in the 830s, Abbot Hugh of Saint-Quentin.

Meanwhile, Louis the German went east, concerned about Lothar's moves toward his territory and therefore intent upon reasserting his authority as king in Bavaria and Saxony. Remember that Louis was already in a weak position, cowed repeatedly over the past few years by Louis the Pious and Adalbert of Metz. His kingdom had been taken from him; his nobles outside Bavaria were understandably unsure how the coming confrontation with Lothar would play out. But the wind was now at Louis's back. Using both carrot (grants of lands and privileges) and stick (threats and actual violence), he gathered significant support from those east of the Rhine, meaning Saxons, Alemans, Thuringians, and others in that part of the empire. He also made sure that he appeared physically in the various regions to convince potential supporters that Lothar's rumor that Louis was injured and Charles dead was another lie.

It was good for Louis that he moved constantly within his kingdom to reassure his supporters in July and August 841, because Lothar had another plan to neutralize him. During the 830s and 840s, both Frankish and Saxon elites in the eastern part of the empire had split their loyalties, some siding with the Emperor Louis the Pious and others with Louis the German. Both groups switched sides when it suited their purposes.

Lothar saw an opening. First he marched east, hoping to isolate Louis and meet him in battle alone. Lothar was unable to cross the

Rhine in sufficient force, but he did leave his ally, Louis the German's old enemy Archbishop Otgar of Mainz (Adalbert of Metz wasn't available, being dead and all), to keep Louis bottled up east of the Rhine. That bought Lothar time to look for more allies. He did so in Saxony, sending some loyal nobles from the region to make an offer to a fascinating group of people: the *Stellinga*.

During Charlemagne's reign, the Franks had conquered (and massacred) the Saxons in waves, imposing on them not just Christianity but also Frankish laws regarding property ownership, judicial procedure, obligations of laborers to landowners, and so forth. The conquest had been completed by circa 800, and so, by the 840s, not only had many Frankish elites been granted lands and rights over Saxon communities, but many Saxon elites had been fully integrated into the empire. And why not? Throughout the empire, especially where the people did not necessarily see themselves as Franks or solely as Franks, those groups maintained their own local traditions alongside the Frankish ones. Integration did not require cultural annihilation.

Holding multiple, oftentimes overlapping identities that might seem to conflict but weren't necessarily in conflict was a very medieval way to be. Each medieval person stood at the center of both hierarchical and communal systems and identities. But the recognized existence of overlapping systems doesn't mean they all lived in some perfect harmony; instead, those people and their identities functioned but remained in tension with one another.

So it was in postconquest Saxony. Many elites found power in Frankish law and tried to exert it, while others, ranging from the unfree (there were lots of different ways to be unfree, including abject chattel slavery, but also many more complex statuses) to poor free landowners and even some petty gentry, came together into an intentional community of people that they called comrades, or, in Old Saxon, *stellinga*.

Both medieval and modern historians have characterized the *Stellinga* as a wild polytheistic peasant revolt. But there was nothing violent about their mere existence. The group had been around for quite some time before 841, and its members were focused primarily on preserving local customs, assisting one another in myriad ways, and, essential to our story, overseeing the use of customary law in dispensing justice. In other words, they were a normal part of Saxon society, a very typical regional collection of people within the Frankish Empire. And so Lothar made them an offer: back his claim against his brother Louis, and he would give them the right to practice whatever law or customs they chose. In effect, he was saying he would elevate customary Saxon law above the Frankish law imposed by Charlemagne and his descendants. That was a good deal. The *Stellinga* launched attacks against Louis's supporters. That distraction in Saxony would allow Lothar—he hoped—to invade from the west while his internal supporters weakened Louis's support.

With Otgar of Mainz holding the Rhine and the *Stellinga* attacking Louis the German on his other flank, Lothar saw a chance to regain the footing lost at Fontenoy. He tried the same tactic elsewhere in July and August 841, looking for external allies to distract and frustrate Louis and Charles. For example, he tried to draw the duke of Brittany to his cause but failed. He summoned a Danish lord who had been an ally of Louis the Pious and asked him to raid his brothers' lands. All of those moves were attempts to bring the fringes of the empire into the fray on his behalf, requiring his brothers to defend their own borders, while Lothar assembled his own force and tried to track down Charles.

But it wasn't to be. Once again Lothar was defeated by his greatest nemesis: a river. When he arrived in the west to confront Charles the Bald directly, he found him vulnerable. Charles's army was outnumbered by Lothar's force. But Charles was on the north of the Seine and Lothar on the south. At Fontenoy, everyone had wanted to fight, so they had fought. Now Charles knew he needed to avoid battle, so he did everything possible to keep Lothar's army from crossing the river: stalling until winter with negotiations over a peace treaty or offering to fight in the spring. Lothar declined, turned south, and reunited with Pepin, then turned back north to attack Charles in force (Charles had crossed to the south of the Seine but was still mobile). But unless a foe was caught by surprise or made a terrible blunder, battle happened only when both sides were seeking it. Lothar was; Charles wasn't. What had started so promisingly by putting his younger brother on the back foot became a wild goose chase that only resulted in Lothar's tiring out his men and convincing Pepin II that he was better off back in Aquitaine.

Charles the Bald, though suffering setbacks of his own (it likely wasn't fun to be chased around Francia by your older brother and his larger army), was able at the same time to draw some important supporters to his cause. His uncle Hugh of Saint-Quentin wasn't the only one of Charlemagne's descendants to join with Charles. Hildegard, Charles's half sister but full sister to Lothar and Louis, had become the abbess of a convent in the city of Laon. She was on Lothar's side initially and had taken one of Charles the Bald's most loyal retainers prisoner. After Lothar had given up his pursuit in the winter, Charles had decided to get his loyal follower back, so he had led his men on a forced march through the bitter cold night. Before dawn, lookouts on Laon's walls were horrified to see an army approaching, preparing to cut off all escape routes and then assault the city. The city begged to surrender. Maybe its officials remembered what Lothar had done to Chalon-sur-Saône in a similar situation in 834; maybe Hildegard remembered what had happened to Bernard of Septimania's sister, the nun Gerberga, at that time. Charles's men, exhausted but eager for plunder, were said to have been prepared to attack anyway. Their king gradually persuaded (and threatened) them until they stood down, and he peacefully took control of the city. Hildegard, we are told, saw the error of her ways and switched her support to Charles—amazing how persuasive an army can be.

Fresh off that new victory, Charles marched to his older brother's aid. Otgar of Mainz was now sandwiched between two hostile armies. He thought better of his chances and fled. Louis the German crossed the Rhine, and the brothers met on the banks of the river in Strasbourg on February 14, 842. Lothar's plan had failed.

The Battle of Fontenoy had not been decisive. Although it had been a victory in the moment for Charles and Louis, nothing had really changed over the next seven months. Charles was struggling to capitalize on the aftermath; Pepin II was still marauding around Aquitaine. Louis had to shore up his base and then defend against an internal rebellion based in Saxony, one carefully targeted at his loyalists. Lothar had skulked (or tactically retreated) back to Aachen but then seemed for a moment to have the upper hand; it was he who pursued Charles around as Louis was occupied elsewhere, only for even that advantage to turn to nothing within just a few months. The brothers now all understood that the conflict would be prolonged. But now Charles and Louis had reunited and were ready to take the fight to the emperor.

In the middle of the ninth century, an unknown poet told a whopper of an epic story that has everything to do with the aftermath of the Battle of Fontenoy. In ways not dissimilar to the visionary literature that had so troubled the empire in the 820s and 830s, the poem called out a warning to those who could listen and understand. The slaughter at Fontenoy might not have immediately scrambled the politics of the empire, but it had scrambled the Franks' intellectual world. Their initial horror had been followed by a ritual attempt at absolution. But that had clearly failed. Over the next few decades, the Franks began to change how they thought about violence, about war, and about their very identity as Franks.

The tale, known as the *Waltharius*, opens with Attila the Hun raging across Europe. Instead of uniting with the other rulers against the Hun, the Frankish king immediately surrenders and sends vast treasure and also his best warrior, Hagen, as a hostage. The kings of Burgundy and Aquitaine then follow the Franks' lead. The Burgundians send the king's only daughter, Hildigund, while the Aquitanians send their king's son Walter (hence *Waltharius*).

Attila's court, however, turns out to be pretty great; Hildigund becomes Attila's queen, and both men become Attila's greatest warriors and best pals with each other. But the Frankish king dies, and Hagen flees back to Francia, breaking his oath as a hostage. Then, as one might predict in an epic poem, Walter and Hildigund fall in love and betray Attila. They get Attila and his men drunk, steal a lot of treasure, and flee west.

Alas, news of a big warrior loaded with treasure reaches the Franks' court and they greedily decide to take it, setting out with Hagen and then cornering Walter and demanding that he surrender the wealth. Walter offers to trade some of the wealth for safe passage and Hagen advises the Franks to take the offer, but their king is too greedy and attacks. Walter slays all but the king and Hagen. The battle is fierce and everyone left alive is maimed, not unlike Monty Python's Black Knight. Indeed, they do eventually call it a draw. As they're healing, Walter and Hagen reconcile more because of exhaustion than anything else, then go their separate ways. The poem closes with Walter and Hildigund marrying and ruling Aquitaine happily ever after.

The story of Walter, Hagen, Hildigund, and Attila would have been well known in both oral and written cultures at the time of composition, which means that it perhaps reflects the view in the villages, the towns, the stories told over ale and wine in taverns by veterans to a crowd of young men still eager for death and glory. It seems like a tall tale about the ancient past. But this version of the epic, composed in the ninth century, like the dream visions we've already encountered, contains an embedded criticism of bad kings, in this case taking aim at the sons of Louis the Pious. The cowardly Frankish king is meant to be Louis the Pious, and his son, whose greed to seize all the wealth lies at the heart of the ultimate maimings and death, is Lothar. This poem, then, is a commentary on contemporary events, a way of cloaking critique behind allegory and allusion while still making sure the message comes across. But it's also coming from a specific angle, from someone who didn't like Lothar, of course, but also someone who was increasingly skeptical of Carolingian kingship generally. Fontenoy, like the final battle of the poem, was a waste—a stalemate and tragedy that was caused by unforgivable greed and a battle that really changed nothing.

And the poet doesn't mean to say only that the greed of kings leads to bloodshed but that greed pairs with cowardice. Lothar, greedy, rides into battle at Fontenoy instead of avoiding it but then flees, much as the Frankish king of the poem, greedy, leads his men into battle against Walter but then flees. That flight leads to more rounds of conflict instead of resolution; by the end of the epic, everyone is maimed and no one is spared culpability. Walter, especially, is much too eager to seek battle but does at least, after his initial victory, hold funeral rites for the fallen that should be reminiscent of the rituals we opened this chapter with.

After Fontenoy, there were no more heroes. Good men are presented with impossible choices and end up killing one another or suffering grievously. Every king is a failure due to cowardice, greed, or bloodthirstiness. The lesson is that warriors should be good to one another while navigating the impossible choices presented to them by their leaders, understanding that at the end, one might have to cut the lips off a friend whether he wants to or not. So much for the grand project of the Franks.

The *Waltharius* is far from alone in regarding the fraternal slaughter at Fontenoy as a turning point that moved things from bad to worse, though our many pessimistic sources divide along two lines. One, epitomized by Nithard's telling, predicted that things—as bad as they were—were only going to get worse. Nithard ended his history of the sons of Louis the Pious in 843. He'd been commissioned to write it by his cousin Charles the Bald, but his attitude changed as he was writing so that by the end, the work had become a lament, even a screed, against the dissolution of his own time. Book IV, the final book of his *Histories*, closes by saying:

> In the time of Charles the Great of good memory, who died almost thirty years ago, peace and concord ruled everywhere because our people were treading the one proper way, the way of the common welfare, and thus the way of God. But now since each goes his separate way, dissension and struggle abound. Once there was abundance and happiness everywhere, now everywhere there is want and sadness. Once even the elements smiled on everything and now they threaten. . . . About this time . . . , a great deal of snow fell in the same night and the

THE EARTH RECOILS IN HORROR

just judgment of God, as I said before, filled every heart with sorrow. I mention this because rapine and wrongs of every sort were rampant on all sides and now the unseasonable weather killed the last hope of any good to come.

Nithard had lost hope. Nothing would improve. Even nature agreed. When brother kills brother, God turns His face away.

But other supporters of Lothar, men who still believed in an empire and an emperor to rule it, took a different position. The theologian Florus of Lyons wrote a poem that made explicit in both style and substance the comparison between the ninth-century Franks and the ancient Israelites. But the allegory isn't meant to reassure. The poem draws on the Book of Amos, which informed the Israelites that God expected them to be pure, and in their sinful nature, God would scourge them. Florus uses this admonition to hinge his poem on Fontenoy, saying of the battle:

We know [we saw just recently] a savage war
in which Christian peoples wickedly attacked one another with
   swords,
and the bonds of duty were severed by kinsmen's blades,
both wild beasts and birds devouring their goodly limbs,
when terrible comets burned so often in the sky,
foreboding disaster and destruction for mankind.

God was, Florus saw, clearly punishing the Franks for their sins. Only that could explain the division of the empire, the disasters that washed over them in waves. But by the end of the poem, there is still hope because the disasters will repurify the Franks and bring them back to the proper path. If the Franks can win "through to the port of peace by Your guidance, we may pluck sweet fruit grown from this dismal seed, and sing again in perpetual praise of Your triumphs!"

But for Lothar, those triumphs wouldn't come.

❖

There's a description of life in the European Middle Ages that still echoes these many centuries later: nasty, brutish, and short. We are made to understand that violence was everywhere all the time, war a constant companion, great slaughter commonplace.

Certainly, there was plenty of violence and war, but we can read the pessimism, the woe, after the Battle of Fontenoy not as a sign of the brutality of the era but rather as the opposite. The Franks' recognition of the scale of the disaster, the moral crisis caused by fraternal warfare, is a sign that they had not dehumanized their foes so as to celebrate the destruction of the enemy without remorse. They had not surrendered their own humanity but rather saw in the horror a sign that they had gone too far, that they needed to pull back. In the years to come, as the next series of battles began anew, the lessons of Fontenoy would stay with the Franks as a cautionary tale.

The Battle of Fontenoy did not have to take place, as evidenced by the avoidance of further fighting in the years before and after the battle. But it did take place. The slaughter of a retreating foe wasn't necessary. But the slaughter of retreating foes did take place. And the slaughter didn't lead to a decisive victory that ended the war. The war continued. The deaths had been for nothing. And the repercussions of those deaths would linger for generations, irreparable.

CHAPTER 10

Oathmakers

February–December 842

In February 842, in the city of Strasbourg, just eight months after the Battle of Fontenoy, the civil war that pitted Emperor Lothar against his younger brothers raged on. Charles the Bald and Louis the German had been pressed by the emperor's machinations—Louis dealing with the *Stellinga* revolt and Charles pursued by the imperial army. But the pressure on them had been released, and it was time to reaffirm the bond between the siblings in their struggle against their elder brother. So they decided to play a game.

In the fields outside Strasbourg, the armies of Louis the German and Charles the Bald faced each other, weapons drawn. A few hundred East Frankish infantry moved first, keeping tight formation as they advanced but at the last minute charging forward at a full run, breaking free from the heavily armed and armored cavalry that surrounded their king to close rapidly with the foe. A phalanx of West Franks from across the way countered, advancing with shields high. But as the Saxons began to charge, the Bretons' courage seemed to fail them and they turned to run, all discipline forgotten. They slung their shields over their backs as they fled, desperate to block arrow fire from the pursuing enemy. All seemed lost, but maybe, just maybe, if they reached their companions at the other side of the field, they might be safe.

Suddenly the commander of the West Franks wheeled and his army, as one, turned to face the onrushers. Shields clattered, and the whoosh of a hundred spears thrown in unison caused a noticeable breeze. The westerners judged that the enemy had overextended themselves, breaking discipline in their eagerness to claim victory, and so gave a new order to charge their onrushing opponents. Their formation re-formed nearly instantly as they charged back toward their pursuers. Now it was the turn of the easterners to flee back across the field with their shields on their backs, the tables turned, until again a commander judged that the westerners had broken discipline sufficiently and so ordered the easterners to reform and turn to charge and chase their foes. The infantry forces on both sides charged back and forth. Eventually, a force of cavalry pursued all sides, dashing back and forth, the kings mounted on their horses, taking the field together, their young men around them, cheering, shouting, driving their horses, extending their lances far ahead of them, forcing the infantry to retreat, then retreating themselves when the foot soldiers charged.

At last, exhausted, both armies returned to their camps. "It was a show worth seeing," wrote Nithard, "because of its excellent execution and discipline; not one in such a large crowd and among such different people dared to hurt or abuse each other." Neither side had lost a single man or seen one killed. It was all just fun and games. Because it wasn't a battle; it was instead a demonstration of friendship and solidarity among the younger grandsons of Charlemagne, Charles the Bald and Louis the German, reunited at last. Still pursued by Lothar, even after their victory at Fontenoy, they once more cemented their shared cause by preparing for a renewal of the war.

❖

We need to remember that at no point in the 830s or in the disorder of the previous two years had either of these Carolingians claimed the imperial title, nor did either argue that he deserved to be his father's sole heir. And Lothar never claimed that his brothers weren't kings! Every argument going back at least to the second coup attempt in 833, if not a bit before, has been about how the hierarchy between an emperor and a king should function (but then it was complicated much further because everyone involved was family: father, son, or brother).

That dispute had led to slaughter. But the slaughter hadn't ended the dispute. It's easy to look across that period and see all kinds of ways that things might have turned out differently in the year that followed the Battle of Fontenoy: a victory for Charles in Aquitaine, more help from the Bretons for Lothar, a battle at the Seine or Rhine in which Lothar crossed a river, defeated a brother, and reset the board. Instead, the reunification of the brothers in Strasbourg proved to be the decisive moment in setting up a beginning of the end of the civil war.

Charles and Louis hadn't seen each other since the days right after Fontenoy. They had both escaped their brother the emperor's clutches and reunited in high spirits. But doubts must have lingered. They and their followers asked themselves if God could really have favored Charles and Louis, particularly in light of Lothar's continued resistance and the setbacks those kings had seen in the wake of Fontenoy. Indeed, had the slaughter of their fellow Franks near the Brook of the Burgundians accomplished anything? Was there a plan that might bring peace to the realm, that might bring final victory?

There was—or so Louis and Charles and their closest advisers hoped.

One of the biggest problems any hope for peace faced was that loyal retainers on both sides, once united by common causes—marriage, royal hunts, attending Louis the Pious together—no longer trusted one another. The old bonds that held them, the old oaths they had made (and broken) no longer seemed to hold any weight. So the brothers and their advisers came up with a new oath with new stakes, as well as a new ritual for the oath taking. In so doing they were creating a new kind of threat to the potential oathbreaker that, they hoped, might both assuage the concerns of their followers and keep the two sides working together.

And so, not long after the two kings had arrived in Strasbourg, they gathered their forces together into a great assembly outside the city walls. Their armies would have been composed primarily of men of fighting age, but a king's court traveled with him and would have included his churchman, the queen and her attendants (including, in Charles's case, his mother, the former empress), and the mass of servants that had to attend such a large gathering. All witnessed the spectacle.

Louis the German, the elder brother, spoke first. He started by addressing the grim cloud still hanging over the throng; it was the first time he spoke publicly about Fontenoy. He proclaimed that the battle had been fought only because Lothar had decided to wipe the brothers out, to seize the whole empire, forcing him and Charles the Bald to come together to (according to Nithard) "submit the matter to the judgment of Almighty God." They had won the battle; God's judgment, therefore, was clear. Louis was reiterating the judgment of the bishops that had been given on the battlefield itself.

But there remained the little problem of all the dead Franks and a war that wouldn't end. In his speech, Louis tried to emphasize the role that he and Charles had played in stopping the slaughter, saying that because they had been "moved by brotherly love and compassion for our Christian people, we did not want to pursue and annihilate our opponents." It was Lothar who was resisting God's will, and Louis cast his retreat and subsequent reorganization as a threat now returning to "ruin our people by fire, plunder, and slaughter." Louis and Charles's decision not to pursue Lothar toward Aachen was an act of mercy, he insisted. But perhaps he was protesting too much, reiterating talking points and actually acknowledging Fontenoy as a strategic blunder that had left bodies strewn across a field in France with no real road map for what would come after.

He next turned to the immediate problem, saying to the assembled nobles and churchmen that "you doubt that our brotherly love is strong and that our loyalty will last. We have both decided to swear an oath before your eyes." And they did. Louis and Charles the Bald pledged their loyalty to each other and their enmity to Lothar. That was all standard procedure. The public swearing of oaths was a normal but important political ritual for medieval people. The ritual had to be public, and it rested on a sense of trust that deed would match word. Oathtakers would say before the assembled throng (and the holy, as the relics of saints were often present) that they would or would not do a certain thing and ask for punishment if they went back on their word. All assembled had performed that kind of act before, but several things were different this time around.

While the other oaths we've seen focused on releasing the opposite party from his vows in case of a breach, this time if the other party violated an oath, he would release his *own* vassals from their vows of obedience. In other words, whereas previous oaths taken by the brothers were about external consequences for actions—if one ruler did this, his opponents' followers could do that—the oath at Strasbourg tried to shift the consequences of oathbreaking to the internal politics of each brother's own kingdom. Instead of allowing the other brother to attack and claim the moral high ground, oathbreaking by one would now, in theory, lead to a dissolution of the bonds of promise and obligation that held his own kingdom together. In other words, breaking this oath would justify—even necessitate—rebellion against their rule.

Moreover, rather than just the kings' swearing an oath, this time they made the magnates who surrounded them into participants in it. It was a collective action. They turned to their followers, demanding that they swear that if their lord ever broke his promise and attacked the other, they wouldn't help. The ritual was an attempt to reentangle the Franks, strengthen the ties that bound, and reassure everyone on all sides that they were united as one until there was a final resolution to the war. The oath, taken in February 842, tried to reset the clock to the "peace" of the Field of Lies, a time before the bloodshed at Fontenoy.

But even as they seemed to wish for that clock to be reset, both Charles the Bald and Louis the German acknowledged that they lived in a new world. Up until that time, oaths among Frankish elites had been taken in Latin, the universal language of Church and empire. That had unified the community of the Franks, and the teaching of Latin was an emphasis on the learning and reform that had emanated from Charlemagne's court a couple of generations previously. But the Oaths of Strasbourg revealed the illusion of Frankish unity: each brother now spoke to his followers in the vernacular.

Louis gave his speech to his followers in vernacular German, and Charles did the same in Romance, a kind of proto-French. Then they turned to the other side: Louis swore his oath in Romance, vowing to aid his brother and never deal with Lothar in any way that might hurt Charles. Charles followed with the same oath but in German. Finally, the ritual was completed when Charles's men swore in Romance to abandon their lord if Charles ever betrayed Louis and Louis's men swore the same in German. Sometime later, Nithard wrote it all down, likely as he had witnessed it himself, in Latin.

The reason that Louis and Charles deployed, then swapped, linguistic vernaculars was that their men already spoke those vernaculars. In many ways, it's more interesting that Latin continued to provide a common linguistic point of reference across the great empire, solidified by the educational reforms under Charlemagne that had created the audience for Nithard's *Histories*. What's more, Nithard's decision to break his Latin narrative and record the oaths in their vernaculars demonstrates the lack of concern among potential elite readers about linguistic drift. The empire was vast, and people spoke different languages in their everyday lives. Lots of people, including Charles and Louis, spoke lots of languages. A thousand years later, nationalist historians in France and Germany would leap on that moment as a birth not only of nations but of peoples, an origin story for modern states and the modern identities of the people who claimed those states. It was an attempt to build a rainbow connection that directly linked the medieval and the modern in a way that erases rather than reveals history. But what mattered for the Franks in the ninth century when it came to oaths was to be sure that all relevant parties fully understood what was going on.

In terms of the civil war right there, right then, the act of oathtaking was significant in that it attempted to heal the lingering distrust that existed even between the purported allies against Lothar. We can see some of that worry in the fullness of Nithard's recounting. Were tensions actually so high between Louis the German and Charles the Bald (and their followers) that everyone involved needed that elaborate ritual? What did the oaths actually *do*?

In short, the display and performance at Strasbourg allowed Louis and Charles to find a way forward. The elaborate ritual provided a message to their supporters that after the carnage of Fontenoy and a frustrating summer, fall, and winter during which defeat had always been waiting in the wings, this was a new beginning. The brothers had been physically divided from each other by mountains and rivers but now had come together and wrapped themselves in chains of alliance. They tried their best to make those chains seem unbreakable.

And it seemed to work. From that position of strength in Strasbourg, they sent messages to their elder brother, the emperor, to tell him that he had no choice but to negotiate. He could keep his title and the middle kingdom, but Charles and Louis were indivisible. That was a threat, but it also gave their supporters hope for peace. Surely this time Lothar would agree. Surely this time the war might soon end.

To some extent, it did. Lothar had been rearming himself and moved his forces just north of the city of Koblenz, where the Rhine and the Moselle—yes, another river—meet. Louis the German sailed down the Rhine from Strasbourg to confront Lothar and stop his advance, accompanied by a large force levied and led by his eldest son, Carloman, now twelve years of age. Charles, taking his best-trained cavalry, led his forces overland in support. At Koblenz on March 18, 842, Charles and Louis, the two united brothers, attended Mass, put on their armor, got onto a boat, crossed the Moselle, and watched Lothar bravely run away. Again.

By the end of March, Lothar had fled to Burgundy and his younger brothers had at last reached Aachen, Charlemagne's city, and were preparing to split the empire between the two of them, cutting Lothar out. He had, after all, run from the chance to defend his position. Charles and Louis gathered bishops together in an echo of the ritual that had followed the battle of Fontenoy, this one confirming God's judgment as shown in battle, that those two were victorious. Each of them took twelve of his most trusted nobles and asked them to come up with the most equitable division of the Kingdom of the Franks between the two brothers.

This is the first time in our story that Louis and Charles tried to write Lothar—the emperor himself—out of the empire. But the attempt wasn't serious. Maybe Charles and Louis would have been delighted with a two-way split, but the move was really about taking a maximalist negotiating stance in order to claim leverage in whatever three-way settlement followed. No one had forgotten that Lothar was still out there, still enjoying wide support. And he was still the emperor.

Indeed, Lothar's position was still strong. Remember how quickly he'd turned the tide on his younger siblings after Fontenoy, rallying support from external allies and drawing wobbling magnates to his side who had initially sat the June 841 battle out. And although he'd fled at Koblenz just now, he continued to supplement his new army. His strategic withdrawal to Aachen after his defeat at Fontenoy had been symbolically important, allowing him to establish himself at the palace in the wake of an unexpected defeat in battle, but that was also where the gold was. The wealth of the treasury at Aachen would, in other words, enable him to buy support and supply troops. Louis's and Charles's partisans may have condemned Lothar for the looting, but cash is always helpful for an emperor, and loyalty can oftentimes be bought.

Lothar also had other assets. Italy, at least once the March snows turned to April showers and opened the passes, was still firmly in his camp, and he could count on support in Burgundy and in the Frankish heartlands from those who still believed in a unitary vision of empire. Indeed, most important, Lothar was the emperor and still a Carolingian. That mattered, not only to Charles and Louis but to all their followers as well. Even during the insurrections of 830 and 833–834, try as the rebels might, Emperor Louis the Pious could not be dethroned. The Franks held an empire, and an empire needed an emperor. Charles and Louis's loudly proclaiming their decision to write Lothar out of the picture was actually warfare by other means, using the threat of exclusion to force Lothar back to the bargaining table.

In any case, whether or not that was Charles and Louis's ideal plan, it worked. By April 842, Lothar had sent envoys asking for a truce. By June, the three brothers had an agreement in principle and a plan to meet again in October to finally resolve their differences and redivide the empire.

Of course, there had been plans for peace before. Again and again over the past three years, the brothers had made arrangements to meet and talk things out, only to shift back to violence when one side or the other saw a potential advantage. Why should this time be different?

The answer was that the rest of the world had taken note of the infighting and had come knocking to see what they could get, too.

The Canche River flows through northwestern France and into the English Channel. Throughout the Carolingian era and surely long before, the mouth of the Canche provided a welcome harbor for English visitors to the continent and was recognized as a place that connected the Frankish kingdom to the trade in goods and ideas that came across the water. In addition, throughout our period, that settlement, named Quentovic, served as one of the coastal *emporia*—trading sites— and mints of coins on the Atlantic coast. The problem with being a wealthy port on the ocean is that opportunity isn't the only thing that can come knocking. In the spring or early summer of 842, not long after the Oaths of Strasbourg and about the time that Lothar was opening negotiations with Charles and Louis, a fleet of longships appeared off Quentovic at dawn. The Vikings had arrived.

According to the *Annals of St-Bertin*, they "plundered [the town] and laid it waste, capturing or massacring the inhabitants of both sexes. They left nothing in it except for those buildings which they were paid to spare." Charles the Bald's kingdom was under attack. To make matters worse, in the same year, the annals continued, in the Mediterranean, Islamic "pirates sailed up the Rhône to near Arles, ravaging everything on their route, and got away again completely unscathed."

It wasn't the first time that pirates had raided the Carolingians from north or south, but it was striking to the chronicler that it had happened at both ends of the empire at roughly the same time. Indeed, they're consecutive sentences in the text; the connection was the point. Moreover, that fact seemed to signal to the author that the raiders were not just mindless plunderers but rather had taken advantage of the ample connections and communication between regions to learn that Charles the Bald's forces were committed elsewhere. And then they struck.

It wasn't the first time. It wouldn't be the last. And while it was possible for locals to bribe the invaders to spare specific buildings, that was cold comfort to those killed, those enslaved, those carried far away. Part of the job of the king was to protect his lands from outside threats, and Charles was letting his people down in the most undeniable way.

To make matters worse, pirates weren't Charles's only concern. He also had internal threats to worry about, especially Pepin II in Aquitaine. Pepin hadn't given up on his desire to retake his father's inheritance, which had been snatched away capriciously by his grandfather Louis the Pious. Pepin used Charles the Bald's distraction at Strasbourg and Aachen in early 842 to mobilize his forces and reestablish himself in Aquitaine.

Charles therefore left Aachen and marched to Aquitaine with an army. As we've seen so many times, it takes two to have a battle, and Pepin didn't want one. He realized he was outnumbered and fled, knowing that Charles wouldn't be able to stay in the area long because he'd need to return to negotiate with his brothers. It worked. Again. In late summer 841, after Fontenoy, Pepin II had split from Lothar and sought his homelands, skirting the edges of Charles the Bald's pursuing forces. Charles had to give up and head toward Paris, where he was almost (saved by a flooded river!) caught out by Lothar. Now, in early 842, Pepin used the same strategy. He and his army ducked and weaved and forced Charles to give up again. Charles headed back to Aachen, having accomplished nothing and left a bit of a mess in his kingdom behind him.

For Louis the German, dealing with internal threats meant reasserting his control of Saxony. After Lothar's retreat and the initial discussion of a new peace, Louis moved east to repress the *Stellinga* during the summer campaigning season. The Saxons did not, it turned out, want to be repressed, and they responded with open rebellion. With Lothar preoccupied and Charles the Bald trying to catch Pepin II, Louis the German went to war in Saxony. The *Annals of St-Bertin* say:

> *Louis marched throughout Saxony and by force and terror he completely crushed all who still resisted him: having captured all the ringleaders of that dreadful example of insubordination—men who had all but abandoned the Christian faith and had resisted Louis and his faithful men so fiercely—he punished 140 of them by beheading, hanged fourteen, maimed countless numbers by chopping off their limbs, and left no one able to carry on any further opposition to him.*

To be clear, this text, like all those that described the uprising after the fact, was praising Louis for his violence. This is a far cry from the descriptions of Fontenoy. In this telling, the Saxons were outsiders; the *Stellinga*, who rejected Frankish law, even more so. As such, they deserved the savagery visited upon them. Pay attention to how the annalist portrays them as *almost* apostates. This is a tell on the part of the annalist, one of many in the ex post facto accounts of the uprising. Had the Saxons really reverted to their earlier polytheism, the annalist would have said "pagans," not almost outside the faith. Instead, they are in the text described as being similar to pagans as a way of othering them, of linking their treachery to the history of Frankish violence inflicted on the Saxons under Charlemagne, and so signaling Louis the German's actions as justified.

That violence worked. The *Stellinga* were for the moment suppressed. Drenched in blood, Louis went west to finish negotiations.

❖

Louis and Charles weren't, of course, the only players in that drama. Lothar was still out there with his history of successfully mobilizing allies to help when things seemed grim. And it just so happened that at the time, the Byzantine emperor Theophilos had problems great and small with which he might need help and that might present Lothar with an opportunity to reset the board. Theophilos's really big problem was the expanding Abassid Caliphate based in Baghdad, against which he had been waging epic campaigns across Anatolia and into the Middle East; campaigns he had mostly lost. But he had plenty of other problems, too: he was fighting the Bulgars to the west and was watching Arab raiders in the Mediterranean turn into Arab conquerors, sweeping Sicily away from the empire and threatening to close off the Adriatic to Byzantine shipping.

Theophilos had few solutions to his problems, too often being low on soldiers, ships, and money. What he did have was prestige, enough to spare, so he sent missions across the region to try to find allies. First, in 839, he sent an embassy to the court of the Umayyad caliph of Spain, praising the legitimacy of his rule from Iberia all the way to Damascus and hoping for help against the Abbasids based in Baghdad. That plan didn't work. Next he tried to contact a group that the *Annals of St-Bertin* called "the Rhos," who may have come either from western Asia (what would later become Kievan Rus) or from Scandinavia. But that plan also didn't work out. Theophilos tried again. The following year, in 840, he dispatched an emissary to Venice to seek naval help against the recent conquerors of Taranto at the mouth of the Adriatic. Venice agreed to help. Venetians and Byzantines both sent out fleets against their common enemy. But they didn't coordinate. The Venetians got there first and were defeated. The Byzantines then arrived and were also defeated. Zero for three so far.

But Theophilos was pleased that at least something had come from his emissary to Venice, so in May 841—that is to say, just weeks before the Battle of Fontenoy—he dispatched another emissary to the Franks to meet with the emperor. But travel could be delayed by weather, by sickness, by a preference for the cuttlefish in Venice, by any number of things, so that Byzantine diplomat didn't arrive in the north until the middle of 842. He found a very different world than he had been expecting. By that point, Fontenoy and the Oaths of Strasbourg had taken place, and Lothar had formally agreed with his brothers to negotiate a just division of the empire and end the war. But that agreement—like all the promises—was provisional. Anything could happen. Lothar was down but not out, and he was determined to hang on to his supporters and his status as emperor by any means necessary.

And so on August 29, 842, Lothar was in Trier, in modern Germany, to sign a diploma that gave control of a monastery to the archbishop of Trier, taking it away from one of his supporters in Italy. The charter included a formal recognition of Lothar's failures to follow "divine admonition," blaming the civil war on "human affairs" and promising to do better. It was a ritual gesture of humility for a ruler and not altogether uncommon in those types of documents, especially ones produced by the son of Louis the Pious, who made them a kind of habit. But the document is important for us because it described the arrival of the imperial delegation from Constantinople. It wasn't the first time that emissaries of the Byzantine emperor Theophilos had arrived at odd moments and met with Emperor Lothar; not long after Theophilos had taken the throne in 829, his emissaries had arrived at Compiègne in 833, looking for Louis the Pious but finding his son, just after the Field of Lies, on the throne instead. In 842, the emissaries might not have been as surprised as they had been in 833, but an emperor was still an emperor and potential ally.

Lothar and Theophilos agreed that Lothar's eldest son, the seventeen-year-old Louis II of Italy, would marry Theophilos's daughter. That was marriage diplomacy at the highest level and a strategic alliance that would benefit both parties. In 839, as Louis the Pious was casting off Louis the German and bringing Lothar back into the fold, the emperor had designated Louis II king of Italy. We don't hear much about him in the sources, but all evidence indicates that when he reached his majority in 840, he was active throughout the peninsula and constantly dealing with the Byzantines, at least by proxy. The marriage alliance, spelled out in a much decayed papyrus diplomatic document known as the *Kaiserbrief* (Imperial Letter) of Saint-Denis, specified that Louis II would lead forces overland to attack the new Muslim rulers of Sicily, while Byzantium would provide naval support.

The *Kaiserbrief* is an important document to look at a bit more closely. First, the fact that it survives at all is remarkable. Byzantines used papyrus because it harkened back to antiquity, giving even their missives a kind of gravitas. But it does not endure well over the eons in the wetter conditions of northern Germany and France. Second, the text called for a joint campaign against their common enemies. In other words, the effort proposed by the *Kaiserbrief* reflected grandiose ambition on both sides, connections between peoples over vast cultural and material differences, and tensions between the newly emerging states in the Mediterranean that would influence the region for centuries. In theory, it was a resurrection of a vision first proposed by the failed marriage alliance between Charlemagne and Empress Irene back in the 780s.

That contact between Byzantium and the Franks reminds us that throughout our story, there was always a bigger world out there. It could arrive in the form of Viking or Muslim raiders or a distinct group of people such as the *Stellinga* seeking liberation from imperial law. A diplomat from across the Mediterranean might arrive at court at a particular moment. During the Carolingian Civil War, even when our perspective narrows to a single field of France, a river crossing in the Rhineland, an altar, a throne, a single document, that wasn't the only storyline, and actions far away might eventually—directly or indirectly, sooner or later—impact what was happening in other realms, ours included. Here, the mostly futile diplomacy of a Byzantine emperor on the edge of death offered Lothar a chance to stage his own imperial performance as he attempted to claw his way back to relevance in the story of the Franks.

But it all came to nothing—again.

By the time the Byzantine emissaries reached Trier and met with Lothar, Emperor Theophilos was already dead and had been succeeded by his two-year-old son, Michael III. Other matters intervened, the Byzantines lost interest, and Lothar wasn't in a strong enough position to enforce the terms of the agreement. The winds of a Mediterranean alliance that had seemed to fill Lothar's sails died suddenly. The marriage that would have united the Eastern and Western Roman

Empires once more and perhaps tip the scales back in Lothar's favor never took place. All eyes turned back to the coming negotiations between the brothers.

※

By October, winter was coming, and the fall harvest had not been good. People would be hungry that year, and another year of war might mean starvation; it would certainly mean distraction from the threats at the borders. Frankish warfare often lasted for a campaign season. The weather was nice, you sent your army out, it won, it came back with plunder, and it disbanded. All three brothers and their nephew, along with most of the empire's nobility, had by October 842 been more or less in the field for more than two years. Everyone was exhausted. No one could force a resolution because any one party could always outmaneuver the others to avoid fighting if they wanted to, but more important, no one wanted another Fontenoy. Too many of God's new chosen people had been killing one another recently.

After Lothar's retreat at Koblenz, Charles the Bald and Louis the German had tried another tactic to settle things: they had banged their diplomatic drums and said that if the eldest wanted to be intransigent, Charles and Louis would simply exclude him. But that was no more than bluster. They were still kings, and their brother was still the emperor. A great victory in battle in June 841 hadn't settled their dispute but sparked a protracted civil war.

By October 842, none of the brothers could see a path forward on his own, so they sent forty nobles each to Koblenz, to the very church where Louis and Charles had celebrated Mass, then put on their armor to drive Lothar from the field one final time. That they sent emissaries and didn't go themselves speaks to their desperation, as well as their distrust of one another at that point. And as if that sense of distrust weren't clear enough, the meeting of the nobles had to take place in the Church of St. Castor in Koblenz, at the confluence of the Moselle and Rhine rivers.

Lothar's army camped, watching the church from the other side of the Moselle. Charles's and Louis's armies camped, watching them, watching the church, from the other side of the Rhine. Each side's nobles were allowed to cross over to the church only by boat.

Together, in that tense atmosphere, the 120 Franks had a clear task: to divide up the realm into three parts. That was easier said than done. The Frankish Empire was massive—a bit contracted from its height under Charlemagne but still extending from the Iberian Peninsula into Denmark, then from around Rome in Italy to the borders of Brittany and all the way into the Balkans. No one—no group—could know the details of the whole empire, let alone the relative value of every part of the realm, including all major benefices, settlements, revenue-generating lands, properties (including enslaved people), and so forth. So yet another delay took place as the kings agreed to send agents throughout the realm to make a careful description of the whole empire. The brothers would reconvene after the emissaries had done their work, some months hence. Then, and only then, would they be able to divide it into three equally valuable parts, and Lothar, as the eldest, as the emperor, would get first choice. No one knew if the attempt at making peace would work, but it was worth a shot.

At that point, anything was worth a shot. Lothar's initial hope of subjugating his younger brothers into submission by using the awesome projection of his imperial status had failed in late 840 and early 841. Charles the Bald and Louis the German's swift, horrifying victory at Fontenoy hadn't chastened their (to their minds) prideful older brother. And throughout, the nobility followed the kings, politicked, grumbled, and mourned dead loved ones.

An extraordinary letter that likely dates to 842 reveals some of that experience. It's addressed to Lothar's wife, Ermengard, and although we're not sure of the author's identity, circumstantial evidence points to a man named Adalard. He was the same man who had commanded the third wing of Charles the Bald's army at Fontenoy just the previous year and had, before that, been Louis the Pious's seneschal beginning just after the first coup attempt in 830. As such, he would have been with Louis the Pious as he (and Lothar) tried to stitch the empire back together after Pepin I, Matfrid, and Hugh had almost broken it apart in 830. Maybe he was one of the few who had stayed with Louis the Pious on the Field of Lies during the second insurrection in 833, or perhaps he had fled in the night to Lothar. Regardless, toward the end of the 830s, he was a node connecting Louis the Pious and Charles the Bald as the latter was establishing himself as king in his own right and attempting to pacify Aquitaine.

If the letter was indeed written by Adalard (as seems likely), that supposedly long-term antagonist of Lothar was writing to his opponent's wife. The letter says it's a response to an initial letter from Empress Ermengard. She said that she had heard that the whole civil war was Adalard's fault, that he was the one who'd stirred up discord between the brother kings. That, she went on, had surely been the work of demons. Einhard's imagined demon named Wiggo from the early 830s apparently had a very long reach. But, Adalard protested, that was slander. The only demons at work were the men who were slandering him to the empress. And he could prove it: demons want war, and Adalard wanted only peace.

Adalard reminded Ermengard of the many times he'd defended Lothar to Louis the Pious, saying that that principled stand had cost him dearly. Moreover, he continued, he'd been the one pressing Charles the Bald to reach concord with his elder sibling. He said he loved Lothar but wouldn't abandon Charles, because if he were to do so, "just for the sake of some fleeting material gain, I would never be acceptable after that either to him [Lothar] or to any right-thinking man." In other words, Adalard (with what must have been some weariness) understood that both of the Carolingian brothers kept trying the same tactics that had already failed, every time expecting different results. They would remain in conflict as long as they continued to listen to "infantile advice." Adalard concluded with a (biting and sarcastic) hope that if Charles and Lothar didn't listen to him, maybe peace would come through "those brave foreign advisers—I mean those enemies that surround us on all sides."

Letters in the European Middle Ages were never private correspondence; they were public performances, meant to be circulated and read aloud. Adalard's letter therefore made a case not only in his own defense but to challenge those in Lothar's camp to press their patron toward peace. He was summoning his authority as a former adviser to the father of the warring brothers, calling on the ties that had used to bind the aristocracy together so tightly (but whose members now found themselves on opposite sides). We see once again how interconnected all our players were, how so many of them had known one another intimately for decades at Aachen before the beginning of the war in summer 840, and how those ties still bound them. We see, too, more importantly, the toll that the war had taken on them all.

Adalard, like his audience, saw the long lines of history and grievance back into the 830s that were constantly being summoned into the present to prolong the civil war among the sons of Louis the Pious. And all he saw was cynical and greedy men—the real demons—flitting among the rival armies to fill their bellies and their pockets, unable or unwilling to see that the real threat to the Franks were the Vikings and Saxons ravaging the countryside. Adalard, like his audience, was tired and frustrated. There cannot be another Fontenoy, he pleaded.

We can't know how the letter was received but, judging by their actions, maybe Adalard's epistolary message was heard by the brothers. As winter 842 arrived, the three brothers left the 120 nobles to their work (under the watchful eyes of small armies) and retreated to their respective kingdoms. All, weary of fighting, perhaps saw the dawning of spring with something close to hope. Maybe the association of nobles would come up with a workable plan. Maybe the end was in sight. Lothar waited patiently, and Louis had to deal with the fallout of his repression of the *Stellinga*.

Charles, however, had other plans: he was going to get married.

CHAPTER II

Grieving Empire and Grieving Mothers

December 842–August 843

W hen Charles and his retinue—which included his mother, Judith, of course—arrived at the palace of Quierzy in December 842, they found it richly decorated with frescoes depicting pastoral scenes, along with moments of biblical and Frankish history. Dried flowers hung along the archways added a fragrance that mixed with the heady aroma of the roasted meats as every servant from kitchen to stable scurried to prepare. It was time not just for the annual winter celebrations but for a much more important party: Charles was getting married.

On the blessed day, Charles and his bride, a young Frankish noble named Ermentrude, wore richly embroidered mantles, worked with gold and perhaps depicting biblical scenes, as they proceeded into the central hall. First there was a feast: a banquet with drinks, rich meats, cheeses, breads, and roasted root vegetables. Wild game was mixed on the table with beef, pork, and lamb, with perhaps something more exotic (such as peacock) reserved for the royal palate. Wine would have flowed freely, alongside beer and mead. Tales were swapped about past conquests, about the loss of loved ones in the war. If the guests spoke about Fontenoy, it was only to emphasize the villainy and cowardice of Lothar and the heroism of those gathered around the table. Music, mostly stringed instruments and drums, filled the room.

But then, as night broke and candles flickered, the music quieted and the crowd hushed. Bride and groom stood and publicly declared to all assembled their consent to the union. Judith confirmed her assent. The bride's family did the same, and the couple retired to consummate the union. Only one last step remained: they were met at the bedroom door by churchmen, bishops in Charles's entourage—many of whom had been on the field at Fontenoy—who blessed the couple and prayed for their fertility.

Why a wedding? Why now, when the fate of the empire still hung in the balance, the treaty agreed to but not yet finalized, with no reason to be sure that this time peace would hold? As we've seen throughout, weddings, like warfare, can be politics conducted by other means. In winter 842, Charles had just left his brother Louis the German at Worms, both of them preparing for the coming meeting of all three brothers for the first time in years (maybe since 833, when Charles had been made a prisoner by the rest of his brothers). So he had returned to this place of power, to the site where, in 838, Louis the Pious had celebrated Charles's ascent to manhood by ritually girding a sword onto his then fifteen-year-old son. Through his marriage four years later, Charles could further demonstrate his manhood to all concerned.

His wife, Ermentrude—maybe as young as twelve (the legal age of maturity for the Franks) but more likely in her middle teens—was the daughter of Odo of Orléans and a niece of Adalard the Seneschal. These are names we recognize. Both had risen to prominence in the late 820s alongside Bernard of Septimania. Odo and Adalard had stayed loyal to Louis the Pious and supported Judith and her young son, Charles, during the first insurrection of 830. Adalard had served as seneschal to Louis the Pious, then commanded part of Charles and Louis's army at Fontenoy. Ermentrude's father, Odo, was the same man who, as Bernard of Septimania's cousin, had taken over Matfrid's county in 829 after the latter had fallen from grace, the same Odo who had then been vengefully slain in 834 by Matfrid, one of

Lothar's biggest supporters in the second insurrection of 833. How intricately interwoven all those families were! Even here, at the end of our story, the same names, the same families, the same lineages of violence carried forward across generations into the civil war of the early 840s.

After her father's death, the young Ermentrude had been protected by her uncle Adalard, likely at court in Aachen, where she had grown up maybe knowing the young Charles. The union was therefore not spur-of-the-moment but a long-planned, strategic joining. It united a king with the family of one of his biggest supporters. Moreover, Charles meant for the wedding to link him back to his father—elevating those who had likewise been elevated in Louis the Pious's imperial court—to justify his position as the legitimate heir to Aquitaine and Western Francia and to reward those who'd stayed loyal to Louis the Pious and Judith through the first and second coup attempts. But the hope was also that the new queen, Ermentrude, could take over the official role of queen at his court, which had for so long been shouldered by Judith. The empress, the woman who had played that role for so long, ever since her marriage to Louis the Pious in 819, was ailing.

The details of the matriarchal transition are not well recorded. Judith seems to have retired immediately from court upon Ermentrude's arrival. One grumpy former member of Louis the Pious's court (therefore likely a beneficiary of Judith's position there) said that Charles had forced her out of court to take her wealth, but more charitably, we know that Judith had been sick off and on over the previous year, perhaps because of hard travel, difficult conditions, or simply the stress of watching her son repeatedly almost die.

Regardless, the new court of King Charles took shape. Adalard became the great lord of Charles's court, doling out favors and controlling access to the king. New men rose with him. Others fell from favor. Nithard, our faithful chronicler throughout those turbulent times, had been a client of Adalard's patronage but lost that patronage shortly after the reshuffling of Charles the Bald's court. Nithard, and surely others who'd stood by Charles since the late 830s at least, felt abandoned. The very last pages of Nithard's *Histories* devolve into bitter griping, accusing Charles of the same kind of oathbreaking that he had previously ascribed only to Lothar and Bernard of Septimania.

Nithard had once, just after the Battle of Fontenoy in summer 841, tried to lay down his quill and end his story. This time, at the dawn of 843, he did so for good. Echoing in some ways the critiques that Lothar's wife, Ermengard, had leveled at Adalard, Nithard said that the new great man at Charles's court had convinced Louis the Pious to abandon the public good and was now doing it again with Charles the Bald. Nithard thus left court and closed his codex in disgust. Some of his last words record Charles and his new queen heading toward Aquitaine after their wedding, most likely to shepherd Judith, in her ill health, to her retirement. Fittingly, the king and his mother chose Tours, in the Loire Valley region, and specifically the famous Cloister of Saint Martin there. That was no accident; Adalard was that church's special patron and protector. The reshuffling of power centers around Charles was already beginning.

One young noble, a fifteen-year-old named William, accompanied Charles south after his wedding. But unlike Nithard, who wanted to be there but wasn't, William almost certainly would have preferred to be anywhere else. Immediately after Fontenoy, very shortly after the Mass among the corpses had been sung, William had been given to Charles as a hostage by his father, Bernard of Septimania.

Bernard had been allied with Pepin II of Aquitaine through the late 830s and a direct opponent of Charles the Bald. According to some accounts, he had been the person responsible for urging Pepin to rebel against Louis the Pious in 839. That alliance between Bernard and Pepin had held until June 841, when suddenly the stakes had escalated and bloodshed was on the horizon. Bernard had taken his substantial army toward Fontenoy but not to the battle itself. Instead of honoring his commitments to Lothar and Pepin II, he had held back his forces until the victor was clear. He had then switched sides and pledged his loyalty to Charles the Bald, saying that he would bring Pepin II to heel and offering his eldest son, William, as a hostage as an assurance.

William's mother, Dhouda, had had no say in that, as recorded in an extraordinary letter sent to her absent son in February 843, the same month Charles, Ermentrude, Adalard, and Judith arrived at Tours after the king's wedding. The text opens a largely unparalleled window into the potential opportunities and perils encountered by the nobility and of life during the civil war for those who were directly impacted by it.

❖

Unfortunately, we don't know much about Dhuoda, having to rely on biographical details we can glean from her own writing. She likely came from important petty nobility east of the Rhine, tied in some way to Empress Judith and perhaps in her service. This theory is given weight by her Germanic name (it can also be spelled "Tota"), as well as her account of being wed to Bernard of Septimania at Aachen in 824 (and we have every reason to believe her). Here's another marriage that would have lasting repercussions, no less real, no less painful than those caused by marriages of kings and emperors. A wedding at Aachen would have been a tremendous honor for the couple. Bernard was, before becoming the bane of everyone's existence around 830, at that point first and foremost Louis the Pious's godson and cousin. And if Dhuoda was attached to Judith, their marriage at Aachen would have made perfect sense.

As Bernard stewed about his fall from grace in the early 830s and fomented rebellion here and there, trying to seize power in the court and kingdom, it was left to Dhuoda to administer the lands still under their family's control, and Bernard trusted her to do so—a not unusual pattern of responsibility for a Frankish noble husband and wife.

In May or June 840, Bernard returned to Dhuoda and took his eldest son with him when he left. William was rapidly approaching adulthood, so his upcoming fifteenth birthday would be an opportunity for Bernard to plot and scheme and use his son as a bargaining chip to win favor back from Charles the Bald (which he did after Fontenoy). The pattern was repeated not long after their second son was born in 841. Bishop Elefantus of Uzès (yes, his real name, and yes, it probably does mean "Elephant") took that baby—before he was even baptized, before he was even named, according to Dhuoda—away from his mother and gave him into his father's sole possession. That action, too, was "practical." Because William had been given to Charles the Bald after Fontenoy as a guarantee of Bernard of Septimania's loyalty, Bernard wanted to make sure he still had one son and, if things went badly for William, an heir safely at hand. Dhuoda was in agony.

We focus here, near the end of the book, on Dhuoda because we need to turn our gaze away from kings and armies and remember how wars touch populations far beyond their combatants. Civilian populations always suffer. Hundreds of people must have been killed when Lothar ransacked Chalons-sur-Saône during the second insurrection of 834, and there must have been dozens of punitive attacks on settlements following the campaigns of summer 841 that were passed over in silence by our written sources. We are often left only with infuriating hints at such violence, such as at a small village called Entrains-sur-Nohain, where scholars found twenty to thirty bodies—men, women, and children as young as three or four—at the bottom of a well.

The carbon dating of the bodies, an imprecise science but one that can ascribe an age range to bones, traced them to the ninth or tenth century. The town itself is on an old Roman road that leads to Auxerre. Taking that road north, one passes directly through Fontenoy, only fourteen miles away. Those poor people, who lived and loved more than a millennium ago, were without question victims of a massacre, but could they have been caught in the frenzy of pursuit after the battle in June 841? We cannot know for sure, but maybe. Lothar fled north, but as Pepin II fled south toward home in Aquitaine, he may well have gone directly through Entrains-sur-Nohain.

The reason this tantalizing, if infuriatingly speculative, evidence matters is that we cannot lose sight of the fact that wars break families. This can happen in horrifying, spectacular ways such as the massacre at Entrains-sur-Nohain. But it can also be seen in the more banal, everyday violence of life "as usual" during wartime, the terror of wondering if your distant child is alive or dead. At that critical moment, even as we know from hindsight that the war was coming to an end, its participants continued to feel that pain.

Dhuoda had had both of her sons taken from her. She feared for them. And so she wrote, picking up her quill in November 841, after news of Fontenoy and William's status as a hostage reached her. She addressed the text to her eldest son but often asked him to pass on its "meager wisdom" to his younger brother, who "was still tiny and had not yet received the grace of baptism when Bernard, my lord and the father of you both, had the baby brought to him." This reveals the circumstances of the composition, but it also is our first hint at a larger truth: that Dhuoda's letter to William is not a letter in the sense we think of today.

Medieval couriers would carry documents, oftentimes sealed, but could also carry oral messages to supplement or clarify the written ones. In this case, we see that the manual was explicitly both a public and a private document, much like Adalard's letter to Empress Ermengard. Dhuoda's missive was absolutely intended for her son, but the author and recipient were quite aware that it would circulate at court. Indeed, she mentioned that several times throughout the work. She knew that William was a hostage at the court of Charles the Bald. She knew the history between that king—all the warring kings—and her family. For her, for her son and the rest of their family, therein lay the danger. She wrote to keep her son safe, to guide him through his time at court, and to complete the moral and political instruction she had begun when they had been together in Uzès.

The manual as a whole is a sophisticated work of subtle learning and even subtler messaging. Dhuoda's document can be seen as part of a loose Carolingian genre of texts called *lay mirrors*. Taking their model from Christian Old Testament prophets speaking difficult truths to the Israelite kings, those Frankish texts offered advice for how to live in a godly society. Earlier, some of the most learned figures of the Frankish palace schools had written guides for the lay nobility about how to function in a godly society. Some had expanded the genre to write guides specific to kings. One of those, for example, had been given to Louis the Pious just before he had succeeded his father, another to Pepin I of Aquitaine in 831 (chastising him for his revolt in the previous year). In all cases, the texts drew heavily from other guides—often to the monastic life—that the authors had written beforehand. In all cases, the texts placed a central emphasis on moral guidance and the administration of justice. Dhuoda's text is no different.

Also like the other texts in this genre, her work was filled with poetry, biblical citations and commentary, practical advice, and moral lessons. She was familiar with the foundations upon which Carolingian learning was built and cited freely—and deftly—from famous early Christian thinkers such as Augustine of Hippo and Pope Gregory the Great, as well as more contemporary authors who populated the court schools of Charlemagne and Louis the Pious.

But her letter is different from those above, of course, in that it was written by a laywoman. The clear and consistent citations she uses are important not only for any analysis of her argument but because they help us see that women participated in the very same literary and intellectual culture that pervaded the Frankish world. The thing that Dhuoda wanted William to learn first and foremost was loyalty. At first glance, this might seem ironic given her husband's actions over the course of his entire career, yet she wasn't counseling blind faith in those above one's station. There was a clear hierarchy of those to whom a noble owed his loyalty and in addition, sometimes, in the face of a tyrant, Dhuoda suggested to her son that a person could break his oath.

We can and should read Dhuoda's work as a commentary on recent Frankish history, and we should realize that everyone who perused its pages would have recognized it as such. The many pages she devoted to the proper godly relationship between father and son were attacks—not so subtle—on the Franks of the 830s, on Lothar and Louis the German. Her discussion of the magnates and priests found those groups, at least in part, culpable for the disorder of their times—acknowledging them as bad models and bad counselors. Ebbo, Matfrid, Hugh, and their ilk still lingered in the memory.

And memory provided not only warnings from the past but also hope for the future. There's a moment when the manual is coming to its end when Dhuoda became reflective, saying that until that moment "the sweetness of my great love for you [William] and my desire for your beauty have made me all but forget my own situation." But, she continued, she was suffering. She asked him to pray for her soul because she was ill and worried about her salvation. That had led her, she continued, to reflect on the past when she suffered "danger from my lineage, danger from the people." She embedded biblical quotations, selecting from a section in 2 Corinthians 11:26 when Paul says that he was nearly killed for spreading the Gospel— beaten, stoned, and shipwrecked. She and her lineage had suffered similarly; she used Latin words for "escape" and "liberation" to conjure up allusions to jailbreaks and desperate flights to safety. It wasn't hyperbole, or at least not very much so, because she and her family had been living in a war zone for years. Lothar had attacked Bernard's and therefore Dhuoda's family, killing or blinding his cousins and his brother, seizing Bernard's sister Gerberga from her convent, sealing her into a barrel, and drowning her in the river. Peace seemed potentially nigh, but the trauma of what had happened to her family leaked through the pages of her letter to William, down through the centuries, down to us. For Dhuoda, who had seen how the magnates and priests poisoned the realm, how the sons of Louis the Pious were driven by greed and neglected the common good, it was as if the demon Wiggo's words once again came true. The powerful, she said, "abuse the higher place, which they received that they might justly rule their subjects, giving themselves up to pride and vainglory; hatred and malice they direct not only against those who are far off but against their neighbors and those with whom they are allied; friend mistrusts friend, brother hates brother, and father has no love for son."

But also, like Einhard when writing that tall tale about Wiggo, Dhuoda was defiant. Her counsel for William was an antidote to

the ills diagnosed by Einhard a decade before. The world was beset
by dishonor and disloyalty, and so she explained to her absent son
how to counter those problems, how to restore a godly society and
bring peace to the Franks: Honor God. Honor your father. Honor
your king. Give good counsel. Pray for the dead. Show mercy. Our
story has largely focused, for obvious reasons, on the sons of Charlemagne, the sons of Louis the Pious, their closest relatives, and their
spouses. But a civil war is not only, not even mostly, about would-be
kings. Instead, it's about the countless people whose lives were
broken and the nearly countless numbers of those who died or who
mourned those who died. We do not have letters from the common
soldiers to folks back home. We cannot hear the stories being told
on campaign, in taverns, or at funerals. Surely the farmers lamented
their fields being filled with soldiers rather than grain when they
and their children starved as their food was taken by an army on the
march, leaving them nothing. But if we don't have the sources to tell
all these stories, we do at least have Dhouda's letter—her desperate
attempt to keep her children safe in the face of the relentless violence
created by nobles and kings.

Dhuoda finished her work in February 843, closing by asking
William to keep it close to him, to keep her in his prayers. She has
completed her labor. The last two words of her manual are *"Consum-
matum est"*—"It is consummated"—the final words spoken by Jesus
before His death on the cross. Remember your mother; she has done
all she can.

William probably received the manual from his mother sometime
in early summer 843. He kept it with him when he accompanied
Charles northeast toward the small town of Verdun in July. They
had deviated from their southern route quite suddenly when they'd
heard the news. The council of 120 Frankish nobles selected from
the retinues of all three brothers had completed their survey of the
empire. The brothers needed to meet as agreed the previous year,

review the nobles' work, set the bounds of their respective kingdoms, and, perhaps, end the civil war.

Verdun wasn't a particularly important place in that period. It had a bishop but not one who wielded considerable secular power outside the local region. It was, however, centrally located among the warring sons of Louis the Pious and able to host not only three kings but the nobles who had overseen the description and division of the realm, every additional noble who wanted to attend, their households, their retinues, and all the people required to support the suddenly arriving throng. Plus all their horses, which could feed on the abundant farmland surrounding the town. They had all had months to prepare; still, the meeting required a logistical labor equivalent to supporting a large military levy. Verdun, it's safe to say, was packed.

We can't really know what each of the sons of Louis the Pious hoped to get out of the gathering. But it's clear that no one wanted a fight. The kings' puffed-out chests could no longer unilaterally impose order on an increasingly fragmented realm; though it might better be said that the disparate regions of the Frankish Empire had finally sloughed off the veneer of unity that had fused them together under Charlemagne and Louis the Pious. Maybe they hoped it would bring an end at last to the enmity that had riven the Franks and massacred thousands of God's new chosen people. But everyone involved remembered the previous decade well and especially the past few years. No one trusted anyone else anymore, so a long-term solution to the fraught fate of the Franks seemed quite distant. At the very least, everyone involved hoped for a pause, a truce of at least a few years so they could lick their wounds and deal with some of the pressing internal and external threats in their respective territories.

In August 843, a document was drawn up. We assume. We have to assume because although surely such a literate culture would have produced a lot of paperwork, including an actual signed treaty or truce that specifically delineated who got which territories, nothing survives. There must also have been a written description of the empire that captured the work produced by the agents sent out between the previous October and July, the results of which would have informed who got what in the end. That, too, alas, doesn't survive. We are left only with descriptions of the division produced by those who may have seen the originals or otherwise knew their contents. Whatever document was produced, it must have been clear; we know that no one in the aftermath seemed to argue about what the borders were, even as many rulers and demagogues would try over the next decades and centuries to exploit the division of the empire into separate (at least quasi-independent) kingdoms to their personal advantage.

Each brother had a kingdom that everyone present acknowledged was theirs: Lothar—Italy; Louis—Bavaria; Charles—Aquitaine. (Note: everyone *present*. Pepin II was not present and also didn't get anything.) That hadn't really been in dispute beforehand. So what was settled at Verdun, when it came to territory, was the wealth of central Francia. Louis the German managed to push his claim to the banks of the Rhine and even, when it came to control over the cities of Mainz, Worms, and Speyer, over to the west bank. He'd finally won the argument he'd had with his father that had bitterly divided them and brought them to the brink of violence in 838. So, too, the rivers, always rivers. River cities meant revenue. River cities also meant ease of crossing. Charles, meanwhile, secured the entire Seine basin, a similarly economically and culturally vibrant slice of the Carolingian world, while also reaching his influence down as far as Barcelona and including the whole of Septimania. Bernard and his captive son, William, must have been pleased.

Lothar got everything in the middle.

It's easy to focus on what Lothar lost, and lose he did. His claim to power over his brothers was gone, and his middle kingdom didn't endure for long. But no one could predict that at the time. The later collapse of what became known as Lotharingia wasn't inevitable, and Lotharingia has its own story, as contingent and wild as anything we've written thus far. What matters is that the goal of the agreement wasn't to create something unrulable for Lothar. He still had ample resources, loyal nobles, all of Italy, and the two imperial capitals of Aachen and Rome. It wasn't so bad.

The real transition marked by Verdun, then, wasn't the division of empire into France, Germany, and something weird in the middle, because that wasn't what happened. Instead, it was about the reformation of the empire in a way that removed even the theoretical control over the various kingdoms from the man who had claimed the imperial title. Lothar had been promised overlordship of the whole Frankish realm in 817, then again in 839–840, and that now seemed to be gone. His father's changeability, looking to shake up his court in the wake of the Barcelona fiasco of 827–828, then his anger after the insurrections of the early 830s, had initially dashed those hopes. Then Fontenoy had drowned those hopes in the bathtub. Charlemagne and Louis the Pious had created new kingdoms and bequeathed them to their sons, but those kingdoms were still part of the empire, still sub–political units under the overlordship of the Frankish emperor. They were still imperial lands. After Verdun, the fiction of imperial unity—a useful fiction to prop up the dream of the Franks as God's chosen people and the empire as a manifestation of that status—could be maintained only as an aspiration. Lothar was still emperor, but Charles and Louis were sovereign within their own kingdoms. They no longer bowed to their elder brother.

The problem for the resulting kingdoms wasn't that they were now so distinct but rather how easily they remained entangled. Noble families and the great Church institutions still maintained control or had family across the borders in ways that would inevitably lead to messy politics and even violent conflicts. Almost certainly, no one saw the situation as a permanent solution. How many times had the empire been carved up under Louis the Pious? The promises made to Bernard of Italy in 814, to Louis the German in 838, and to many others had been nullified so easily. Many people suspected that that moment at Verdun would be much the same. Borders were fluid and moved to where a ruler's effective power extended, waxing and waning depending on circumstances. None of the nobles felt the need to divest himself from one kingdom to remain wholly in another.

But no one could come up with a pathway back to a more unified empire, either. Lothar and Louis had adult children who were eager to rule in their own right and so were creating independent dynasties of their own. Charles was married now, and everyone expected that he would soon have heirs. In fact, his queen, Ermentrude, was already pregnant in August 843 at Verdun, soon to bear her first child (a daughter named Judith after her grandmother, as it turned out). And there was still Pepin II, of course, a nephew omitted from the division of the empire just as Bernard of Italy had been in 817—and one who had, also like Bernard of Italy, been promised something by the current emperor. The events of Verdun had promised so much, perhaps the empire stitched back together in a new form. But by 843, there were just too many legitimate descendants of Charlemagne around. And of course, the Carolingians were not alone in the world. Vikings and other raiders, would-be conquerors, political rivals, and fractious conquered peoples lurked around the edges of the empire, there all along.

Verdun may have brought peace between the brothers, but the regions of the empire they ruled over remained constantly at war.

It's easy to focus, in the years immediately following Verdun, on the dire threats that external (often non-Christian) enemies posed to the Franks. And they were indeed dire. Muslims, moving across the Mediterranean most likely from Sicily, attacked Rome in 846. The large force decimated the garrison at Ostia before moving inland and defeating a small, panicked Frankish army sent to meet them. The Romans stayed inside the Aurelian Walls, but St. Peter's Basilica and the Basilica of St. Paul Outside the Walls, which were beyond those walls' protection, were thoroughly sacked. The Islamic force thought better of mounting a full-on assault on the city, though, and wandered away to the south. Lothar, horrified, levied an army and placed it under the command of his eldest son, but the raiders were long gone by the time the army arrived.

At the other end of Europe, Charles the Bald had the Vikings to deal with. In 845, they sailed up the Seine, meeting only local resistance (they likely killed Nithard, who was defending his lands near Saint-Quentin) and arriving unexpectedly at the very walls of Paris. The annals written at the Monastery of Xanten say that Charles couldn't be bothered to fight them off, blaming the king's "slothfulness" (*desidia*) and saying that he had bribed them to go away. It worked, for the moment. The Viking leader, Ragnar Lodbrok, decided—not unlike what later happened at Rome—that he would take the money and spare Paris but that anything outside the city was fair game. His forces pillaged the Monastery of Saint-Germain-des-Prés before retreating back toward the coast.

Those weren't the only threats to the Frankish borders in those years. Charlemagne had expanded the empire by assimilation. Some conquered groups, such as the Lombards in northern Italy and the Saxons in northeastern Germany, had been made part of the empire proper—their people forcibly converted to Christianity when necessary, their local customs more or less effaced, and their nobility made part of the Frankish political class. Other groups farther out on the fringes had been allowed to retain their nominal independence but required to send tribute and remain allied with the empire. Louis the Pious had continued that policy, but several groups had seized the chaos of the civil war to break their bonds and assert their independence. Louis the German faced a revolt among the Slavic peoples to the north in 843–846, and the Bretons troubled Charles the Bald for many years in the 840s.

Apart from dealing with the pressures at the periphery, the brothers also had to administer their realms and appease an increasingly restless nobility that could move easily across Europe, leveraging the same networks of familial relationships that stretched across the empire's new borders. Lothar put down a short-lived but quite serious rebellion in Provence in 845, led by a disaffected count who hinted at creating an independent kingdom. In 846, a second civil war nearly erupted when a count under Charles the Bald abducted one of Lothar's daughters and fled to Pepin II of Aquitaine. It was extortion, pure and simple. The count had bet on the wrong horse, switching sides after Fontenoy in 841 from Lothar to Charles, but then had seen his lands placed in Lothar's middle kingdom at Verdun in 843. Lothar hadn't forgotten the betrayal, so had given his lands to someone else. That had made the count angry and launched his abduction scheme; the desperate gamble ended up paying off for him in the long run, as he and Lothar were reconciled in 848.

Throughout 846–847, Charles the Bald and Louis the German desperately sought to assure Lothar that they hadn't been behind the abduction. *The Annals of Fulda* recorded that 847 was "a year free of wars," but that likely means that there weren't any significant external campaigns, because all three brothers were worried that they'd have to fight one another again. The situation was finally resolved at a meeting that year, when the hatchet was buried and Lothar was convinced of Charles's innocence in the plot. Lothar, Louis the German, and Charles the Bald resolved not to let their nobles foment discord among them and to enlist those nobles to restore good governance (including, not surprisingly given the reason for the meeting, specifically punishing those who abducted women). Lothar also agreed to stop plotting with his magnates to weaken Charles's rule in Aquitaine, a recognition that the plotting and scheming had continued. Most important at that meeting, though, the three rulers agreed that the division of Verdun would hold—that their respective sons would inherit their fathers' kingdoms "according to the clearly defined partitions existing at this time."

Six years after the Battle of Fontenoy and four years after the Treaty of Verdun, everything had changed and nothing had changed; another agreement on succession that had revealed as much tension as it did comity and that had seemed to solve a problem in reality had simply ignored it. Left out of the discussions, omitted altogether, was the other Carolingian in the room: Pepin II of Aquitaine.

And indeed, Charles the Bald and Pepin II remained at war throughout. In 844, Pepin took the important city of Toulouse, and Charles responded by marching with a small army, intending to pin his enemies down in the city, leaving it to his magnates to gather the larger expeditionary force and meet up with him later. Bernard of Septimania came to Charles's camp, though whether he'd been captured or was arriving voluntarily—maybe with another offer to "help"—is unclear. Regardless, according to the *Annals of St-Bertin*, Bernard was put on trial, condemned of treason "by the judgment of the Franks," and executed. Suddenly the story of Bernard of Septimania, a story we began tracking with the battles over Barcelona in the reign of Louis the Pious, came to an end. That wasn't great news, of course, for William, the hostage son. He fled, likely after he heard his father had been captured but before the execution, escaping from Charles the Bald's court and finding his way to Pepin II in the region around Barcelona. William raised an army in revolt. For those counting, here's the second nickel.

As Charles the Bald held court at a monastery just outside the city walls of Toulouse and waited for reinforcements to arrive, Pepin II and William circled around Charles's army and headed north. They hoped to intercept the king's relief force before it arrived and thereby break the siege of Toulouse. As we saw in the buildup to Fontenoy, smaller forces often traveled with their kings, but larger expeditions were cumbersome; they took time and planning to gather. Pepin and William deployed their scouts, their spies, and learned that the army would be big, assembled by Charles's leading magnates, and that it would gather first at his stronghold at Poitiers. They prepared an ambush. When Charles's relief force marched south from Poitiers toward Toulouse in June 844, somewhere near Angoulême (if they were, as is most likely, following the old Roman road), that army found Pepin II and William waiting. The region is relatively flat but would have been wooded, and at some point the army moving south or southwest would have had to cross the Charente River. That may have been, as with so many times before, where disaster struck. The *Annals of St-Bertin* pulled no punches, recording that Pepin and William "in a short time and without casualties amongst [their] own men, scattered [Charles's army] so completely that once the leaders had been killed, the rest who had started to flee even before battle was joined, with the exception of a very few who got away, were either taken prisoner or allowed to return home only after being stripped of all they had and bound by solemn oaths." Among the dead were several important counts and churchmen, including Abbot Hugh of Saint-Quentin, Charlemagne's son and a half brother of Louis the Pious.

Angelbert's lament from Fontenoy, "brother readies death for his brother, an uncle for his nephew," takes on special resonance here. An anonymous poem from about that time recorded the death of Abbot Hugh, saying he had been run through with a lance. Pepin II, surveying his victory afterward, found his great-uncle naked, his garments looted by soldiers, and wept over the corpse.

The victory of Pepin and William would be short lived, though, as Charles swore vengeance. Charles the Bald took back Toulouse. He drove his enemies south, across the Pyrenees. Arabic sources from the period mention a "William, son of Bernard" who arrived as an emissary to 'Abd al-Rahman II in Córdoba to try to secure support against the Franks and other Muslims who were rebelling against the authority of the emir. With Islamic help, William captured Barcelona in 848. That city had been his father's path to prominence, but it turned out to be the son's tomb. In 850, William captured some of Charles's loyal counts by a trick, but "he himself was captured by a still craftier trick and was killed"—most likely, like his father, executed for oathbreaking and treachery at Charles's orders in his now-reclaimed city of Barcelona. Verdun had offered hope that the interfamilial killing would stop. But in the woods south of Poitiers, and in a city south of the Pyrenees, that hope died along with the fallen descendants of Charlemagne. All of Dhouda's worst fears had come to pass.

Lothar died in 855 at the monastery of Prüm. Soon afterward, Louis the German and Charles the Bald conspired against Lothar's sons and, by 870, split almost all of Lothar's lands north of the Alps between them. After the last of Lothar's sons died in 875, Charles the Bald seized Italy and then the next year invaded East Francia after the death of Louis the German. Charles the Bald had claimed the imperial title just that year and so was looking to, ironically, finish the work of reuniting the empire under one person's rule that Lothar had started. He, too, failed. At the Battle of Andernach in 876, Charles found himself on the wrong side of a river battle—a viciously bloody defeat for Charles the Bald from which he barely escaped. The Frankish Empire would never be reunited, even if it remained a nostalgic dream and separate successor kingdoms emerged into what would someday—in several hundred years—become France and Germany.

For those who came after, those who saw Charlemagne's realm crumble, the Battle of Fontenoy was the moment it all turned, the moment an empire shattered. The violence was staggering, and "the power of the Franks was so diminished, and their famous manhood so weakened, that thereafter they were incapable not only of expanding the kingdom, but also of defending its frontiers." As our story of the early-ninth-century civil war comes to an end, it turns out that the monster of the story was never the political hybrid that the sons of Louis the Pious created with ink and oaths at Verdun but rather, as in *Frankenstein*, was the Franks themselves, who continued to plot and scheme and kill one another as if nothing had changed. The forces that made medieval Europe, that etched political borders into the soil, that lettered the texts that narrated its histories, that fertilized its grounds with blood were all in some ways outgrowths of that civil war and the crashing thunder of hooves at Fontenoy.

Monument to the Ghosts of Empire

Circa 1860

Today, the fields around Fontenoy unroll before you in soft, undulating waves. The farmland is abundant, and the region is peaceful, quiet. In April and May, fields of flowering rapeseed paint the landscape yellow, while in other well-organized fields thousands of sunflowers stretch their colors toward the sky. A few small stone houses can be seen in the distance, connected by a smattering of one- and two-lane roads that crisscross the flatland. If you climb one of the gentle rises, you can see for miles in almost every direction.

Few remnants of the ninth-century landscape remain. The town of Fontenoy hosts a small museum, alongside a restaurant, butcher, and small church. To the south, the wooded Bois de Briotte, where the first action of the battle occurred, still stands, albeit in much shrunken form. The hamlet of Solmet, where Nithard fought, is to the southeast, now little more than a lane flanked by quaint stone houses. The Brook of the Burgundians meanders lazily off a bit to the east. If one drives south out of the town along the Rue des Corbiers, the road slowly climbs to a lovely vantage point, and at that crest, as the countryside expands to the horizon, next to the road, surrounded by low hedges, stands a simple gray stone obelisk.

Inspired in large part by European colonialist encounters with Egypt, the obelisk as a monument began to appear across Europe during the eighteenth and nineteenth centuries. Although not as popular across the Atlantic, they made their presence felt in the United States as well. The Bunker Hill monument commemorating that revolutionary battle was begun in 1827 and the Washington Monument in 1848. The small, remote monument at Fontenoy was erected not too long after that, in 1860. On it, two inscriptions—one in Latin, the other in French—commemorate the ninth-century battle.

The Latin inscription at the top simply says "The Battle of Fontenoy, 25 June 841." Underneath, in French, it reads "Here, on 25 June 841, the Battle of Fontenoy was fought between the children of Louis the Pious. The victory of Charles the Bald separated France from the Western Empire and founded the independence of the French nationality" (French: *et fonda l'indépendance de la nationalité française*).

Here, at the end of our story, this version of the battle might give us pause. Was it Charles the Bald's victory alone? Did the battle finally separate the western part of the Frankish realm from imperial control? And more ideologically, did Fontenoy really create France and a French nationality if the next decade, as we know, was filled with Charles's struggle against Pepin II and his efforts to secure the imperial title for himself? The resounding answer—no—asks us to rethink how, exactly, we remember. And whom does the remembrance serve?

We get a better sense of what the obelisk and its inscription are trying to do when we consider the context of its creation. Funds were set aside for its construction in 1857 as a bequest from the estate of a local nobleman, a Napoleonic prefect. But the final decision to erect the monument was likely inspired by the French victory in the 1859 Franco-Austrian War, which expanded France's borders and seemed to be a replay of past victories over a Germanic empire.

In 1851, Louis-Napoléon Bonaparte refused to step down from the presidency of France and dissolved the National Assembly with the help of the army. In December 1852, the now self-declared Napoleon III gave himself the title of emperor and made the position hereditary. In foreign affairs, the Second Empire aimed to emulate the first and current emperor, his uncle Napoleon Bonaparte. France was often at war in that period, first in the Crimea and then, as just noted, in 1859 in northern Italy. In that year, the French allied with the Kingdom of Sardinia to expel the Austrian Empire from northern Italy. It was a tremendous success for France, leading to the annexation of the duchy of Savoy and the city of Nice.

In a speech related to the obelisk's dedication in June 1860, the director of the local historical society explained that the battle at Fontenoy was worth commemorating because it, "so fierce and so deadly, was, according to the historians, the beginning of the transformation of the Franks and their subjects in Gaul into the French nation." In other words, the June 841 battle of Fontenoy was, the speaker reaching his crescendo said, the beginning of France. Indeed, the mass death of the Franks (which the speaker called a "Germanic race") in that battle forced them to merge with the native Gauls and prioritize the French language, which was used at the Oaths of Strasbourg.

Those are nineteenth-century claims, not ninth-century ones. In other words, the obelisk at Fontenoy was not erected at the direct behest of the French Second Empire or Napoleon III himself but rather almost certainly as a local act of nationalism. The two events, separated though they were by more than a thousand years, were inextricably linked in the minds of the obelisk's creators. It cannot be a coincidence that the 1860 obelisk's inscription and dedication both emphasize the fact that in the battle, a French ruler defeated a Germanic empire and secured the freedom of the nation and her people. That was the story Napoleon III would have told of his most recent war as well.

Monuments attempt to cement a particular understanding of the past into the popular consciousness. They seek to eliminate debate, to paper over the messiness of history and the choices people made in the past that could have turned out differently. The erection of monuments is about creating a moral consensus of interpretation, a place where people who visit "remember" the memories of other people.

We're far removed from Nithard's apologetic history and the anguish of Angelbert. At least for a moment, in the Department of Yonne, in the middle of the nineteenth century, the Battle of Fontenoy, which had shattered an empire and seen brothers draw brothers' blood, was a cause of celebration.

❖

The very idea of the nation-state came into its fullest flower during the nineteenth century, and the architects of the idea quite often looked to the medieval past for its legitimacy. The "science" of philology—the discipline concerned largely with the historical development of languages—as well as the new academic discipline of history, were both put into the service of the state. At first, the academic work functioned much as monuments do, and so it shouldn't surprise us that the same period that saw the rise of those disciplines was also a period of "statuemania." In all cases, the study of the past—its events, its monuments, its languages—became a study of genealogy, a way of connecting the nineteenth-century present to the past to make the present look like destiny. To put it another way, they went hunting through the past, looking for mirror images of themselves.

Those moderns often found what they were looking for in medieval Europe and more specifically, for the mythographers of nation-states in nineteenth-century France and Germany, in the history of the Carolingians. The civil war and the breakdown of the empire, they claimed, had birthed their nations. For example, the great French historian Jules Michelet wrote about the Battle of Fontenoy in 1833, in volume one of his mammoth multivolume *Histoire de France*. He concluded that the battle had been a disaster but without significance in and of itself, writing:

> If the historians are to be believed, the battle was fierce and bloody; so bloody that it exhausted the military population of the Empire and left it defenseless against the ravages of the barbarians. Such a massacre, difficult to believe at any time, is least of all so in this era of lethargy and of ecclesiastical influence. . . . [T]he reign of Charlemagne and of his first successors became, for the men of the deplorable times that followed, a heroic era, the glory of which they loved to exalt by means of fables as

patriotic as they were insipid. It was, moreover, impossible for the men of that age to explain, by political causes, the depopulation of the West and the decay of the military spirit. It was both easier and more poetic to suppose that all the brave men had perished in a single battle and that nothing had been left but cowards.

Charles the Bald and Louis the German may have been victors, but nothing had been settled, Michelet argued (that part, at least, was correct). The only positive outcome for Michelet was that it had forced the two brothers back into cooperation and that at Strasbourg in 842, they had taken an oath that would endure in languages that would endure. Those "solemn words pronounced on the banks of the Rhine, on the border of the two peoples," Michelet continued, were *"le premier monument de leur nationalité"*—the first monument of their nationality. The Treaty of Verdun, then, according to Michelet, had been little more than a formal application of the oaths—the language—that really created both France and Germany.

Notice the difference in tone from but similarity in language to that of the Fontenoy obelisk. Both memorializations, one in text and the other in stone, depict the events of 841–843 to have been the origin points of the French as a people (their *nationalité*). Michelet, writing with the heady optimism of the constitutional July Monarchy of the 1830s, looked with disdain on the violence of the battle, on the pointlessness of a civil war, and instead saw diplomacy as the critical moment in the beginnings of the nation. The obelisk was created later, after the overthrow of the republic by Napoleon III and the establishment of the Second Empire in 1851. That government saw glory in battle, both medieval and modern, and Napoleon III himself likely chose Compiègne as one of his primary palaces because it had been one of the favored seats of Charles the Bald in the second half of the ninth century. The obelisk says that France was forged in war and the nation's father was Charles the Bald.

On the other side of the Rhine, in the 1880s, the historian Leopold von Ranke discussed Fontenoy near the end of his life, in his nine-volume *World History*. He said of the battle:

The battle was not as intense as one might imagine; the most important thing about the event was that it happened. The [Carolingian] army, which had dominated Europe for a long period, was seized by the dissensions of the brothers and was destroyed by a day of battle that could never be repaired. The two younger brothers secured their place. And the great question at hand had been decided primarily through the battle. It concerned the relationship between the empire and the hereditary powers; it was decided in favor of the latter.

Note the first sentence: "the most important thing about the event was that it happened." Indeed, Ranke goes on in the rest of the chapter to discuss how little the battle actually changed—that the war between the brothers had continued apace.

The real event of significance, as Michelet argued from his side of the Rhine, was the moment of oathtaking at Strasbourg. Also similar to Michelet, those oaths were important to Ranke because they marked a moment of "emerging nationalities" (German: *werdenden Nationalitäten*). The civil war, Ranke continued, hadn't been intended to overthrow the empire but rather to restructure it. It had been, in other words, a failed moment of national consciousness—France and Germany, via Charles the Bald and Louis the German, hadn't yet been evolved enough to create themselves. Instead, and happily for Ranke, the empire had endured. The division at Verdun was a codification of the Oaths of Strasbourg, but more importantly was what Charlemagne had wanted all along—all the way back to the *Divisio regnorum* of 806. The oaths at Strasbourg and Verdun were sworn in the region's "natural" languages, enabling the beginnings of Germany (which held the lineage of empire) and, to the west, France (though he mostly called it "Aquitaine" in a way that only a nineteenth-century German could to throw shade at their rivals).

There is not much to separate Michelet and Ranke, save the latter's emphasis on the continuity of the empire (not surprising, given Ranke's political conservatism and support of the First German Empire proclaimed in 1871). Both historians understood the Battle of Fontenoy primarily as a mistake and one to be regarded with disdain at that. The erectors of the Fontenoy obelisk disagreed and saw it as a heroic victory for "their side." But the one thing they all agreed upon was that it had been destined to happen, setting into motion a necessary civil war that had created those nineteenth-century interpreters in their modernity.

❖

Ninth-century Frankish sources universally saw the Battle of Fontenoy as a biblical catastrophe. The Franks under the Carolingians had created an ideology of rulership so successfully that it shocked everyone when it was revealed as the fiction it was. Empires are built on lies, and lies eventually begin to crumble. Charlemagne played a messy game of dynastic succession with his sons by different wives and could have lost his throne to his eldest in 792. Louis the Pious did the same thing with his sons and came even closer to losing his throne in 830 and then again 833. In this sense, the civil war of the early 840s was business as usual. A Carolingian was a Carolingian was a Carolingian, and in 841 all four (lest we forget, Pepin II was himself a Carolingian) had legitimate claims to a royal title, at least according to the Franks themselves. But that reality ended up being irreconcilable with the ideology of a unified empire. Alliances formed and broke and reformed among the warring parties, as rulers sought to gain and maintain their own power. Perpetual oathmakers, perpetual oathbreakers.

In that way, the nineteenth-century understanding of those events was right in one regard—the civil war and oaths made afterward among the rulers would lead, after a long and winding path, to the division of Europe. But what the modern historians missed, or chose not to acknowledge, was that it all could have turned out so differently; the borders of European countries are not a given. And even the most ordinary day set events into motion that gave us the outcome with which we now live.

What if Carloman hadn't been rebaptized as Pepin in 781, thereby effectively disinheriting Pepin the Hunchback? What if the Franks had honored the *Ordinatio imperii* of 817, instead of Louis the Pious trying to rewrite it so many times after the birth of his youngest son? What if Matfrid and Hugh hadn't been dismissed in 828 and Bernard of Septimania summoned to replace them? What if Louis the German hadn't said whatever it was he said to his father in June 838, an argument that cost him his father's favor and perhaps an empire? What if Adalbert of Metz had held Louis the German at the Rhine, as he had several times before, in spring 841, and prevented Louis's alliance with Charles the Bald on the fields of Fontenoy? What if Dhuoda had kept William close and her husband had been forced to honor his oath to Pepin II at Fontenoy, charging into battle on behalf of the king of Aquitaine and Lothar I, catching Charles the Bald unaware, and ending the civil war there and then? We know what happened in all of those instances, the choices that were made, the lucky and unlucky breaks, but a single decision otherwise among any of those forking paths might have led to somewhere very different.

In the aftermath of Fontenoy, as Angelbert wept for the carnage he'd seen, as Nithard began to despair of the rampant greed he saw among his kings and magnates, as Florus of Lyons welcomed the scourging of the Franks for their sins, the brothers—the sons of Louis the Pious, grandsons of Charlemagne, kings all—kept right along, as if little had changed. They fought, they made deals, then made other deals. Eventually, they died and their children did just the same. The magnates followed their kings under that bright, shining lie about the necessity of the Carolingian family. And behind that blind adherence to despots and tyrants lay an ever-extending trail of blood, betrayals, and broken families.

The story of the Franks as it was experienced in the ninth century was one of imperial coronations and solemn oaths taken by nobles and churchmen to honor their rulers, but it was also one of broken promises and decisions made by the powerful for their own benefit. It's a story not only of kings and nobles but also of wives, mothers, and orphaned sons. But it's most importantly a story that was created by the Franks and for the Franks, and one so powerful that they forgot it was a lie. Until one bright summer morning in June 841 as spears clashed and hooves thundered, leaving a feast for vultures and wolves.

ACKNOWLEDGMENTS

To write a book about the history of a civil war, betrayal, and the collapse of an empire at a moment when so much feels so fragile all around us, right here and now, has required support from so many different people, and it's impossible to thank them all. This project wouldn't have happened without the support of our agent, William Callahan, and our editor, Sarah Haugen. We couldn't ask for better collaborators, both of whom always seem to ask just the right questions at the right moments to drive forward the story we're trying to tell. In addition, we must thank our colleagues at the University of Minnesota and Virginia Tech. In particular, a grant from the Virginia Tech Center for Humanities enabled us to hire Rachael Vause as a research assistant; her efforts early in the project helped us launch. Matthew spent autumn 2023 in the Department of Mediaeval History at the University of St Andrews, sharing his thoughts with James T. Palmer, Alex Woolf, Simon MacLean, and Frances Andrews (among others). David thanks for their particular assistance Adam Stemple, Bruce Schneier, and Christopher Flynn. Their insights were invaluable. But most of all, we thank our families, who smiled when we told them we were going to write another book, cheered our successes, supported us when the going seemed hard, and without whom nothing—least of all this book—would be possible.

NOTES

Prologue: A Feast for Vultures and Wolves

1 "Let not that accursed": The whole poem can be found in Angelbert, "At the Battle of Fontenoy," in *Carolingian Civilization: A Reader*, trans. Paul Edward Dutton, 2nd ed. (Toronto: University of Toronto Press, 2004), 332–33.

5 "in this battle": Regino of Prüm, *Chronicle*, in *History and Politics in Late Carolingian and Ottonian Europe: The Chronicle of Regino of Prüm and Adalbert of Magdeburg*, trans. Simon MacLean (Manchester, UK: Manchester University Press, 2009), 131–32.

5 "a great outpouring": Hugh of Flavigny, *Chronicon*, ed. G. H. Pertz, *Monumenta Germaniae Historica: Scriptores*, vol. 8 (Hanover: Hahn, 1848), 481.

Introduction: Origin Stories, 732–750

10 deeper into Gaul: For what follows, see the summary in James T. Palmer, *Merovingian Worlds* (Cambridge, UK: Cambridge University Press, 2024).

13 the Frankish army defeated: James Palmer, "The Making of a World Historical Moment: The Battle of Tours (732/3) in the Nineteenth Century," *postmedieval* 10, no. 2 (2019): 206–18.

15 just as much ferocity: Thomas F. X. Noble, *Images, Iconoclasm, and the Carolingians* (Philadelphia: University of Pennsylvania Press, 2009), 6–9.

16 as a tragedy: See Courtney M. Booker, *Past Convictions: The Penance of Louis the Pious and the Decline of the Carolingians* (Philadelphia: University of Pennsylvania Press, 2009).

17 writing in order to ensure: On this topic, see, e.g., Rosamond McKitterick, *History and Memory in the Carolingian World* (Cambridge, UK: Cambridge University Press, 2004), and Matthew Gabriele, *An Empire of Memory: The Legend of Charlemagne, the Franks, and Jerusalem Before the First Crusade* (Oxford, UK: Oxford University Press, 2011), among many other works.

18 "Although I am besieged": Dhuoda, *Handbook for William: A Carolingian Woman's Counsel for Her Son*, trans. Carol Neel (Washington, DC: Catholic University of America Press, 1999), 6.

Chapter 1: Discontent and Disinheritance, 750–792

25 Notker the Stammerer: For a readily available English translation, see Notker the Stammerer, *Charlemagne*, in *Two Lives of Charlemagne*, trans. Lewis Thorpe (London: Penguin, 1969), 93–172.

26 the Carolingian dynasty rested: Carl I. Hammer, "Pipinus Rex: Pippin's Plot of 792 and Bavaria," *Traditio* 63 (2008): 235–76.

27 Instead, the text was written: Paul Edward Dutton, *The Politics of Dreaming in the Carolingian Empire* (Lincoln: University of Nebraska Press, 1994), 86–87.

27 the text was almost certainly: We know that the text was the product of a succession of at least three or four continuators probably beginning at the very end of the eighth century and continuing until about 830. See Rosamond McKitterick, *History and Memory in the Carolingian World* (Cambridge, UK: Cambridge University Press, 2004), 101–104.

28 Pepin's decision to maneuver: Paul Fouracre, "The Long Shadow of the Merovingians," in *Charlemagne: Empire and Society*, ed. Joanna Story (Manchester, UK: Manchester University Press, 2005), 5–21.

29 had almost never been used: Fouracre, "The Long Shadow of the Merovingians."

30 "a brood hardly human": "Pope Stephen Scolds Charlemagne and Carloman," in *Carolingian Civilization: A Reader*, ed. Paul Edward Dutton, 2nd ed. (Toronto: University of Toronto Press, 2004), 25–26.

33 Both pope and king got: Courtney M. Booker, "By Any Other Name? Charlemagne, Nomenclature, and Performativity," in *Charlemagne: Les temps, les espaces, les hommes. Construction et déconstruction d'un règne*, ed. Rolf Grosse and Michel Sot (Turnhout, Belgium: Brepols, 2018), 409–26.

35 The latter King Pepin: Hammer, "Pipinus Rex."

36 It was added: Roger Collins, "The 'Reviser' Revisited: Another Look at the Alternate Version of the *Annales Regni Francorum*," in *After Rome's Fall: Narrators and Sources of Early Medieval History*, ed. Alexander Callander Murray (Toronto: University of Toronto Press, 1998), 191–213.

37 Perhaps Fardulf was: Hammer, "Pipinus Rex," 263.

Chapter 2: Fathers and Sons, 800–814

39 Charlemagne had been invited: On this campaign in the eighth century, see Sam Ottewill-Soulsby, *The Emperor and the Elephant: Christians and Muslims in the Age of Charlemagne* (Princeton, NJ: Princeton University Press, 2023), 159–70. For an accessible English translation of the twelfth-century poem, we suggest Glyn Burgess, trans., *The Song of Roland* (London: Penguin, 1990).

41 "Charles the most serene augustus": Janet L. Nelson, *King and Emperor: A New Life of Charlemagne* (Oakland: University of California Press, 2019), 384–85.

41 things didn't radically change: See, e.g., Nelson, *King and Emperor*;
Rosamond McKitterick, *Charlemagne: The Formation of a European Identity*
(Cambridge, UK: Cambridge University Press, 2008); and Jennifer R. Davis,
Charlemagne's Practice of Empire (Cambridge, UK: Cambridge University
Press, 2015).

45 "keys of the Lord's Sepulcher": *Royal Frankish Annals*, in *Carolingian
Chronicles*, trans. Bernhard Walter Scholz and Barbara Rogers (Ann Arbor:
University of Michigan Press, 1970), 81.

46 that was now happening again: See more in Ottewill-Soulsby, *The
Emperor and the Elephant*. On the relationship with Jerusalem specifically,
see Michael McCormick, *Charlemagne's Survey of the Holy Land: Wealth,
Personnel, and Buildings of a Mediterranean Church Between Antiquity and
the Middle Ages* (Cambridge, MA: Harvard University Press, 2011); and
Matthew Gabriele, *An Empire of Memory: The Legend of Charlemagne, the
Franks, and Jerusalem Before the First Crusade* (Oxford, UK: Oxford University
Press, 2011).

47 "the alms that had": McCormick, *Charlemagne's Survey of the Holy Land*.

49 Charlemagne and his court: For a new understanding of how
Charlemagne ruled in practice, see Davis, *Charlemagne's Practice of Empire*.

53 It seems clear: Janet L. Nelson, "Women at the Court of Charlemagne: A
Case of a Monstrous Regiment?," in Nelson, *The Frankish World, 750–900*
(London: Hambledon Press, 1996), 223–42.

55 That coin: Simon Coupland, "A Coin of Queen Fastrada and Charlemagne,"
Early Medieval Europe 31, no. 4 (2023): 585–97.

57 That title was reserved: "Divisio regnorum," in *Carolingian Civilization: A
Reader*, ed. Paul Edward Dutton, 2nd ed. (Toronto: University of Toronto
Press, 2004), 146–51.

58 Our eyebrows are duly raised: For more on the cattle plague and its
potential move from animal to human, see Timothy Newfield, "A Great
Carolingian Panzootic: The Probable Extent, Diagnosis and Impact of an
Early Ninth-Century Cattle Pestilence," *Argos* 46 (2012): 200–210.

Chapter 3: Sisters and Nephews, 814–823

62 "a few who were particularly": The Astronomer, *The Life of Emperor
Louis*, in *Charlemagne and Louis the Pious: Lives by Einhard, Notker, Ermoldus,
Thegan, and the Astronomer*, trans. Thomas F. X. Noble (University Park:
Pennsylvania State University Press, 2009), 247.

71 the emperor's primary concern: See Courtney M. Booker, *Past
Convictions: The Penance of Louis the Pious and the Decline of the Carolingians*
(Philadelphia: University of Pennsylvania Press, 2009); Mayke de Jong, *The
Penitential State: Authority and Atonement in the Age of Louis the Pious, 814–840*
(Cambridge, UK: Cambridge University Press, 2009); and others.

73 "was partly true": *Royal Frankish Annals*, in *Carolingian Chronicles*, trans. Bernhard Walter Scholz and Barbara Rogers (Ann Arbor: University of Michigan Press, 1970), 103.

75 "in the district of Laon": On the importance of visionary literature in this period, see Paul Edward Dutton, *The Politics of Dreaming in the Carolingian Empire* (Lincoln: University of Nebraska Press, 1994).

76 The Poor Woman: "The Vision of the Poor Woman of Laon," in *Carolingian Civilization: A Reader*, ed. Paul Edward Dutton, 2nd ed. (Toronto: University of Toronto Press, 2004), 203–204.

77 "to make one powerful friend": Dutton, *The Politics of Dreaming*, 72.

78 Looking back from his perch: Mayke de Jong, "Bride Shows Revisited: Praise, Slander and Exegesis in the Reign of the Empress Judith," in *Gender in the Early Medieval World: East and West, 300–900*, ed. L. Brubaker and J.M.H. Smith (Cambridge, UK: Cambridge University Press, 2004), 257–77.

78 "the most pious emperor": *Royal Frankish Annals*, in *Carolingian Chronicles*, trans. Bernhard Walter Scholz and Barbara Rogers (Ann Arbor: University of Michigan Press, 1970), 109–10.

79 The Astronomer (again, writing decades later): See the wonderful analysis in Andrew J. Romig, *Be a Perfect Man: Christian Masculinity and the Carolingian Aristocracy* (Philadelphia: University of Pennsylvania Press, 2017).

80 A recently unearthed manuscript: Philippe Depreux, "The Penance of Attigny (822) and the Leadership of the Bishops in Amending Carolingian Society," in *Religious Franks: Religion and Power in the Frankish Kingdoms: Studies in Honour of Mayke de Jong*, ed. Rob Meens et al. (Manchester, UK: Manchester University Press, 2016), 370–85.

81 "At about that time": The Astronomer, *The Life of Emperor Louis*, 266.

Chapter 4: Sex, Witchcraft, and Angry Nobles, 828–831

85 The demon called itself Wiggo: The complete story about Wiggo is translated in Einhard, "The Translation and Miracles of Marcellinus and Peter," in *Charlemagne's Courtier: The Complete Einhard*, trans. Paul Edward Dutton (Toronto: University of Toronto Press, 1998), 103–105.

91 access to the imperial bedroom: A late-ninth-century text that plausibly claims to be based on an earlier example describes the chamberlain's duties. See the English translation in Hincmar of Rheims, "On the Governance of the Palace," in *Carolingian Civilization: A Reader*, ed. Paul Edward Dutton, 2nd ed. (Toronto: University of Toronto Press, 2004), 525.

95 cuckolded the emperor: Thegan, *The Deeds of Emperor Louis*, in *Charlemagne and Louis the Pious: The Lives by Einhard, Notker, Ermoldus, Thegan, and the Astronomer*, trans. Thomas F. X. Noble (University Park: Pennsylvania State University Press, 2009), 209; and Agobard of Lyons, *Liber apologeticus*

I, in *Opera Omnia*, ed. L. van Acker, *Corpus Christianorum Continuatio Mediaevalis*, vol. 52 (Turnhout, Belgium: Brepols, 1981), 309–10.

95 Writing later, in the 850s: The full text has been translated in Paschasius Radbertus, "Epitaph for Arsenius," in *Confronting Crisis in the Carolingian Empire: Paschasius Radbertus' Funeral Oration for Wala of Corbie*, trans. Mayke de Jong and Justin Lake (Manchester, UK: Manchester University Press, 2020), 49–223.

98 Perhaps the rebellion: An analysis suggested in Roger Collins, "Pippin I and the Kingdom of Aquitaine," in *Charlemagne's Heir: New Perspectives on the Reign of Louis the Pious (814–840)*, ed. Peter Godman and Roger Collins (London: Clarendon Press, 1990), 380–81.

98 "does not seem": The Astronomer, *The Life of Emperor Louis*, in *Charlemagne and Louis the Pious: Lives by Einhard, Notker, Ermoldus, Thegan, and the Astronomer*, trans. Thomas F. X. Noble (University Park: Pennsylvania State University Press, 2009), 276.

Chapter 5: Deposed, 833–834

102 "*collactaneus et conscholasticus*": Flodoard of Reims, *Historia Remensis Ecclesiae*, in *Monumenta Germaniae Historica: Scriptores*, vol. 36 (Hanover: Hahnsche Buchhandlung, 1998), 175. Their relationship is also discussed in Peter R. McKeon, "Archbishop Ebbo of Reims (816–835): A Study in Carolingian Empire and Church," *Church History* 43, no. 4 (1974): 437–47.

104 Pharaoh, King Saul, even Antichrist: Our analysis of this particular image follows Bart Jaski, "The Ruler with the Sword in the Utrecht Psalter," in *Religious Franks: Religion and Power in the Frankish Kingdoms: Studies in Honour of Mayke de Jong*, ed. Rob Meens et al. (Manchester, UK: Manchester University Press, 2016), 72–91.

109 "Go to my sons": Thegan, *The Deeds of Emperor Louis*, in *Charlemagne and Louis the Pious: The Lives by Einhard, Notker, Ermoldus, Thegan, and the Astronomer*, trans. Thomas F. X. Noble (University Park: Pennsylvania State University Press, 2009), 210–11.

112 A manuscript composed afterward: Translated in Courtney M. Booker, *Past Convictions: The Penance of Louis the Pious and the Decline of the Carolingians* (Philadelphia: University of Pennsylvania Press, 2009), 257–64.

114 "kept thinking over": Janet L. Nelson, trans., *Annals of St-Bertin* (Manchester, UK: Manchester University Press, 1991), 28.

115 Thegan captured some: Thegan, *The Deeds of Emperor Louis*, 211–13.

116 As he waited: John B. Gillingham, "Fontenoy and After: Pursuing Enemies to Death in France Between the Ninth and the Eleventh Centuries," in *Frankland: The Franks and the World of the Early Middle Ages. Essays in Honour of Dame Jinty Nelson*, ed. Paul J. Fouracre and David Ganz (Manchester, UK: Manchester University Press, 2008), 242–65.

117 Heartened, Lothar headed north: Thegan, *The Deeds of Emperor Louis*, 215–16.

118 The rebels' single-minded pursuit: See especially Booker, *Past Convictions*; Mayke de Jong, *The Penitential State: Authority and Atonement in the Age of Louis the Pious, 814–840* (Cambridge, UK: Cambridge University Press, 2009).

Chapter 6: The King Is Dead, Long Live the Kings, 835–840

119 In the middle of the Easter celebration: The Astronomer, *The Life of Emperor Louis*, in *Charlemagne and Louis the Pious: Lives by Einhard, Notker, Ermoldus, Thegan, and the Astronomer*, trans. Thomas F. X. Noble (University Park: Pennsylvania State University Press, 2009), 292–93.

128 "there was a great argument": Janet L. Nelson, trans., *Annals of St-Bertin* (Manchester, UK: Manchester University Press, 1991), 39.

129 As the assembly opened: Eric J. Goldberg, *Struggle for Empire: Kingship and Conflict Under Louis the German, 817–876* (Ithaca, NY: Cornell University Press, 2006), 82–90.

131 Hastily, a new assembly: "Excavations at Quierzy in 1916–17 revealed traces of a large hall, brightly painted walls and ceramics, concentric walls around the enclosure and, nearby, a monastery, possibly serving as a palace-church." Janet L. Nelson, *King and Emperor: A New Life of Charlemagne* (London: Allen Lane, 2019), 24, 495–96. See also Janet L. Nelson, *Charles the Bald* (London: Longman, 1992), 96–98.

136 "in a cone": Timothy Reuter, trans., *The Annals of Fulda* (Manchester, UK: Manchester University Press, 1992), 17.

137 "should not forget": The Astronomer, *The Life of Emperor Louis*, 301.

Chapter 7: Feints and Provocations, June 840–June 841

140 On the blade were four words: "The Vision of Charlemagne," in *Carolingian Civilization: A Reader*, ed. Paul Edward Dutton, 2nd ed. (Toronto: University of Toronto Press, 2004), 456–57.

143 All of the leaders shared: Bernard Bachrach, "The Practical Use of Vegetius' 'De Re Militari' During the Early Middle Ages," *Historian* 47, no. 2 (1985): 239–55; and throughout Bernard Bachrach, *Early Carolingian Warfare: Prelude to Empire* (Philadelphia: University of Pennsylvania Press, 2001).

143 Within the Frankish realm: Bachrach, *Early Carolingian Warfare*, 55–73.

144 "teams of equal numbers": Nithard, *Histories*, in *Carolingian Chronicles*, trans. Bernhard Walter Scholz and Barbara Rogers (Ann Arbor: University of Michigan Press, 1970), 164.

145 Across the whole of the empire: Christopher Flynn, "'Unconquered Louis Rejoiced in Iron': Military History in East Francia Under King Louis the

German (c. 825–876)," (PhD diss., University of Minnesota, 2020), 169,
https://conservancy.umn.edu/items/c8c42ce4-4fc6-4042-b73e
-ca38b8f08514.

147 At the moment of crisis: Flynn, "'Unconquered Louis Rejoiced in Iron,'"
221.

150 "pitched their camps": Nithard, *Histories*, 142.

151 Instead, he went off: Nithard, *Histories*, 142–43.

155 Louis the German now did: Flynn, "'Unconquered Louis Rejoiced in
Iron,'" 161–62.

155 He sent out his scouts: On battlefield intelligence gathering, see Bernard
Bachrach and David Bachrach, "Military Intelligence and Long-Term
Planning in the Ninth Century: The Carolingians and Their Adversaries,"
Mediaevistik 33, no. 1 (2020): 101–104.

Chapter 8: Fontenoy: Saturday, June 25, 841

168 those armies could each: Christopher Flynn, "'Unconquered Louis
Rejoiced in Iron': Military History in East Francia Under King Louis the
German (c. 825–876)," (PhD diss., University of Minnesota, 2020), 170,
https://conservancy.umn.edu/items/c8c42ce4-4fc6-4042-b73e
-ca38b8f08514.

173 But at Fontenoy: See John B. Gillingham, "Fontenoy and After: Pursuing
Enemies to Death in France Between the Ninth and the Eleventh
Centuries," in *Frankland: The Franks and the World of the Early Middle Ages.
Essays in Honour of Dame Jinty Nelson*, ed. Paul J. Fouracre and David Ganz
(Manchester, UK: Manchester University Press, 2008), 242–65.

174 "Louis and Charles deliberated": Nithard, *Histories*, in *Carolingian
Chronicles*, trans. Bernhard Walter Scholz and Barbara Rogers (Ann Arbor:
University of Michigan Press, 1970), 155. See also David S. Bachrach and
Bernard S. Bachrach, "Nithard as a Military Historian of the Carolingian
Empire c. 833–843," in Bachrach and Bachrach, *Writing the Military History
of Pre-Crusade Europe* (London: Routledge, 2020), 29–55.

174 "the slaughter of the fugitives": Janet L. Nelson, trans., *Annals of St-Bertin*
(Manchester, UK: Manchester University Press, 1991), 50.

175 Nithard was therefore forced: See Bachrach and Bachrach, "Nithard as a
Military Historian," 29–55.

176 "many were slain": Nelson, trans., *Annals of St-Bertin*, 50–51.

177 Agnellus described the armies: The key phrase in Agnellus is *lucida tela*,
which seems to be taken from the Roman author Lucretius. Goldberg's
translation of the passage comes closest to its sense. See Eric J. Goldberg,
Struggle for Empire: Kingship and Conflict Under Louis the German, 817–876
(Ithaca, NY: Cornell University Press, 2006), 101.

177 "fought alone like ten men": Agnellus of Ravenna, *The Book of the*

Pontiffs of the Church of Ravenna, trans. Deborah Mauskopf Deliyannis (Washington, DC: Catholic University of America Press, 2004), 301.

179 "I, Angelbert, fighting": Angelbert, "At the Battle of Fontenoy," in *Carolingian Civilization: A Reader*, ed. Paul Edward Dutton, 2nd ed. (Toronto: University of Toronto Press, 2004), 332–33.

180 "fought each other like madmen": B. de Simson, ed., *Annales Xantenses et Annales Vedestini, Monumentis Germaniae Historicis: Scriptores rerum Germanicarum*, vol. 12 (Hanover: Hahnsche Buchhandlung, 1909), 11.

180 "there was such a slaughter": Timothy Reuter, trans., *The Annals of Fulda* (Manchester, UK: Manchester University Press, 1992), 19.

Chapter 9: The Earth Recoils in Horror, June 841–February 842

182 "O what grief and wailing!": Angelbert, "At the Battle of Fontenoy," in *Carolingian Civilization: A Reader*, ed. Paul Edward Dutton, 2nd ed. (Toronto: University of Toronto Press, 2004), 332–33.

184 The priests erect a portable altar: On portable altars, see Sarah Luginbill, "The Medieval Portable Altar Database," *Material Religion* 16, no. 5 (2020): 683–85.

185 We have abundant evidence: Drew Gilpin Faust, *This Republic of Suffering: Death and the American Civil War* (London: Penguin, 2009); see also the experiences of soldiers in Vietnam in Karl Marlantes, *What It Is Like to Go to War* (New York: Grove Atlantic, 2011).

188 "a purple robe": Agnellus of Ravenna, *The Book of the Pontiffs of the Church of Ravenna*, trans. Deborah Mauskopf Deliyannis (Washington, DC: Catholic University of America Press, 2004), 302–303.

192 Lothar issued charter after charter: Elina Screen, "The Importance of an Emperor: Lothar I and the Frankish Civil War, 840–843," *Early Medieval Europe* 12, no. 1 (2003): 25–51.

195 The group had been around: Ingrid Rembold, *Conquest and Christianization: Saxony and the Carolingian World, 772–888* (Cambridge, UK: Cambridge University Press, 2017).

196 He summoned a Danish lord: Simon Coupland, "From Poachers to Gamekeepers: Scandinavian Warlords and Carolingian Kings," *Early Medieval Europe* 7, no. 1 (1998): 85–114.

198 In the middle of the ninth century: See Alice Rio, "Waltharius at Fontenoy? Epic Heroism and Carolingian Political Thought," *Viator* 46, no. 2 (2015): 41–64.

200 "In the time of Charles the Great": Nithard, *Histories*, in *Carolingian Chronicles*, trans. Bernhard Walter Scholz and Barbara Rogers (Ann Arbor: University of Michigan Press, 1970), 174.

201 "We know": Florus of Lyons, "Lament on the Division of the Empire," in *Poetry of the Carolingian Renaissance*, trans. Peter Godman (Norman: University of Oklahoma Press, 1985), 264–73.

201 "through to the port of peace": Florus of Lyons, "Lament on the Division of the Empire."

Chapter 10: Oathmakers, February–December 842

203 So they decided to play a game: On war games, see Christopher Flynn, "'Unconquered Louis Rejoiced in Iron': Military History in East Francia Under King Louis the German (c. 825–876)," (PhD diss., University of Minnesota, 2020), 268, https://conservancy.umn.edu/items/c8c42ce4 -4fc6-4042-b73e-ca38b8f08514.

204 "It was a show": Nithard, *Histories*, in *Carolingian Chronicles*, trans. Bernhard Walter Scholz and Barbara Rogers (Ann Arbor: University of Michigan Press, 1970), 164.

206 Louis the German: For the speeches, see Nithard, *Histories*, 161–62.

208 their men already spoke those vernaculars: Sara S. Poor, "The Curious Multilingual Prehistory of French and German Monolingualism," *German Studies Review* 41, no. 3 (2018): 465–85.

210 the move was really about: Janet L. Nelson, *Charles the Bald* (London: Longman, 1992), 124–25.

211 that settlement, named Quentovic: See Simon Coupland, "Trading Places: Quentovic and Dorestad Reassessed," *Early Medieval Europe* 11, no. 3 (2002): 209–32.

211 "plundered [the town]": Janet L. Nelson, trans., *Annals of St-Bertin* (Manchester, UK: Manchester University Press, 1991), 53.

213 "Louis marched throughout Saxony": Nelson, trans., *Annals of St-Bertin*, 54.

213 In this telling: Ingrid Rembold, *Conquest and Christianization: Saxony and the Carolingian World, 772–888* (Cambridge, UK: Cambridge University Press, 2017).

214 Next he tried to contact: Jonathan Shepard. "Revisiting the Rus Visitors to Louis the Pious," *Byzantinoslavica* 80, nos. 1–2 (2022): 59–87.

215 And so on August 29, 842: Elina Screen, "The Importance of an Emperor: Lothar I and the Frankish Civil War, 840–843," *Early Medieval Europe* 12, no. 1 (2003): 25–51.

219 "just for the sake": Translation from Janet L. Nelson, "The Search for Peace in a Time of War: The Carolingian Brüderkrieg, 840–843," in *Träger und Instrumentarien des Friedens im hohen und späten Mittelalter*, ed. Johannes Fried (Ostfildern, Germany: Jan Thorbecke Verlag, 1996), 103. See also the comments about the translation in Courtney M. Booker, "Imitator Daemon Cicor: Adalhard the Seneschal, Mistranslations, and Misrepresentations," *Jahrbuch für Internationale Germanistik* 33 (2001): 114–26.

Chapter 11: Grieving Empire and Grieving Mothers, December 842–August 843

221 they found it richly decorated: "Excavations at Quierzy in 1916–17 revealed traces of a large hall, brightly painted walls and ceramics, concentric

walls around the enclosure and, nearby, a monastery, possibly serving as a palace-church." Janet L. Nelson, *King and Emperor: A New Life of Charlemagne* (Oakland: University of California Press, 2019), 24, 495–96.

221 First there was a feast: On Carolingian food, see Cullen J. Chandler, "Charlemagne's Table: The Carolingian Royal Court and Food Culture," *Viator* 50, no. 1 (2019): 1–30.

222 But then, as night broke: Andrea Maraschi, "Rules for Attending Wedding Banquets in Early Medieval Europe: A Matter of Fun, Excess, and Moral Integrity," *Food & History* 20, no. 2 (2022): 9–30. We don't have specific evidence about how Frankish royal weddings were conducted, unfortunately.

223 Nithard, our faithful chronicler: On this relationship, see Janet L. Nelson, "Public Histories and Private History in the Work of Nithard," *Speculum* 60, no. 2 (1985): 251–93.

226 scholars found twenty to thirty bodies: We discuss this discovery briefly in "Bodies at the Bottom of a Well," Modern Medieval, https://buttondown .email/ModernMedieval/archive/bodies-at-the-bottom-of-a-well/.

227 "meager wisdom": Full text available in English translation; see Dhuoda, *Handbook for William: A Carolingian Woman's Counsel for Her Son*, trans. Carol Neel (Washington, DC: Catholic University of America Press, 1999).

228 We can and should read: Régine Le Jan, "The Multiple Identities of Dhuoda," in *Ego Trouble: Authors and Their Identities in the Early Middle Ages*, ed. Richard Corradini et al. (Vienna: Austrian Academy of Sciences Press, 2010), 211–20.

232 The later collapse: See, e.g., Charles West, *The Fall of a Carolingian Kingdom: Lotharingia, 855–869* (Toronto: University of Toronto Press, 2023).

233 The problem for the resulting kingdoms: Stuart Airlie, *Making and Unmaking the Carolingians: 751–888* (London: Bloomsbury Academic, 2020), 173–74.

236 "a year free of wars": Timothy Reuter, trans., *The Annals of Fulda* (Manchester, UK: Manchester University Press, 1992), 26.

236 "according to the clearly defined": See summary in Eric J. Goldberg, *Struggle for Empire: Kingship and Conflict Under Louis the German, 817–876* (Ithaca, NY: Cornell University Press, 2006), 152–53.

237 "in a short time": Janet L. Nelson, trans., *Annals of St-Bertin* (Manchester, UK: Manchester University Press, 1991), 58–59.

239 become France and Germany: On the transition of the nostalgic dream, see Matthew Gabriele, *Empire of Memory: The Legend of Charlemagne, the Franks, and Jerusalem Before the First Crusade* (Oxford, UK: Oxford University Press, 2011). On the dynasties and end of the Carolingians, see among others Simon MacLean, *Kingship and Politics in the Late Ninth Century: Charles the Fat and the End of the Carolingian Empire* (Cambridge, UK:

Cambridge University Press, 2003); and Justine Firnhaber-Baker, *House of Lilies: The Dynasty That Made Medieval France* (New York: Basic Books, 2024). Oddly, there's no good one-volume history of the Ottonians in English, but Hagen Keller, *Die Ottonen* (Munich: C. H. Beck, 2021), is useful.

239 "the power of the Franks": Regino of Prüm, *Chronicle*, in *History and Politics in Late Carolingian and Ottonian Europe: The Chronicle of Regino of Prüm and Adalbert of Magdeburg*, trans. Simon MacLean (Manchester, UK: Manchester University Press, 2009), 131–32.

Epilogue: Monument to the Ghosts of Empire, circa 1860

242 In a speech: Printed in *Bulletin de la Société des sciences historiques et naturelles de l'Yonne* 14 (1860): 44–76.

242 The erection of monuments: Jay Winter, "Sites of Memory," in *Memory: History, Theories, Debates*, ed. Susannah Radstone and Bill Schwarz (New York: Fordham University Press, 2010), 312–24.

243 "statuemania": Maurice Agulhon, "La 'statuomanie' et l'histoire," *Ethnologie française* 8, nos. 2–3 (1978): 145–72.

243 "If the historians": Jules Michelet, *Histoire de France*, vol. 2 (Paris: Champion, 1833), 18–21.

245 "The battle was not": Leopold von Ranke, *Weltgeschichte*, vol. 6 (Leipzig: Verlag von Duncker & Humblot, 1885), 102–103.

SELECTED BIBLIOGRAPHY

The scholarly literature on the Franks, the Carolingians, and the various peoples across three continents who had dealings with them is vast. What appears here, therefore, is just a selection of all the materials that we consulted during the writing of the book. That said, this bibliography does include everything cited in the endnotes and most primary sources from the eighth and ninth centuries that are available in translation. Indeed, the list below includes mostly works in English, but much, if not most, scholarship on the Carolingians, going back more than a century, is in French, German, and Italian. There are hints of that below as well.

As with *The Bright Ages*, we aimed in this book to tell a compelling story about a very knowable medieval European world. But all stories are incomplete, each story emerging out of other tales in the past, leading toward tales of the future, and always taking place in a complicated, expansive world with lots of people making all sorts of different history. There is much more to discover, much more to learn, and so we hope that you, the reader, will take this bibliography as first and foremost an invitation to participate in a wider conversation. We hope you'll explore what's below to discover a period just as human as our own.

In every case, our colleagues and our medieval informants allow us to hear some version of the past's voices. Those voices tell us about an empire, about the wonders of an elephant roaming the German countryside and the triumphs the Franks celebrated as they expanded their borders. But the works below also—reluctantly—reveal the lies upon which the empire rested and how, when those lies were revealed, their writers were horrified as they watched brother fighting brother to leave a feast for vultures and wolves.

Agnellus of Ravenna. *The Book of the Pontiffs of the Church of Ravenna.* Translated by Deborah Mauskopf Deliyannis. Washington, DC: Catholic University of America Press, 2004.

Agobard of Lyons. *Liber apologeticus I.* In *Opera Omnia*, edited by L. van Acker, 309–19. *Corpus Christianorum Continuatio Mediaevalis*, vol. 52. Turnhout, Belgium: Brepols, 1981.

Agulhon, Maurice. "La 'statuomanie' et l'histoire." *Ethnologie française* 8, nos. 2–3 (1978): 145–72.

Airlie, Stuart. *Making and Unmaking the Carolingians: 751–888.* London: Bloomsbury Academic, 2020.

Angelbert. "At the Battle of Fontenoy." In *Carolingian Civilization: A Reader*, translated by Paul Edward Dutton, 2nd ed., 332–33. Toronto: University of Toronto Press, 2004.

Astronomer, The. "The Life of Emperor Louis." In *Charlemagne and Louis the Pious: The Lives by Einhard, Notker, Ermoldus, Thegan, and the Astronomer*, translated by Thomas F. X. Noble, 226–302. University Park: Pennsylvania State University Press, 2009.

Bachrach, Bernard S. *Early Carolingian Warfare: Prelude to Empire.* Philadelphia: University of Pennsylvania Press, 2001.

———. "The Practical Use of Vegetius' 'De Re Militari' During the Early Middle Ages." *Historian* 47, no. 2 (1985): 239–55.

Bachrach, Bernard S., and Bachrach, David S. "Military Intelligence and Long-Term Planning in the Ninth Century: The Carolingians and Their Adversaries." *Mediaevistik* 33, no. 1 (2020): 89–112.

Bachrach, David S., and Bachrach, Bernard S. "Nithard as a Military Historian of the Carolingian Empire c. 833–843." In Bachrach and Bachrach, *Writing the Military History of Pre-Crusade Europe*, 29–55. London: Routledge, 2020.

Booker, Courtney M. "By Any Other Name? Charlemagne, Nomenclature, and Performativity." In *Charlemagne: les temps, les espaces, les hommes. Construction et déconstruction d'un règne*, edited by Rolf Grosse and Michel Sot, 409–26. Turnhout, Belgium: Brepols, 2018.

———. "Histrionic History, Demanding Drama: The Penance of Louis the Pious in 833, Memory, and Emplotment." In *Vergangenheit und Vergegenwärtigung: Frühes Mittelalter und europäische Erinnerungskultur*, edited by Helmut Reimitz and Bernhard Zeller, 103–27. Vienna: Austrian Academy of Sciences Press, 2009.

———. "Imitator Daemon Dicor: Adalhard the Seneschal, Mistranslations, and Misrepresentations." *Jahrbuch für Internationale Germanistik* 33 (2001): 114–26.

———. *Past Convictions: The Penance of Louis the Pious and the Decline of the Carolingians.* Philadelphia: University of Pennsylvania Press, 2009.

———. "The Two Sorrows of Nithard." In *In This Modern Age: Medieval Studies in Honor of Paul Edward Dutton*, edited by Courtney M. Booker and Anne A. Latowsky, 97–142. Budapest: Trivent Publishing, 2023.

Bulletin de la Société des sciences historiques et naturelles de l'Yonne 14 (1860): 44–76.

Burgess, Glyn, trans. *The Song of Roland*. London: Penguin, 1990.

Chandler, Cullen J. "Charlemagne's Table: The Carolingian Royal Court and Food Culture." *Viator* 50, no. 1 (2019): 1–30.

Choy, Renie S. *Intercessory Prayer and the Monastic Ideal in the Time of the Carolingian Reforms*. Oxford, UK: Oxford University Press, 2016.

Claussen, M. A. "Fathers of Power and Mothers of Authority: Dhuoda and the Liber manualis." *French Historical Studies* 19, no. 3 (1996): 785–809.

Collins, Roger. "Pippin I and the Kingdom of Aquitaine." In *Charlemagne's Heir: New Perspectives on the Reign of Louis the Pious (814–840)*, edited by Peter Godman and Roger Collins, 363–89. London: Clarendon Press, 1990.

———. "The 'Reviser' Revisited: Another Look at the Alternate Version of the Annales Regni Francorum." In *After Rome's Fall: Narrators and Sources of Early Medieval History*, edited by Alexander Callander Murray, 191–213. Toronto: University of Toronto Press, 1998.

Costambeys, Marios, Matthew Innes, and Simon MacLean. *The Carolingian World*. Cambridge, UK: Cambridge University Press, 2011.

Coupland, Simon. "A Coin of Queen Fastrada and Charlemagne," *Early Medieval Europe*, 31, no. 4 (2023): 585–97.

———. "From Poachers to Gamekeepers: Scandinavian Warlords and Carolingian Kings." *Early Medieval Europe* 7, no. 1 (1998): 85–114.

———. "Holy Ground? The Plundering and Burning of Churches by Vikings and Franks in the Ninth Century." *Viator* 45, no. 1 (2014): 73–98.

———. "Trading Places: Quentovic and Dorestad Reassessed." *Early Medieval Europe* 11, no. 3 (2002): 209–32.

Czock, Miriam. "Arguing for Improvement: The Last Judgment, Time and the Future in Dhuoda's Liber Manualis." In *Cultures of Eschatology: Time, Death and Afterlife in Medieval Christian, Islamic and Buddhist Communities*, edited by Veronik Wieser et al., vol. 2, 509–27. Berlin: De Gruyter, 2020.

Davis, Jennifer R. *Charlemagne's Practice of Empire*. Cambridge, UK: Cambridge University Press, 2015.

de Jong, Mayke. "Bride Shows Revisited: Praise, Slander, and Exegesis in the Reign of the Empress Judith." In *Gender in the Early Medieval World: East and West, 300–900*, edited by Leslie Brubaker and Julia M. H. Smith, 257–77. Cambridge, UK: Cambridge University Press, 2004.

———. *Epitaph for an Era: Politics and Rhetoric in the Carolingian World*. Cambridge, UK: Cambridge University Press, 2019.

———. *The Penitential State: Authority and Atonement in the Age of Louis the Pious, 814–840*. Cambridge, UK: Cambridge University Press, 2009.

Depreux, Philippe. "The Penance of Attigny (822) and the Leadership of the Bishops in Amending Carolingian Society." In *Religious Franks: Religion and Power in the Frankish Kingdoms: Studies in Honour of Mayke de Jong*, edited by

Rob Meens et al., 370–85. Manchester, UK: Manchester University Press, 2016.

———. *Prosopographie de l'entourage de Louis le Pieux (781–840).* Ostfildern, Germany: Jan Thorbecke Verlag, 1997.

Dhuoda. *Handbook for William: A Carolingian Woman's Counsel for Her Son.* Translated by Carol Neel. Washington, DC: Catholic University of America Press, 1999.

Divisio regnorum. In *Carolingian Civilization: A Reader,* translated by Paul Edward Dutton, 2nd ed., 146–51. Toronto: University of Toronto Press, 2004.

Dutton, Paul Edward. *Charlemagne's Mustache and Other Cultural Clusters of a Dark Age.* London: Palgrave Macmillan, 2004.

———. *The Politics of Dreaming in the Carolingian Empire.* Lincoln: University of Nebraska Press, 1994.

Einhard. *The Life of Charlemagne.* In *Two Lives of Charlemagne,* translated by Lewis Thorpe, 49–90. London: Penguin, 1969.

———. "The Translation and Miracles of Marcellinus and Peter." In *Charlemagne's Courtier: The Complete Einhard,* edited and translated by Paul Edward Dutton, 69–130. Toronto: University of Toronto Press, 1998.

Faust, Drew Gilpin. *This Republic of Suffering: Death and the American Civil War.* London: Penguin, 2009.

Firnhaber-Baker, Justine. *House of Lilies: The Dynasty That Made Medieval France.* New York: Basic Books, 2024.

Flodoard of Reims. *Historia Remensis Ecclesiae. Monumenta Germaniae Historica: Scriptores,* vol. 36. Hanover: Hahnsche Buchhandlung, 1998.

Florus of Lyons. "Lament on the Division of the Empire." In *Poetry of the Carolingian Renaissance,* translated by Peter Godman, 264–73. Norman: University of Oklahoma Press, 1985.

Flynn, Christopher. "Fontenoy and the Justification of Battle-Seeking Strategy in the Ninth Century." *Mediaevistik* 35, no. 1 (2022): 89–110.

———. "'Unconquered Louis Rejoiced in Iron': Military History in East Francia Under King Louis the German (c. 825–876)." PhD diss., University of Minnesota, 2020, https://conservancy.umn.edu/items/c8c42ce4-4fc6-4042 -b73e-ca38b8f08514.

Folz, Robert. *The Coronation of Charlemagne, 25 December 800.* Translated by J. E. Anderson. London: Routledge, 1974.

Fouracre, Paul. "The Long Shadow of the Merovingians." In *Charlemagne: Empire and Society,* edited by Joanna Story, 5–21. Manchester, UK: Manchester University Press, 2005.

Gabriele, Matthew. *Between Prophecy and Apocalypse: The Burden of Sacred Time and the Making of History in Early Medieval Europe.* Oxford, UK: Oxford University Press, 2024.

———. *An Empire of Memory: The Legend of Charlemagne, the Franks, and Jerusalem Before the First Crusade.* Oxford, UK: Oxford University Press, 2011.

Gabriele, Matthew, and David M. Perry. *The Bright Ages: A New History of Medieval Europe.* New York: Harper, 2021.

Garver, Valerie L. *Women and Aristocratic Culture in the Carolingian World.* Ithaca, NY: Cornell University Press, 2009.

Gillingham, John B. "Fontenoy and After: Pursuing Enemies to Death in France Between the Ninth and the Eleventh Centuries." In *Frankland: The Franks and the World of the Early Middle Ages. Essays in Honour of Dame Jinty Nelson*, edited by Paul J. Fouracre and David Ganz, 242–65. Manchester, UK: Manchester University Press, 2008).

Gillis, Matthew Bryan. *Religious Horror and Holy War in Viking Age Francia.* Budapest: Trivent Publishing, 2021.

———, ed. *Carolingian Experiments.* Turnhout, Belgium: Brepols, 2022.

Godman, Peter. *Poetry of the Carolingian Renaissance.* Norman: University of Oklahoma Press, 1985

Goldberg, Eric J. "Popular Revolt, Dynastic Politics, and Aristocratic Factionalism in the Early Middle Ages: The Saxon Stellinga Reconsidered." *Speculum* 70, no. 3 (1995): 467–501.

———. *Struggle for Empire: Kingship and Conflict Under Louis the German, 817–876.* Ithaca, NY: Cornell University Press, 2006.

Hammer, Carl I. "Christmas Day 800: Charles the Younger, Alcuin and the Frankish Royal Succession." *English Historical Review* 127, no. 524 (2012): 1–23.

———. "'Pipinus Rex': Pippin's Plot of 792 and Bavaria." *Traditio* 63 (2008): 235–76.

Heinzle, Georg Friedrich. "Le souvenir de nos gloires: Überlegungen zur Schlacht von Fontenoy (841) in der französischen Erinnerung des Spätmittelalters und des 19. Jahrhunderts." In *Wissen im Mythos? Die Mythisierung von Personen, Institutionen und Ereignissen sowie deren Wahrnehmung im wissenschaftlichen Diskurs*, edited by Christina Bröker et al., 189–216. Munich: Akademische Verlagsgemeinschaft München, 2017.

Hincmar of Rheims. "On the Governance of the Palace." In *Carolingian Civilization: A Reader*, edited by Paul Edward Dutton, 2nd ed., 516–32. Toronto: University of Toronto Press, 2004.

Hugh of Flavigny. *Chronicon.* Edited by G. H. Pertz. *Monumenta Germaniae Historica: Scriptores*, vol. 8. Hanover: Hahn, 1848.

Jaski, Bart. "The Ruler with the Sword in the Utrecht Psalter." In *Religious Franks: Religion and Power in the Frankish Kingdoms: Studies in Honour of Mayke de Jong*, edited by Rob Meens et al., 72–91. Manchester, UK: Manchester University Press, 2016.

Keller, Hagen. *Die Ottonen.* Munich: C. H. Beck, 2021.

Kramer, Rutger. *Rethinking Authority in the Carolingian Empire: Ideals and Expectations During the Reign of Louis the Pious (813–828).* Amsterdam: Amsterdam University Press, 2019.

Le Jan, Régine. "The Multiple Identities of Dhuoda." In *Ego Trouble: Authors and Their Identities in the Early Middle Ages*, edited by Richard Corradini et al., 211–20. Vienna: Austrian Academy of Sciences Press, 2010.

Luginbill, Sarah. "The Medieval Portable Altar Database." *Material Religion* 16, no. 5 (2020): 683–85.

MacLean, Simon. *Kingship and Politics in the Late Ninth Century: Charles the Fat and the End of the Carolingian Empire*. Cambridge, UK: Cambridge University Press, 2003.

Maraschi, Andrea. "Rules for Attending Wedding Banquets in Early Medieval Europe: A Matter of Fun, Excess, and Moral Integrity." *Food and History* 20 (2022): 9–30.

Marlantes, Karl. *What It Is Like to Go to War*. New York: Grove Atlantic, 2011.

McCormick, Michael. *Charlemagne's Survey of the Holy Land: Wealth, Personnel, and Buildings of a Mediterranean Church Between Antiquity and the Middle Ages*. Washington, DC: Dumbarton Oaks Research Library and Collection, 2011.

McKeon, Peter R. "Archbishop Ebbo of Reims (816–835): A Study in the Carolingian Empire and Church." *Church History* 43, no. 4 (1974), 437–47.

McKitterick, Rosamond. *Charlemagne: The Formation of a European Identity*. Cambridge, UK: Cambridge University Press, 2008.

———. *The Frankish Kingdoms Under the Carolingians, 751–987*. London: Longman, 1983.

———. *History and Memory in the Carolingian World*. Cambridge, UK: Cambridge University Press, 2004.

Michelet, Jules. *Histoire de France*, vol. 2. Paris: Champion, 1833.

Neel, Carol. "Mother, Father, King: Dhuoda and Carolingian Patriarchy." In *On the Shoulders of Giants: Essays in Honor of Glenn W. Olsen*, edited by David Appleby and Teresa Olsen Pierre, 23–39. Turnhout, Belgium: Brepols, 2016.

Nelson, Janet L., trans. *Annals of St-Bertin*. Manchester, UK: Manchester University Press, 1991.

———. *Charles the Bald*. London: Longman, 1992.

———. "Dhuoda on Dreams." In *Motherhood, Religion, and Society in Medieval Europe, 400–1400: Essays Presented to Henrietta Leyser*, edited by Lesley Smith and Conrad Leyser, 41–53. London: Routledge, 2016.

———. *King and Emperor: A New Life of Charlemagne*. Oakland: University of California Press, 2019.

———. "The Last Years of Louis the Pious." In Nelson, *The Frankish World, 750–900*, 37–50. London: Hambledon Press, 1996.

———. "Public Histories and Private History in the Work of Nithard." *Speculum* 60, no. 2 (1985): 251–93.

———. "The Search for Peace in a Time of War: The Carolingian Brüderkrieg, 840–843." In *Träger und Instrumentarien des Friedens im hohen und späten Mittelalter*, edited by Johannes Fried, 87–114. Ostfildern, Germany: Jan Thorbecke Verlag, 1996.

———. "Violence in the Carolingian World and the Ritualization of Ninth-

Century Warfare." In *Violence and Society in the Early Medieval West*, edited by Guy Halsall, 90–107. Martlesham, UK: Boydell and Brewer, 2002.

———. "Women at the Court of Charlemagne: A Case of Monstrous Regiment?" In Nelson, *The Frankish World, 750–900*, 223–42. London: Hambledon Press, 1996.

Newfield, Timothy. "A Great Carolingian Panzootic: The Probable Extent, Diagnosis and Impact of an Early Ninth-Century Cattle Pestilence." *Argos* 46 (2012): 200–210.

Nithard. *Histories*. In *Carolingian Chronicles*. translated by Bernhard Walter Scholz, 129–74. Ann Arbor: University of Michigan Press, 1970.

Noble, Thomas F. X. *Images, Iconoclasm, and the Carolingians*. Philadelphia: University of Pennsylvania Press, 2009.

Noga-Banai, Galit. "The Sarcophagus of Louis the Pious at Metz: A Roman Memory Reused." *Frühmittelalterliche Studien* 45 (2016): 37–50.

Notker the Stammerer. *Charlemagne*. In *Two Lives of Charlemagne*, translated by Lewis Thorpe, 93–172. London: Penguin, 1969.

Ottewill-Soulsby, Sam. *The Emperor and the Elephant: Christians and Muslims in the Age of Charlemagne*. Princeton, NJ: Princeton University Press, 2023.

Palmer, James T. *The Apocalypse in the Early Middle Ages*. Cambridge, UK: Cambridge University Press, 2014.

———. "Gaul, Francia, and the Wider Early Medieval World." In *Routledge Handbook of French History*, edited by David Andress, 21–30. London: Routledge, 2023.

———. "The Making of a World Historical Moment: The Battle of Tours (732/3) in the Nineteenth Century." *Postmedieval* 10 (2019): 206–18.

———. *Merovingian Worlds*. Cambridge, UK: Cambridge University Press, 2024.

Paschasius Radbertus. "Epitaph for Arsenius." In *Confronting Crisis in the Carolingian Empire: Paschasius Radbertus' Funeral Oration for Wala of Corbie*, translated by Mayke de Jong and Justin Lake, 49–223. Manchester, UK: Manchester University Press, 2020.

Phelan, Owen M. "The Scope of Fidelity in Nithard's Ninth Century." *Viator* 48, no. 2 (2017): 21–47.

Poor, Sara S. "The Curious Multilingual Prehistory of French and German Monolingualism." *German Studies Review* 41, no. 2 (2018): 465–85.

Ranke, Leopold von. *Weltgeschichte*, vol. 6. Leipzig: Verlag von Duncker & Humblot, 1885.

Regino of Prüm. *Chronicle*. In *History and Politics in Late Carolingian and Ottonian Europe: The Chronicle of Regino of Prüm and Adalbert of Magdeburg*, translated by Simon MacLean, 61–231. Manchester, UK: Manchester University Press, 2009.

Rembold, Ingrid. *Conquest and Christianization: Saxony and the Carolingian World, 772–888*. Cambridge, UK: Cambridge University Press, 2017.

Renoux, Annie. "Du palais impérial aux palais royaux et princiers en Francie occidentale (c 843–1100)." In *The Emperor's House: Palaces from Augustus to the Age of Absolutism*, edited by Michael Featherstone et al., 93–106. Berlin: De Gruyter, 2015.

Reuter, Timothy, trans. *Annals of Fulda*. Manchester, UK: Manchester University Press, 1992.

Riché, Pierre. *Daily Life in the World of Charlemagne*, 2nd English ed. Translated by JoAnn McNamara. Philadelphia: University of Pennsylvania Press, 1988.

Rio, Alice. "Waltharius at Fontenoy? Epic Heroism and Carolingian Political Thought." *Viator* 46, no. 2 (2015): 41–64.

Romano, John F. "The Coronation of Charlemagne as a Liturgical Event." *Mediaeval Studies* 82 (2020): 149–81.

Romig, Andrew J. *Be a Perfect Man: Christian Masculinity and the Carolingian Aristocracy*. Philadelphia: University of Pennsylvania Press, 2017.

Royal Frankish Annals. In *Carolingian Chronicles*, translated by Bernhard Walter Scholz and Barbara Rogers, 37–125. Ann Arbor: University of Michigan Press, 1970.

Screen, Elina. "The Importance of an Emperor: Lothar I and the Frankish Civil War, 840–843." *Early Medieval Europe* 12, no. 1 (2003): 25–51.

Shepard, Jonathan. "Revisiting the Rus Visitors to Louis the Pious." *Byzantinoslavica* 80, nos. 1–2 (2022): 59–87.

Simson, B. de, ed., *Annals of Xantenses, Monumenta Germaniae Historica: Scriptores rerum Germanicarum*, vol. 12. Hanover: Hahnsche Buchhandlung, 1909.

Sorber, Andrew H. *Prophecy and Politics in the Early Carolingian World*. London: Routledge, 2024.

Stone, Rachel. *Morality and Masculinity in the Carolingian Empire*. Cambridge, UK: Cambridge University Press, 2012.

Story, Joanna, ed. *Charlemagne: Empire and Society*. Manchester, UK: Manchester University Press, 2005.

Thegan. "The Deeds of Emperor Louis." In *Charlemagne and Louis the Pious: The Lives by Einhard, Notker, Ermoldus, Thegan, and the Astronomer*, translated by Thomas F. X. Noble, 194–218. University Park: Pennsylvania State University Press, 2009.

Ubl, Karl. "Carolingian Mirrors for Princes: Texts, Contents, Impact." In *A Critical Companion to the "Mirrors for Princes" Literature*, edited by Noëlle-Laetitia Perret and Stéphane Péquignot, 74–107. Leiden, The Netherlands: Brill, 2022.

van Renswoude, Irene. *The Rhetoric of Free Speech in Late Antiquity and the Early Middle Ages*. Cambridge, UK: Cambridge University Press, 2019.

"The Vision of Charlemagne." In *Carolingian Civilization: A Reader*. edited by Paul Edward Dutton. 2nd ed., 456–57. Toronto: University of Toronto Press, 2004.

"The Vision of the Poor Woman of Laon," In *Carolingian Civilization: A Reader*, edited by Paul Edward Dutton. 2nd ed., 203–204. Toronto: University of Toronto Press, 2004.

Ward, Elizabeth. "Caesar's Wife: The Career of the Empress Judith, 819–829."
   In *Charlemagne's Heir: New Perspectives on the Reign of Louis the Pious (814–840)*,
   edited by Peter Godman and Roger Collins, 205–27. London: Clarendon
   Press, 1990.

Ward, Elizabeth F. "The Career of the Empress Judith, 819–843." PhD diss.,
   King's College, University of London, 2002, https://kclpure.kcl.ac.uk/ws
   /portalfiles/portal/2929040/402576.pdf.

West, Charles. *The Fall of a Carolingian Kingdom: Lotharingia, 855–869.* Toronto:
   University of Toronto Press, 2023.

Winter, Jay. "Sites of Memory." In *Memory: History, Theories, Debates*, edited by
   Susannah Radstone and Bill Schwarz, 312–24. New York: Fordham University
   Press, 2010.

Matthew Gabriele is a professor of medieval studies at Virginia Tech and coauthor with David M. Perry of *The Bright Ages: A New History of Medieval Europe*, alongside several other academic books. His research generally is on religion and violence, nostalgia and apocalypse, and how people tell stories about the past. His public writing has appeared in numerous newspapers and magazines, and interviews with him have aired locally, nationally, and internationally.

David M. Perry is a journalist, a medieval historian, and the associate director of undergraduate studies in the history department at the University of Minnesota. He was formerly a professor of history at Dominican University. Perry is the author of *Sacred Plunder: Venice and the Aftermath of the Fourth Crusade* and coauthor of *The Bright Ages: A New History of Medieval Europe*. His writing on history, disability, politics, parenting, and other topics has appeared in the *New York Times*, the *Washington Post*, the *Nation*, the *Atlantic*, and CNN. com, among other outlets.